BASEBALL'S OUTCAST

BASEBALL'S OUTCAST

The Story of Ron LeFlore

ADAM HENIG

BLOOMSBURY ACADEMIC
NEW YORK · LONDON · OXFORD · NEW DELHI · SYDNEY

BLOOMSBURY ACADEMIC

Bloomsbury Publishing Inc, 1359 Broadway, New York, NY 10018, USA
Bloomsbury Publishing Plc, 50 Bedford Square, London, WC1B 3DP, UK
Bloomsbury Publishing Ireland, 29 Earlsfort Terrace, Dublin 2, D02 AY28, Ireland

BLOOMSBURY, BLOOMSBURY ACADEMIC and the Diana logo are trademarks of Bloomsbury Publishing Plc

First published in the United States of America 2026

Copyright © Adam Henig, 2026

Cover design: Devin Watson
Cover image: © Getty Images Sport/Focus On Sport

All rights reserved. No part of this publication may be: i) reproduced or transmitted in any form, electronic or mechanical, including photocopying, recording or by means of any information storage or retrieval system without prior permission in writing from the publishers; or ii) used or reproduced in any way for the training, development or operation of artificial intelligence (AI) technologies, including generative AI technologies. The rights holders expressly reserve this publication from the text and data mining exception as per Article 4(3) of the Digital Single Market Directive (EU) 2019/790.

Bloomsbury Publishing Inc does not have any control over, or responsibility for, any third-party websites referred to or in this book. All internet addresses given in this book were correct at the time of going to press. The author and publisher regret any inconvenience caused if addresses have changed or sites have ceased to exist, but can accept no responsibility for any such changes.

A catalog record for this book is available from the Library of Congress.

ISBN: HB: 978-1-5381-9495-9
ePDF: 979-8-2163-7793-1
eBook: 978-1-5381-9496-6

Typeset by Deanta Global Publishing Services, Chennai, India
Printed and bound in the United States of America

For product safety related questions contact productsafety@bloomsbury.com.

To find out more about our authors and books visit www.bloomsbury.com and sign up for our newsletters.

CONTENTS

Prologue vi

1   The LeFlores   1
2   Harry and Ron   15
3   Young, Uneducated, and Reckless   31
4   Jackson   47
5   Twinkle Toes LeFlore   61
6   The Tryout   79
7   Freedom   95
8   A Story From Day One   115
9   Becoming a Tiger   137
10   A Star Emerges   167
11   One in a Million   193
12   Le Expos   217

Epilogue 241
Acknowledgments 258
Notes 261
Bibliography 286
Index 297

PROLOGUE

In March 1978, the Detroit Tigers were in Lakeland, Florida, for spring training. Gates Brown, the team's hitting instructor, had a message for 29-year-old All-Star outfielder Ron LeFlore. No one on the roster attracted more attention than Ron, who, a month earlier, had published a memoir about his childhood poverty, years in prison, and his recruitment to play Major League Baseball. The book had become an instant bestseller and was in the process of being adapted into a movie featuring one of Hollywood's biggest stars, actor LeVar Burton.

Brown, who had recently retired after thirteen seasons in the majors, where he had been one of baseball's premier pinch hitters and played mostly as a backup outfielder, was unimpressed by the glitz and glamour that surrounded Ron. If anyone in baseball understood Ron's background, it was Brown. He, too, had spent time behind bars prior to becoming a professional athlete: Brown for breaking and entering; Ron for armed robbery.

One day at spring training, Milton Richman, a well-respected syndicated sports columnist who worked for United Press International, was interviewing both men during a moment of downtime. Standing with them behind a batting cage, the veteran journalist asked Ron if he was concerned he would lose focus on the field and be "carried away" by the trappings of fame.

"I don't think it'll affect me," Ron replied.

"You know why it shouldn't?" Brown jumped in with his deep baritone voice. "Because nothing lasts forever. Everything you have now could burn up just as fast as you got it."[1]

Like much of the advice offered to Ron throughout his baseball career, Brown's went unheeded. Ron should have listened to him.

1

The LeFlores

No one knows the exact reason why John LeFlore Jr. left his home in Mississippi in the late 1930s, but he had to go. Once you were in trouble with white people, you either left or were dead. During the first half of the twentieth century, an African American in the South was hanged or buried alive approximately every four days, with no trial or due process for his accused crime. Since this fear was ever-present, John, who was a Black teenager, the demographic most vulnerable to becoming a lynching victim, made a conscious decision not to become a statistic.[1]

Born on November 7, 1920, in Jackson, Mississippi, John LeFlore Jr.—whose ethnic heritage included French and Choctaw Indian, along with African American ancestry—aspired to be an artist. But according to his son, Ron LeFlore, that wasn't realistic for a "young Black man living in the South during the [Great] Depression."[2]

"He could draw and paint anything, people and landscapes," Ron explained decades later. But when "you don't have anyone to support you, you lose out on a talent you really are successful with."[3]

When John was fourteen, his mother died. He dropped out of school, took care of his sister, Geraldine, and worked backbreaking, manual labor jobs to support both of them. He was a large man—six feet three, 250 pounds. Ron heard stories that his father, known as Big John by friends and family, would "whup anyone who came at him. He didn't care what they used—bricks, bats, knives. He simply had no fear."[4] Perhaps John's self-confidence got the best of him, which was why he was on the run.

It was a wise decision for this young man to head to a larger urban center. Since 1920, the population of Memphis, Tennessee, had increased by more than a third over a decade and a half, largely due to an influx of African Americans from rural Tennessee or neighboring states, Mississippi among them. Memphis was the largest city in the Volunteer State and home to Beale Street, best known for its live blues music scene and as a hub for Black business and culture. When John arrived in the late 1930s, however, the Great Depression had decimated Beale Street. And while John struggled to earn a living, it didn't get in the way of him pursuing a love interest.

Georgia Kincade was born in St. Louis, Missouri, in 1921. Her father, Gerald, who had served in the First World War, was stationed there when he met his future wife, Henrietta. Eventually, Gerald moved his family to his hometown of Memphis. Raised in a close, spiritual family, Georgia's parents and grandparents (on her father's side), Will and Georgia Bolden, hosted Sunday church services in a makeshift tent. Their Christian revival sermons were lively, inspiring members to give themselves to God and repent their sins. Although there were few female preachers in the 1920s and 1930s, it didn't prevent Georgia's mother from leading services. Henrietta was devout and preached to as many as 200 parishioners on any given Sunday. Money was always tight in their family, as was the case with most families during the Depression, especially Black families in the South, where economic opportunities were mostly limited to sharecropping and domestic servitude. Going to church offered an escape from the bitter reality of being poor, disenfranchised, and segregated in the former Confederacy.

Although Georgia was only five feet two and weighed 105 pounds, she possessed superior athletic abilities. She could play and dominate any sport when given the opportunity. During this era, sports weren't encouraged for girls, especially Black girls. Despite gender discrimination and her height,

Georgia played basketball for Memphis's Manassas High School, the first Black school in the city to establish a sports program.

When John met Georgia in Memphis during the early 1940s, she was a single mother of two sons, Harry and Marvin Campbell. No one knows what happened to their father, but it didn't dissuade John, who embraced Harry (born in 1937) and Marvin (1939) as his own. When John and Georgia married, he adopted the boys. Soon after, though, he was back on the run.

"Whoever was chasing my father in Mississippi found out he was in Memphis," according to Ron, "and he had to flee again."[5]

When John left Tennessee in 1942, he joined millions of other African Americans in the Great Migration, a mass exodus of those who left their homes in the South, fearing for their safety and wanting to improve their financial potential. Similar to John, those who fled were predominantly young people between the ages of fourteen and thirty-four. "Migration favored the young," award-winning historian Ira Berlin explained in his book, *The Making of African America: The Four Great Migrations*. They "were at once less attached to the South, more willing to take their chances in the North, and eager to escape the constraints that had shaped their parents' lives."[6]

Moving to Detroit, Michigan, was not an arbitrary decision. Since the most popular form of travel was by rail, migrants took the direct route when heading north. If you were coming from the coastal region—eastern Florida, Georgia, or the Carolinas—the line took you along the Atlantic Seaboard to such cities as Philadelphia, New York, or Boston. Those living more inland—the Florida panhandle, Arkansas, or Tennessee—went to Midwestern cities like Chicago, Cleveland, Detroit, or Milwaukee. And if you were coming from Louisiana or Texas, you headed west to Los Angeles or San Francisco.[7] John's younger sister, Geraldine, had already made the trek to Detroit with her husband, Vernon. She was working as a domestic servant; he was a chauffeur. They most likely met through work and were employed by a white family.

John arrived in Detroit during an economic boom sparked by the Second World War, with automobile factories churning out tanks and jeeps instead of sedans and pickup trucks. Jobs were plentiful, even for Black men. John found work at a Zenith factory. Since the turn of the century, the Chicago-based manufacturing company had been a leader in consumer electronics, pioneering the development of the personal radio in the 1920s. When John was hired, Zenith was developing a prototype to mass-produce the personal television. John wouldn't be there once the company finally did; he had moved to another job by then, one that probably paid a higher wage. He went to work for what Detroit was best known for: automobile production.

Within a year of his arrival, John began sending money to Georgia, who was still in Memphis, living with her parents and raising her two sons. John was living with Geraldine and Vernon. Years later, Ron remembered that his aunt Geraldine was "happy-go-lucky . . . and liked her drink."[8]

In 1945, as the Second World War was coming to an end, Detroit still had endless employment opportunities, though circumscribed for Black people. The plan was for Georgia to move to Detroit and find a job. Once there, she and John would have two stable incomes and could send for Harry and Marvin. Leaving her sons in Memphis with her parents was "one of the toughest decisions of her life."[9]

Like Geraldine, Georgia found work as a domestic servant. John might have thought Detroit was more hospitable to Black people than it actually was. He was fortunate that he had arrived when the economy peaked. If he had known more about its past, he would have realized that, under normal economic circumstances, jobs for Black men were severely limited. Detroit was not a land of opportunity for people of color.

Before Michigan became a state in 1837, slavery had flourished. When it joined the Union, human bondage was abolished. Nevertheless, more than a century later, the rights of Black people remained restricted.

Throughout the late nineteenth century, poor European immigrants flocked to Detroit, crowding into ethnic ghettos. People of color, however, were either discouraged or prohibited from entering this thriving community. Whether it was church, work, or housing, Detroit was just as racially segregated as any town in the South. When word spread that it was not hospitable to African Americans, the city's small Black population remained stagnant through the end of the century. Still, Detroit's population swelled from 80,000 residents in 1870 to 286,000 by the end of the century.

Through the production of furniture, railroad parts, and kitchen stoves, the city had emerged as the Midwest's economic center. Factories were popping up everywhere, and they needed white workers, especially if they were cheap and unskilled. Foreigners were ideal; they wouldn't complain about unfair labor practices. Those who resisted could easily be replaced. Poles, Jews, Italians, and Greeks were coming in droves. With an abundance of factories and workers, as well as a perfect location along a major shipping route, Detroit was positioned to seize upon the world's next revolutionary invention: the automobile.

By 1920, automobile production was in full swing. As a result, the population of Detroit—now nicknamed Motor City—exploded during the first two decades of the new century. The number of residents had more than doubled; three-quarters of them were either new to the city or a generation removed. For companies like Ford, Dodge, and Cadillac, the demand for labor was so high that these businesses eased their hiring policies when it came to people of color and sent recruiters to the South.

"Anybody wants to go to Detroit, come and see me," a factory representative would tell Black Southerners.[10]

With little to lose, young African American men were easily persuaded. During the 1920s, Detroit's Black population increased fivefold to 40,000 residents (or 5 percent of the city's population). The area's largest employer, Henry Ford, hired 10,000 workers of color for his massive Rouge plant in nearby Dearborn. But while jobs were plentiful, housing was not. White residents refused to allow African Americans into their communities, shutting them out of nearby suburbs like Dearborn and most of Detroit. There were only two neighborhoods in the city where Black people could find housing during the first half of the twentieth century: Black Bottom and Paradise Valley.

As a result, housing availability was insufficient, with more workers than rooms available. Hundreds of newcomers from the South kept arriving every day but had no place to stay. Some African American families had no other option but to live together in one- or two-room apartments that were inadequately maintained. They were the lucky ones. Most were "forced to live in the stables, outhouses, and the other wobbly sheds that have been thrown together in the filthy service alleys."[11] Despite these conditions, the pace of Black migration didn't slow—no doubt an indicator of how much worse the situation was in the South.

By 1930, more than 120,000 African Americans were living in the Black Bottom neighborhood, which was designed to hold only a third of that number. Those who had the financial means to afford a more desirable residence were barred from living in other communities because of racial discrimination. If they were brave enough to try to rent or buy a home in another neighborhood, they faced the ire of white racists—many of whom were once immigrants and had experienced restrictions themselves when they had arrived from overseas. People of color either were physically prevented from moving in or witnessed burning crosses and men marching in white hoods, all of which meant one thing: Leave or be victimized.

When the Great Depression hit Detroit, the lives of African Americans went from bad to worse. Less than a year after the stock market collapsed in 1929, one-third of auto jobs in the city had disappeared. So did employment for Black men and women, who were the first to be fired—even though they were holding positions white people didn't even want. When it came to municipal jobs, Black people were limited to sanitation positions. In the factories, they were assigned janitorial, paint, and searing foundry jobs, all of which subjected them to the inhalation of toxic fumes. These positions were not only the most dangerous and least desirable but also where the most accidents occurred. Lifelong health problems often ensued.

To make matters worse, landlords charged people of color "high rents for run-down vermin-infested homes" and could do so with impunity.[12] Black people fared no better in terms of medical care. Pneumonia, heart disease, tuberculosis, and venereal diseases were experienced by African Americans in disproportionate numbers. The overall situation was so dire that sociologist Gunnar Myrdal, in his classic 1944 work *An American Dilemma: The Negro Problem and Modern Democracy*, wrote that the physical and mental stress that African Americans experienced from racial discrimination was a "constant threat to their health."[13]

The breaking point inevitably came.

On June 20, 1943, 6,000 federal troops were brought into Detroit to quell the civil unrest between white and Black residents. Among those arrested, 85 percent were Black. Among the thirty-four people who died, two-thirds of them were African American.

This was the Detroit that John and Georgia LeFlore encountered with their hopes and dreams in tow. If they believed they could shield their sons from what was happening around them, they were destined for disappointment.

In the late 1940s, Georgia traveled back and forth between Detroit and Memphis, working in one city, visiting her sons and her parents in the other. During that time, she became pregnant with her third child. On June 16, 1948, she gave birth to Ronald LeFlore in Detroit. He weighed nine pounds and nine ounces. Two years later, on September 1, 1950, Gerald, Georgia's fourth son, was born. Harry and Marvin were still in Memphis. They would continue to live with their grandparents for three more years.

For the LeFlore family of four, their living conditions in East Detroit were barely tolerable. They resided in a one-bedroom apartment at 234 Alfred Street. While the parents slept in the bedroom, Ronald and Gerald slept in a Murphy bed that Georgia would pull out of the living room wall each night. The family contended with bedbugs, which ate away at their skin. Foot-long rats were a common sight, too. Having no choice, the LeFlores had to accept the unacceptable.

"My mother was a very good cook," Ron recalled.[14] Georgia worked as a short-order cook at a restaurant, and when Ron showed an interest in culinary matters, she was happy to oblige. Starting with the basics like baking cookies, Ron worked his way up to meals. His efforts were put to the test when he was five years old. One morning, Georgia woke up sick and could not get out of bed. She was concerned that her husband would come home from work and find no meal on the table. Whenever John came home, he was typically in no mood for small talk. Forced to take the stairs to the top floor of their apartment building since the elevator was out of order, John wanted to do two things: eat and drink.

Ron offered to help his mom. Georgia must have thought he was joking, but he wasn't. He brought the ingredients from the kitchen to his parents' bedroom. Georgia then told him what to use and the necessary quantities. The recipe called for a dash of black-eyed peas, cornbread, and pork neck bones—a popular Southern dish.

When John walked through the door that evening, he smelled the food, and a smile lit up his face. "Georgia, ol' man, am I hungry!" he yelled for everyone to hear. When Ron told his father that he had prepared the meal, John was in shock. "He couldn't believe it," Ron remembered.[15]

The whims of the auto industry meant that those at the bottom of the pecking order—which were almost always African Americans—were most susceptible to layoffs. When John was let go, the family had no choice but to apply for government welfare. To exacerbate matters, John had "spent most of his extra cash on booze." Georgia found a second job working as a maid, trying to keep her family afloat. Although John found work, the family had fallen so far behind on their bills, including rent, that it took some time before they could catch up.

One day, Ron was home with his mother when she told him the landlord was planning to visit. "Why is the landlord coming?" Ron asked. He was under the impression that their financial situation had improved, since his father had been rehired. Georgia didn't want to get into the details, but she promised him that "it would be over soon." When the landlord entered the apartment, Ron recalled, "I watched from my room as he walked into my parents' bedroom. Then the door closed. I knew what was happening inside. It hurt."[16]

Seventy years later, with that memory still vivid in his mind, Ron explained that "all the mothers would do this when they fell behind [on the rent].... Everybody had to do what they had to do."[17]

When Ron was five years old, his parents finally sent for Harry and Marvin, who were living in Memphis and were now in their early teens. Although there was a concern they would be homesick, surprisingly, they were not. In Detroit, they had more freedom than they had when living with their grandparents. For the first time in Harry's and Marvin's lives, Sundays were not spent in church. In addition, they had fun playing with Ron and Gerald, who, in turn, enjoyed having older siblings to entertain them. Harry and Marvin were also helpful around the house, especially with eradicating the pesky rodents. They would hunt them at night using flashlights, then kill them on the spot.

Now a family of six, the LeFlores continued to live in their one-bedroom apartment, which meant Ron and Gerald had less space on the Murphy bed. The crowded conditions resulted in squabbles, especially between Harry and Marvin, who would kick Harry while they were asleep.

"I'm giving you one more warning," Harry threatened Marvin one time. "You better stop kicking me."

Marvin couldn't control himself, though, and kicked his older brother later that night. Harry had had enough. He got Marvin out of bed. They faced each other, and Harry punched his brother in the stomach.

It was the first time Ron saw his oldest sibling throw a punch. "I couldn't believe how hard Harry could punch," he recalled.[18] Marvin buckled and never kicked Harry again.

Eventually, the family settled into a routine. One of those rituals was that no one ate dinner until John was home from work. A bite from Georgia's pot beforehand could result in a quick slap of the hand. Ironically, there were several instances when waiting for John was pointless. He often stopped at a bar on his way home. When he arrived, he was so intoxicated that he'd pass out and fall asleep without having taken a bite.

"It was rough growing up with him. . . . He was drinking so much," Ron looked back sadly. "He used to whip me as a kid. At times, he would whip me because he was thinking I was going to do something." John never used a belt for disciplining his children. It was always with an open hand.

Georgia was also a victim of her husband's aggression. Raising four boys, keeping track of the bills, and working odd jobs, she was frustrated with John and would sometimes complain loudly "about how he didn't bring home enough money to eat and pay rent."[19] Intoxicated, John would beat her in front of their sons. There was no accountability for domestic abuse at the time. The police were of no help. Family counseling and shelters for women and children were not as readily available as they are today. Georgia had no family in Detroit to seek solace with. She was on her own. So were the kids.

It wasn't long before Harry and Marvin went astray. In post–Second World War Detroit, street gangs were thriving, though less violent than they would become decades later. For Harry and Marvin, who were new to the city and had minimal parental oversight, they were prime candidates for gang membership. Whatever their specific reason—to keep themselves safe (from neighborhood thugs), to relieve boredom, or to find a sense of community—a gang offered benefits that no other institution appeared to offer.

During the 1950s, street gangs in Detroit were a common sight. There were white and Black gangs, but they were more often divided by geography than race. Since Harry and Marvin were living on the East Side, they joined the Shakers, the neighborhood's dominant group. Committing petty crimes and getting into fights with rival gangs over street turf, Harry and Marvin equipped themselves with bows and arrows, which they used mostly to hunt rats at night in the alleys. For them, it was a game; whoever killed the biggest rat was the winner. When the Shakers weren't hunting animals, however, they fought opposing street gangs. This usually took place at a playground. Similar to the musical *West Side Story*, the teenagers would rumble using their bare fists. In some cases, they would bring brass knuckles and chains.

One night, Harry and Marvin, now of high school age, came home bloodied from a stabbing. No longer viewing the Shakers as a mild neighborhood disturbance, John took the boys to the hospital and decided that it was time to move. John and Georgia were making more money by then and could cover the seventy-five-dollar-a-month rent.

The family moved into another apartment in the East Side at 5139 Parker Street, located only a few blocks from Pingree Park. The apartment provided more space than the previous one; notably, it had two bedrooms instead of one. The hope was that the move would minimize exposure to gangs and other negative influences. It didn't.

Even Ron, now seven years old and attending nearby M. M. Rose Elementary School, got caught up in the cross fire with a notorious gang member. One night, he was playing house with a girl from the neighborhood. Nobody was home except for him and Gerald. Ron and the girl were sitting in his parents' bedroom, "playing doctor." The two children took their shirts off and continued to play when Georgia unexpectedly walked in. She screamed, horrified and embarrassed by what she saw. The children put their clothes back on, and the girl went running home. Ron likely received a beating from his mom, but that wasn't what he remembered.

A high-ranking Shakers gang member lived in their new neighborhood. His name was Maurice. He was twenty years old, and his younger sister, unbeknownst to Ron, was the girl he'd been playing doctor with. When Maurice found out what had happened, he taunted the LeFlore boys in front of their friends. Harry became upset and intervened. He told Maurice, "It was just stupid kid stuff, so leave it alone. Let it go."

Maurice wouldn't. When John heard about what was happening, his sons pleaded with him not to get involved.

"You think I'm afraid of that piece of trash?" John told his boys. He left the house and looked for Maurice.

"What the hell you want, old man?" Maurice responded after John told him who he was. Once John explained his purpose, Maurice wouldn't have any of it: "Yeah, so what?"

John grabbed him and then hit him. Maurice fell to the ground and took off.

The LeFlore brothers were certain that Maurice would come back with other gang members and hurt their father—and maybe them, too. John, however, smirked. "I fought for my life in Mississippi against white folks. You think that little runt means anything at all to me?"

To show how unconcerned he was, John waited outside their apartment building that night and the night after, showing that he was unafraid. "Come on now," he shouted to anyone he saw on the street who looked like a gang member. "You know where I am. I'm waiting on y'all."[20]

Georgia was no pushover, either. When Ron was in first grade, his mother insisted that he wear a particular pair of shorts to school, which he was adamantly against. "I didn't want to look stupid in front of my friends," he remembered, so he skipped school and spent the day in a shed near his apartment. When the teacher contacted Georgia to find out why Ron didn't attend school that day, he made up a response.

"Don't you tell me no lies, Ronald!" Georgia responded, spanking him.[21]

The next day, she made him wear those shorts again. But this time, Georgia walked him to school. On the way, she stopped at a tree and broke off a branch. They continued their walk to school. When they arrived at Ron's classroom,

Georgia took that branch—also known as a switch—and swatted him in front of his peers.

As embarrassing as it was, the incident seemed to have minimal effect on curbing Ron's defiant behavior. He was caught cheating on tests (even though he excelled in math and reading), looked up girls' dresses, and nearly set his family's apartment complex on fire. But it was during one of the LeFlores' annual trips to Memphis that Ron's fearlessness caused his family the most concern.

Every Christmas, the four brothers and Georgia would visit her parents in Memphis. They would take a Greyhound bus and stay with them through the holidays. Months before the family's 1955 trip, another Black boy from the North named Emmett Till was visiting his relatives in Mississippi. Not knowing the unspoken rules that applied only to African Americans, Emmett made the deadly mistake of whistling at a young white woman. It cost him his life; he was kidnapped, beaten, shot in the head, and had a 150-pound iron fan tied to his neck with barbed wire so that his body would sink when it was thrown into the Tallahatchie River.

During the LeFlores' Christmas visit, Ron—who was seven years old and unaware of the Emmett Till incident—said hello to a white girl in a store, something he would do without hesitation in Detroit. Except he wasn't in Detroit then. He was south of the Mason-Dixon Line. "My grandmother panicked," he recalled nearly seventy years later, "and hurried me up, got me out of the store, took me to the house, and sent me back to Detroit."[22]

If that event was supposed to be a sober reminder to Ron about the consequences of his behavior, it didn't work. At the first elementary school he attended, Ron was expelled for fighting. At the next one, he got into another fight. He had bumped a student—according to Ron, it was an accident—and it escalated. Ron backed away, but then the student threatened to stab him with a drawing compass. A fight ensued, but it was broken up before it got out of hand. The two boys fought again after school, and Ron hit the boy so hard that he broke his nose. School administrators considered expelling Ron until Georgia pleaded with the principal to give her son another chance.

Ron escaped expulsion, but his unstable home life and the violent neighborhood he was growing up in would inevitably have a negative impact on his attitude and behavior. According to the community activitst Useni Eugene Perkins, author of *Home Is a Dirty Street: The Social Oppression of Black Children*, public school administrators and teachers—most of whom were white—lacked the knowledge (or were just indifferent) to the violent environment their African American students were confronted with daily. The child, Perkins wrote, "is expected to be socially adjusted, morally sound and free of so-called anti-social behavior, yet his environment represents the antithesis of these virtues."[23] Discipline, not empathy, was how school officials dealt with unruly behavior.

The reversal of Ron's expulsion was clearly the exception, not the rule. Schools failed to consider that the majority of these students were not receiving a sufficient amount of attention at home. In most cases, only one parent was raising the children, and that parent was rarely home because they (most likely the mother) were working multiple jobs. This was common in underserved communities like Detroit's East Side, considered "the toughest area of the whole city."[24]

Even though Ron's parents were more involved than those of many of his peers, John and Georgia had their shortcomings. The economic stress, the alcoholism, the beatings, the frequent moving, and the gangs created living conditions where positive role models and youth enrichment opportunities were all but nonexistent. Georgia, who was the only constructive influence in Ron's life during his adolescence, could not provide all four of her sons the parental attention they needed to keep them engaged in positive social behavior. As a consequence, Ron was left idle. It was only a matter of time before he got into trouble.

2

Harry and Ron

If there was one person whom young Ron LeFlore idolized, it was his oldest brother, Harry.

By the mid-1950s, Harry had moved on from the Shakers. Instead of getting into street brawls, he channeled his aggression inside a boxing ring. Initially tutored by his stepfather, Harry refined his skills at the Brewster Recreation Center (later renamed the Brewster-Wheeler Recreation Center), located about a mile from the LeFlores' apartment. The center had previously served as the training ground for legendary boxer Joe Louis, who had also grown up in the area. Although it had been two decades since the Brown Bomber had sparred in the center's basement, the venue was still seen as a source of pride for up-and-coming boxers, including Harry. These young boxers—almost all of whom were Black and poor—would refine their moves at Brewster-Wheeler, in hopes of monetizing their talent into a career. The overwhelming majority did not make it beyond recreational competitions. Harry was one of the few who did.

He caught the eye of a coach who encouraged him to fight in bouts outside of the center, a stepping stone in the process of becoming a professional fighter. Sensing his own pathway to success, Harry encouraged Ron to do the same. Although Ron didn't take up boxing (he didn't like getting hit), he played other sports such as basketball and football. Ron's enviable speed—he was so fast that no one could tackle him—brought him popularity in the neighborhood. Everyone wanted him on their team.

Unfortunately, Ron still had a knack for getting in trouble. By the time he was ten years old, he was already smoking marijuana and consuming alcohol, which Harry warned him about. But it was stealing that gave Ron the rush he sought. As he recalled, "I liked people to look up to me. Maybe that was one reason I stole so much when I was a kid."[1] And stole he did.

Ron worked for tips at a local grocery store, helping customers carry their bags. He would steal steak and wine from the store, selling it to friends while consuming some of it himself. At the same market, he observed an employee dropping envelopes into the cash register. He assumed that these envelopes contained money. During a moment when no one was paying attention, he took a small, thin, sturdy branch and attached a piece of used gum at the end. Then he placed the sticky part into a slit within the register—the same slit the employee had used to drop the envelope—and felt around the confined area until he detected an envelope. Once he made contact, he "jabbed it [the stick] so the gum would stick" to an envelope.[2]

After retrieving the envelope, Ron placed it underneath his clothes. He walked out of the store and headed home.

Later, when he saw his younger brother, Gerald, they went to the basement, and Ron showed him the money. They counted $1,500 in cash. "We're rich! We're rich!" he recalled screaming.[3] "Guys who were bigger and older couldn't steal that much unless they used a gun."[4] Ron was twelve years old at the time. Fancying himself as a "Robin Hood," he bought Converse high-tops and other apparel for his friends.[5]

Ron's thievery was kept under wraps, but his physical fearlessness was well-known. He lived in a neighborhood where violence was common. One had to be tough to survive, a lesson learned in early childhood. Ron knew instinctively the need to establish a reputation for being tough among his peers. Whenever a fight seemed inevitable, he would throw the first and final punches. "Don't mess with this guy," word about him had spread. "He's crazy."[6] His plan worked.

Meanwhile, Harry, now eighteen, was making headway in the amateur boxing arena. In December 1955, he fought in the coveted Golden Gloves of America Tournament of Champions in Chicago, where the best young fighters in the Midwest and Far West competed. The first time he fought in the tournament, where he was competing in the 118-pound division, Harry made it to the semifinals. The following year, he made it to the championships. He had quickly become a name in the regional boxing circuit and was known as a "slick-boxing featherweight."[7]

When Harry graduated from Cass Technical High School, he enlisted in the army, where he continued to box. Before he departed for basic training, Harry sat Ron down, sensing that his younger brother was heading in the wrong direction. He reminded him that athleticism ran in the family and that he should use it to his advantage. He told Ron, "Those guys in the gangs were always going to be dressing a little better than me, having a little more fun, and having girls come around. But in the end, their world would come crashing down."[8]

Around that time, the LeFlore family moved again, this time to a small house they rented about a mile south of their previous residence. For the first time, they had a porch, a backyard, and—most importantly—three bedrooms, enough that Ron only had to share his bedroom with his younger brother, Gerald.

Ron tried to follow Harry's advice. They spoke on the phone whenever Harry called home from San José State University, where he attended on a boxing scholarship. Ron was getting high marks in the classroom, something he was proud to tell his older brother. School came easy to him. He did well on tests, even though he didn't study. He could easily absorb a lot of information without much effort. He was gifted—if only he would put in more effort. But he lacked motivation. Sports, on the other hand, was a natural motivator. Plus, it helped that he had someone in his corner, cheering him on.

Ron's half brother, Army Specialist Harry Campbell, in the mid-1950s. (Ron LeFlore's personal collection)

Ron played in a youth basketball league, where he represented his mother's place of worship, the Greater Christ Baptist Church. One of the church's deacons was also the coach, Charles Lewis, who worked for the City of Detroit's Parks and Recreation Department. A lifelong Detroiter, Lewis worked at Pingree Park, close to where the LeFlores lived. Witnessing the rapid decline of organized recreational opportunities for Black youth, Lewis was convinced that sports was an effective way to keep local youngsters out of trouble. Whenever he heard that one of them went astray, his only thought was, "If that young man or young woman had a recreation center open to them, would they have committed that crime?"[9]

Lewis's nurturing attitude and Detroit roots made him a magnet for local wayward youth, including Ron. Known as Coach Lewis, he was so respected in the community that children who could not avoid the pitfalls of gangs and drugs were so embarrassed when they encountered him that "they tried to keep it away from him."[10] As much as Lewis wanted his players to improve on the court, it was more important that they took what they learned and made positive choices off the court.

Ron's quickness and athleticism caught the eye of Coach Lewis, who encouraged him to compete in the citywide youth track-and-field competition. Ron won his event, the long jump. He flew nineteen feet and ten inches, a tremendous mark for a ten-year-old boy. What Ron remembered most about his feat, though, was how Coach Lewis encouraged him every step of the way. It remains one of Ron's fondest childhood memories.

Even with Coach Lewis in his corner, temptation was too much for Ron to overcome. Georgia worked multiple jobs and could not keep a close eye on her second-youngest son, while John continued his drinking and abusive behavior toward his family. Ron dealt with the situation by rebelling. At twelve years old, after his parents were asleep, he would jump from his bedroom window to the front porch without detection and wander the streets. He also continued stealing. He stole money from a local gambler. He stole money from a paperboy. When his mom got him a job delivering newspapers, he quickly realized that he could make more money stealing than tossing rolled-up newspapers onto people's porches.

While spending the day with his younger brother, Gerald, and their friends at Edgewater Park, a popular amusement center in Detroit, Ron noticed an employee carrying a bag to the park office. After she went inside, she left the office without the bag. Ron had a feeling that the bag was filled with cash. When she was out of sight, he went over to the office door to see if it was locked, which it was. He took a "fingernail file," inserted it into the lock, and jostled it.[11] Sure enough, the door opened. He grabbed two bags full of money; one was filled with dollar bills, while the other had coins. Anticipating he might look suspicious while carrying these bags out of the park, Ron told Gerald to fake a fight with one of the other boys to serve as a distraction for the security guard at the exit gate. It worked. Ron walked out with two bags of money that totaled approximately $300.

Without losing sight of Ron's criminal intent, there is something to be said for a twelve-year-old to have observed the employee, figured out her intentions, and come up with a plan to leave the location undetected—all in the heat of the moment. If only his keen observational instincts and strategic thinking could have been recognized and nurtured for more positive purposes, his early trajectory might have been channeled in an entirely different direction.

Clever as he was, Ron was also a show-off. He took risks so that he could impress his peers. Years later, he explained:

A lot of kids wanted to hang around me because I was so bold and gutsy. . . . I was getting away with so much. That made me feel especially proud. I always wanted people to believe I was better than they were, whether we were playing stick ball on the street or stealing. I was always competitive, and I didn't want people to beat me at anything. I had to be first.[12]

It was just a matter of time, though, before he would get caught. When he did, he was taken to the Youth Bureau, a facility for juveniles, where he would sometimes be forced to spend the night before his mother would pick him up. His father stopped coming to take Ron home. Coach Lewis was convinced that if he could intervene in a troubled child's life while they were still young, he had a chance of saving them before irreversible harm could take effect. In some cases, it worked. But Coach Lewis was one person trying to undo a system that, in several respects, had set these youngsters up to fail.

Although Black Detroit benefited economically from the industrial output of the Second World War, those benefits would be fleeting. In 1950, Detroit's population reached 1.85 million. It would never rise above that number again. By the end of the decade, the population declined by more than 10 percent, or by 200,000. The majority of those who left were white, fleeing for the leafy suburbs, which grew from 3 million to 3.8 million during that same period, while Detroit's Black population, by default, increased from 16 percent to 29 percent.

When white people left the city, so did the jobs and tax revenue. The impact was devastating. The automakers moved and built their factories and plants outside city limits, partly to avoid paying higher taxes but mainly to accommodate the white suburban workforce. It was the economic death knell for the East Side, "once the epicenter of the auto industry." That area of the city would soon become "an economic slum," explained Thomas J. Sugrue, author of *The Origins of the Urban Crisis: Race and Inequality in Postwar Detroit*.[13] Black workers like John LeFlore could no longer take a bus, carpool with their spouse, or walk to work. He would need his own car, which he might not have been able to afford (in a city that produced tens of thousands of cars a day).

As white families left the city, the tax revenue that schools were reliant on to hire teachers, maintain facilities, and invest for the future decreased significantly. Already unhappy about the lack of resources and lower wages than their suburban counterparts, Detroit's administrators and educators—most of whom were white—were indifferent, if not hostile, to the racial changes. The lack of funding, the unmotivated instructors, the overcrowded conditions (schools closed in many neighborhoods), and the high concentration of impoverished students led to a rapid decline in the quality of Detroit's public schools. Curriculum standards, many believed, were lowered "to accommodate prevalent white stereotypes of blacks as a class of people unable to learn as fast as whites."[14] Consequently, youth truancy surged, leading to high student dropout rates.

This was the environment Ron LeFlore, his younger brother Gerald, and tens of thousands of other African American children in Detroit were subjected to. They were given a minimal chance to survive, and no opportunity to thrive.

If there was anything that kept Ron tethered, it was the inspiration of his half brother Harry. In the spring of 1960, at San Francisco's Cow Palace Arena, Harry competed for a spot on the 1960 Olympic Boxing Team. Fighting in the 132-pound division, the "lean and limber" fighter was beating up his competition, eventually securing a coveted spot on the team that would feature another up-and-coming boxer, the heavyweight Cassius Clay (later known as Muhammad Ali) of Louisville, Kentucky.[15]

Harry also had a new coach, Bill Young. A boxer during his youth, Young was a former police officer-turned-private detective who worked as a coach for a half dozen promising professional fighters.

Young took a liking to Harry. Perhaps it was a bond they shared, having both been former army paratroopers. If boxing didn't work out, Young told Harry that he had the instincts and intellect to become a detective. In fact, the coach was trying to get him to change his major from physical education to criminal justice: "He has a talent that shouldn't be wasted." Although Harry was offered "fairly sizable sums for his signature to a pro contract" by other managers, he trusted Young, demonstrating shrewd instincts in a sport tainted with criminal influence.[16] The future appeared bright for Harry. From Detroit to San José, to Olympic competition in Rome, Harry had reached the pinnacle of his sport as an amateur boxer.

The 1960 Olympics featured one of the most memorable US teams, which included world decathlon champion Rafer Johnson and the fastest female runner in the world, Wilma Rudolph, both of whom were gold medal winners. But the athlete everyone remembers from the Rome games is Cassius Clay, who won the gold in the light heavyweight division of boxing. Harry wasn't as successful as his teammate. He won his first two fights but lost to Sandro Lopopolo, an Italian, in the quarterfinals. (Lopopolo went on to win the silver in the lightweight division.)

Harry Campbell, Ron's half brother, standing beside his opponent, Sandro Lopopolo of Italy at the 1960 Olympics in Rome. Lopopolo beat Campbell in the quarterfinals in boxing and went on to win the silver in the lightweight division. (Alamy Stock Photo)

Nevertheless, the LeFlore family was proud of Harry. Georgia wanted him to return to college. Boxing was dangerous, she told him. He now had opportunities that most of his peers would never have: an education and a stable career. Harry had different plans. He was twenty-three years old, had represented the United States in the Olympics, and wanted to turn pro. With Marvin off to college (he received a track scholarship from San José State), Georgia was hoping Ron and Gerald would follow in their older brothers' footsteps.

Ron was largely left to his own devices. The neighborhood that he was coming of age in was in worse shape than when Harry and Marvin were growing up. Ron pushed boundaries. He stole money from a local supermarket. Violating the trust of his parents, he sold the silver coins they had given him "for safekeeping."[17] He was having run-ins with the police. Someone needed to intervene.

Fortunately, a Detroit police officer who lived down the street from the LeFlore family took a liking to him. Lieutenant Turner Murphy worked for the Detroit Police Department's Youth Bureau division. Like Coach Lewis (the church deacon who coached Ron in basketball), Murphy tried to steer Ron away from negative influences and into sports. Whenever Ron played football, basketball, or any other sport, it was obvious he had the potential to excel as an athlete.

Murphy observed that Ron was bright and that, unlike his peers, his parents were present, even if one of them had a drinking problem. When Ron was caught committing a petty crime, it was Murphy who visited the LeFlore home and spoke with Georgia and Ron. In later years, Ron referred to him as a "positive influence... [always] persistent in telling me to do the right thing."[18] If only he could replicate the success of Harry, Ron would be on a pathway to a better life, too.

When Harry returned from Rome, he began training for his first professional bout. This time, he would be paid—a boon, considering he was now married and had a son. His first fight was scheduled to take place on November 1, 1960, in San José. With a crowd of 1,000 on hand, most of whom were in Harry's corner, the ex-Olympian knocked out Johnny Guerrero of Sacramento in three rounds. His next opponent was Valentin Rangel of Mexico City in a fight scheduled in San Francisco on November 28. It was another knockout in three rounds. Boxing writers commented that from the beginning of the fight, Harry was "toying" with Rangel.[19] After Harry knocked out his third and fourth opponents, going 4–0, boxing insiders began making comparisons to the legendary boxer Sugar Ray Robinson. Promotor Lou Thomas, who was lining up Harry's matches, told a local reporter, "I think he'll go real big here."[20]

Unfortunately, Harry didn't leave the ring unscathed. He suffered a scratched cornea, which caused his coach to postpone a February bout in Santa Cruz, California, with a Mexican boxer. The plan was for Harry to sit out until his eye healed. When Harry returned to the ring, he continued his unbeaten streak, though it was the first time he failed to knock out his opponent since turning pro.

With five straight wins, Harry was on his way "to the top" of the boxing world, a certainty that did not escape the attention of his former college and Olympic coach, Jules Menendez. "I haven't seen a finer prospect in the last 10 years," Menendez told a *San Francisco Examiner* reporter, who agreed with the assessment, and added that Harry "can box and punch. He is fast and determined. If he has any physical weakness, it's small, soft hands. But he is striving to toughen them. He even carries iron bars in his palms, squeezing them continuously."[21]

While Harry trained for his next fight, the sport was debated across the country. A New York lawmaker, for example, introduced legislation "to suspend or possibly outlaw" boxing in the Empire State.[22] Assembly Representative Bentley Kassal of Manhattan was disturbed by the violent impact the sport was having on its athletes. "We now have hundreds of permanently disabled boxers, unable to support themselves because of injuries incurred in the ring," Kassal emphasized.[23] He believed boxing was "inhumane."[24] If it were to remain, he wanted fighters to be examined before and after each bout. The bill did not pass.

Next up for Harry was Oakland-based lightweight fighter Al Medrano. Medrano was known as an "aggressive fighter," but his record wasn't impressive: six wins, five losses, and one draw.[25] However, three of his wins were knockouts. It was expected to be another easy fight for Harry, though some thought Medrano should not be readily dismissed.

On March 20, 1961, Medrano met Harry in the arena. The fight went the distance—except this time, Medrano was the victor. It was Harry's first loss. In fact, Medrano almost knocked Harry out, but Harry managed to stay on his toes. From the start, Harry had seemed out of sorts. Perhaps his eye had not fully healed? Regardless, it was the sport's biggest upset of the year to date. The boxing world chalked it up as a one-off for the "smooth, skilled 135-pound lightweight" Harry Campbell.[26] A few weeks later, a rematch was announced, set for May 15 at San Francisco's Kezar Pavilion.

For the next two months, Harry trained with a level of intensity he hadn't had before. Would he shake off his first setback? He was still picked as the favorite for the rematch. It's not known whether Harry was reading the local papers leading up to the fight. But if he had, he should have sought the unsolicited advice that boxing columnist Eddie Muller shared with his readers: "[Harry] holds his head too high. He has it out there as an inviting target. And he seems to take the full force of a punch."[27]

Muller's observations proved accurate in the end.

During the May 15 match, Harry would hit the canvas twice in the final round as Medrano pinned him in the corner of the ring. When Harry clinched up, trying to avoid the beating, Medrano threw Harry to the floor and continued to punch him. Vern Bybee, the referee, began his count, but the bell rang before a technical knockout could be called.

Harry got up slowly and walked back to his corner, where he sat down on the stool. Before Bybee could announce that Medrano had won the fight, Harry fell over. Dr. Don Lastreto, the boxing commission's physician, who was at ringside that evening, attended to the collapsed fighter. He checked Harry's vitals. No pulse.

Dr. Lastreto called for a stretcher. "Send him to the emergency room," he told event officials.

Harry was taken to Park Emergency Hospital, located only a hundred yards away from Kezar Pavilion. When he arrived, medical officials discovered there was "extensive brain damage."[28] Park Hospital was an auxiliary medical facility with minimal resources. Harry needed to get to a better-equipped hospital. He was taken to St. Luke's Hospital, about three miles away. Every minute counted.

Harry was prepped to undergo a three-hour operation on his brain at St. Luke's. The neurosurgeon, Dr. Edward Keller, who would operate on Harry, said the fighter's chances of survival were "50-50."[29] That was optimistic. Dr. Lastreto gave Harry a 10 percent chance.

The surgery occurred immediately upon Harry's arrival. Once it was completed, he was in a coma. Dr. Lastreto provided updates to the media throughout the day. Harry's condition did not change; the next forty-eight hours would be critical.

Fifty miles south, San José State students were "glued to radios," waiting for an update.[30] Distraught after the fight, Al Medrano went to St. Luke's. Still in shock, he "felt terrible" about what happened to Harry. "I actually don't think I hit him very hard," he told reporters.[31]

"I don't think any referee in the country would've stopped the fight," referee Vern Bybee said afterward. "When I cleaned off his gloves after the first knockdown, his eyes looked clear."[32]

Back in Detroit, Georgia LeFlore received the call about her son. She caught the next flight to San Francisco.

At 10:30 p.m. on May 17, twenty-four hours after the start of the match, Dr. Lastreto announced that Harry Campbell, the 24-year-old Olympian, had died of a "subdural hematoma," or what is commonly known as a massive brain hemorrhage. "He had almost no chance to live," Dr. Lastreto explained.[33] Georgia arrived in San Francisco an hour after the announcement was made.

The boxer's untimely death was reported in newspapers and magazines throughout the country. Concerns about "whether an underlying disorder was to blame for the death" were circulating widely among fans and journalists.[34] When Harry's autopsy was conducted, it was revealed that the "amount of bleeding and bruises seemed out of proportion to what we would expect results from a professional fight." The coroner was going to "study the brain in detail . . . [to] see whether there was some underlying disorder which would cause such profuse bleeding."[35] (There wasn't. The blows to Harry's head that evening caused bleeding in his brain, which led to his death.)

Georgia stayed for the funeral in California. It was held in a San Francisco chapel two days following the announcement of her son's death. Georgia would not have to cover the expenses, which she probably could not have afforded. They were paid for by the California Boxers and Wrestlers Assistance Fund. The fund's board would later meet to "decide how much money" Harry's family would receive.[36] This was in addition to the amount Harry was owed for the fight; his purse was $533.41 (approximately $6,000 today).

When Georgia returned to Detroit, she delivered the news to her family. She waited for Ron to come home. He was at football practice. His mother, he recalled, "gave me the worst news of my life." Ron could only take it in fragments. He recalled something about Harry's head hitting the ring post in the corner. That Harry had been "knocked out cold and didn't get up." That Harry had gone to the hospital and had brain surgery. That nothing had helped, and "Harry never woke up." By now, Ron was less than a month away from celebrating his thirteenth birthday.

There were two services for Harry: one in California, the other in Memphis. Ron and his family attended both of them. His brother's final resting place was in Memphis, where Georgia's parents still lived. Since he was a veteran, Army Specialist Harry Campbell was buried at Memphis National Cemetery. The entire LeFlore family attended the funeral there. Ron promised himself he would not cry or show any emotion. He was tough. He could handle it. Or so he thought.

Harry's funeral featured an open casket. When Ron went to pay his respects to the older brother he had idolized, his emotions could not be contained. During the operation, the doctor had shaved part of Harry's head

The gravesite of Ron's oldest half brother, Harry Campbell. (Jo Nelson)

to make the incision. "Harry didn't live long enough for the hair to grow back. He had been a handsome man," Ron recalled. Now, he looked like "Frankenstein."[37]

When Ron returned to Detroit, he had numerous dreams about Harry. One moment, he was watching his older brother boxing. The next moment, he was in the locker room with Harry, and they were going to dinner together. Then, Harry was gone.[38]

3

Young, Uneducated, and Reckless

If there was any hope for Ron to make it out of the East Side safely, it would involve sports. It was already in his genes; his mom had been a star basketball player, and Harry had been a successful boxer. During his last year of middle school, Ron asked his parents if he could attend St. Rose of Lima, a Catholic high school in Detroit, and play on their football team. John and Georgia were more than willing to oblige. He was finally engaged in an organized activity that he enjoyed and excelled at. Compared to other youngsters Ron's age, his speed was superior, and he possessed incredible strength. Combined with his huge size, he was a coach's dream. Best of all, sports would keep him out of trouble. Given his brush with the juvenile justice system, any future infractions would not go well for him.

While his sport of choice was football, basketball was a close second. Baseball was nowhere on his radar. His hero was Jim Brown, the Cleveland Browns' fleet-footed running back. Ron would be built just like him. He stood five feet nine and was already lifting weights. His sheer size and athleticism caught the attention of his middle school math teacher, who was also the football coach at St. Rose. Committing a massive violation of the school's athletic rules, the teacher recruited Ron (along with two of his friends) to play on the Catholic high school's team—even though they were still in middle school.

Fully aware of his teacher's subterfuge, Ron "didn't care." He "just wanted to play."[1]

Ron was initially placed on the junior varsity squad, but once his extraordinary speed and overall athleticism became obvious, he was promoted to varsity. During a preseason scrimmage, Ron played defensive back instead of running back his usual position. The coach called for Ron to blitz the quarterback to attack him once the play was in motion. He did so to the chagrin of the offensive linemen, whose job was to protect the quarterback. As upperclassmen, the linemen (who were white) felt humiliated that this young Black rookie ran right through them. Determined to teach him a lesson, on the next play, one beefy lineman unnecessarily piled onto Ron, injuring his shoulder. A stabbing sensation cut through his body. The pain was so severe that Ron, despite his tough upbringing, had to inform the head coach. Instead of investigating the extent of the injury, the coach (who was also white) yelled, "Get the hell back out there, boy. There's nothing wrong with you. Shake it off."[2]

In an age before members of a school athletic staff were required to undergo positive youth coaching training, this type of reaction was common and accepted. Did Ron receive less sympathy from his coach because he was Black? Years later, Ron wasn't sure, but he was certain that the pain he had experienced was excruciating. Nevertheless, he did what he was told. During the next play, the lineman who had knocked him down previously came at Ron again, hitting him on the left arm. This time, the pain worsened to the point that Ron thought he was going to pass out. The coaching staff decided to transport him to the hospital, where doctors determined that his shoulder was fractured. Although the head coach later apologized, Ron would never play another football game in a St. Rose uniform.

After completing his final year in middle school, Ron enrolled at St. Rose, entering the ninth grade. He was hoping to earn a spot on the basketball team, which he easily secured but was unable to maintain because of his poor academic performance. On his own initiative, he tried transferring to

Northeastern High School, which had one of the best basketball programs in the city for a public school. Based on his residence, however, he was ineligible to attend Northeastern. Eastern High School served students in his area. Resourceful as ever, Ron lied about his address and somehow finagled his way into Northeastern, all to no avail. Failing to attend classes at Northeastern, he was expelled.

"We did the best we could . . . [but] when two people are working, trying to make things go, it's tough," was how Ron's mother, Georgia, explained this turn of events in her son's life. "I paid attention to my children. . . . I don't see how a child could get into so much trouble. It just shows you: you don't even know your own children."[3]

Without parental oversight and compounded by a tough living environment, "it wasn't hard to fall through the cracks."[4] Ron ended up at Eastern, an academically underperforming school plagued with poverty and violence. In order to enroll in the school and keep his parents unaware of what was happening, Ron hired a prostitute he knew from his neighborhood to play the role of his mother. "She was convincing," Ron recalled. "She might have been ten years older than me, but with all that wear and tear, she looked like she really *could* have been my mother."[5]

Once enrolled, Ron joined Eastern's basketball team. Even though he was only five feet nine, as he described in his memoir, he was able to "outjump guys" who were well over six feet tall.[6] And, he could dunk!

While he excelled on the court, Ron struggled in the classroom. A chronic truant, he preferred to hang out with his friends, drinking alcohol and playing billiards at a local pool hall. He roamed the streets, on one occasion going across town to Hitsville U.S.A., the nickname given to the Motown Records recording studio on West Grand Boulevard. He and his friends tried to get inside the famous building but were unsuccessful. They did, however, see some of Motown's most famous artists such as Marvin Gaye, Smokey Robinson, and the Temptations.

Ron's failure to attend classes would ultimately catch up with him. Once his coach was made aware of his truancy, he kicked him off the team. Without sports, Ron saw no reason to attend school. As he had done in the past, Ron took it upon himself to decide whether he wanted to pursue an education. Barely a teenager, he dropped out of high school.

It was cheap. It was easy to purchase. It targeted the young. It could be snorted or injected. And, it was addictive. Heroin had become a drug of choice in Detroit, especially within the Black community, as it had in other large American cities in the late 1960s. By the end of the decade, heroin cost the city an estimated tens of millions of taxpaying dollars annually in crime and substance abuse services. The drug was closely associated with shoplifting, prostitution, assaults, holdups, and homicides. According to the Detroit police, assaults were more violent than ever because of heroin's addictive potency. When the *Detroit Free Press* interviewed a municipal court judge about the cases that were coming before her, she estimated "85% of them had some involvement with heroin."[7]

Hanging out on the street, where there was a dope house or two on every block, Ron was fourteen years old when he first tried heroin, snorting the powdery substance. The dryness it left in his nose and his mouth curbed his liking (he would drink lots of soda to kill the taste). His friend Eric convinced him to shoot it, something Ron had witnessed multiple times but had never done so himself. It was appealing, having seen addicts "look completely relaxed, like they had no worries in the world."[8]

When Ron and Eric arrived at a local dope house, they recognized many of the users, who had previously paid them to shoot the drug into their arms, necks, or ankles. They were too stoned to do it themselves. Ron would place a tourniquet on each addict's arm, try to locate a vein, and stick the needle in once the vein became visible. He could perform it on anyone but himself. He wanted his friend to do it for him.

Ron clenched his fist, and Eric stuck the needle in his upper forearm. When the blood became visible in the syringe, Ron immediately felt a tingling sensation enter his body. His muscles were disabled, and he soon passed out. When Ron woke up hours later, he was dizzy and disoriented. He hadn't moved an inch. The needle was still in his arm. He tried pulling it out, but his muscles were too weak.

"Man, I'm gonna die," Ron muttered to himself.

"Naw, you ain't gonna die," other addicts nearby said, overhearing Ron's cries.[9]

Whatever strength Ron could muster, he tapped into it and yanked that needle out of his forearm. Then he threw up.

Ron swore that he would never shoot up again—a pledge that he would not keep.

"There were drug dealers, pimps, and prostitutes in the neighborhood," he remembered. "I would see all these hookers and pimps driving Cadillacs and say to myself, 'Man, I'm going to get involved in this.'"

It was 1964. Ron was sixteen years old, and he had already embraced the street lifestyle. He was hired by local pimps who would pay him to watch their women. The prostitutes would turn to Ron and bribe him to buy drugs for them. It wasn't long before he was pretending to be their pimp. Then he took it a step further. When the unsuspecting white suburbanite cruised through the neighborhood looking for action, Ron lured him into a nearby abandoned house, where he proceeded to rob him.

Although Georgia claimed she had no idea what her son was up to, her husband, John, was no fool when it came to his son's behavior. When he caught Ron at a local dope house, he yelled for him to come outside. When Ron didn't appear, he pulled out a lighter and threatened to light the debris of garbage on the front porch. "I'll burn this sucker down!" he yelled for everyone to hear.[10]

Ron knew his dad wasn't joking, and he came outside.

When they arrived home, John did what he knew best: he slapped Ron. As far as Ron was concerned, if his father could go about drinking himself into oblivion and be abusive to his family, who was he to pass judgment on his son's lifestyle?

One day, when Ron and his friends went to a gas station, he noticed that the attendant inside the convenience store was leaving the front counter to use the restroom. As soon as the attendant was out of sight, Ron "popped" the cash register open and grabbed all the cash he could, unaware the station's owner was watching him.[11] As soon as Ron stole the money, the proprietor grabbed him on the shoulder—the same shoulder that he had injured months earlier playing football. Instead of calling the police, the owner called John and Georgia. Rather than express remorse and seek forgiveness, Ron demonstrated the self-centeredness of a typical teenager. "I was hardheaded," he said years later. At the time, he foolishly believed that his actions were justifiable, since his parents "weren't in a position to give me the things I wanted."[12]

Undaunted, Ron engaged in other unlawful schemes. He managed to get a job as a bagger at A&P, a national chain grocery store. While working there, he figured out how to rip off the store by pocketing the paycheck envelopes. He stole $1,500 (equivalent to $15,000 today) before being caught by the store manager. This time, the police were called. Ron was arrested. Because of his age, he was placed on probation, which was a temporary blessing in disguise.

Lieutenant Murphy, Ron's former neighbor who worked for the Detroit Police Department's Youth Bureau division, encouraged him to stay involved with athletics and stop using drugs. For a brief period, Ron responded positively, even participating in a Police Athletic League-type program. But he needed more oversight if he was going to change his ways. The neighborhood, the constant temptations, and the lack of educational and economic opportunities, coupled with insufficient parental support, proved overwhelming.

Ron's crimes grew in scope and scale. He robbed cases of beer from Stroh Brewery. When he was working at Dairy Queen, he stole from his employer and was fired. He broke into a Sears, Roebuck and Co. department store and ran off with a bunch of clothes that he sold on the black market. He wanted to take a color television, but he and his friends didn't have a car to transport it. Then there was the safe at the wholesale tobacco company.

When Ron was tipped off by his Italian friends about a safe that contained thousands of dollars in cash at a local business where tobacco was processed for distribution, it seemed too good to pass up. It would pay for his growing dependence on heroin and cocaine. Ron and a group of buddies brought two dollies with them when they broke into the building. They located the safe, placed it on the dolly, and rolled it into the street. Then they started kicking it and hitting it with a piece of lumber. No luck.

Someone from the group went to get a sledgehammer. After several blows to the safe, they finally chipped a piece off. There was enough of a hole that Ron could put his arm inside the safe and grab a wad of cash. It was approximately $600—a lot less than he had hoped. When the group heard a noise, they took off, leaving the damaged safe behind.

A few days later, Ron learned a valuable street lesson: know beforehand who you were ripping off. The owner of the company was the most feared crime figure in Detroit—Anthony Giacalone, who would later be connected with the disappearance of union leader Jimmy Hoffa. Fearing the mob more than the police, Ron kept a low profile... until an unexpected knock sounded on the family's front door.

When the safe had been discovered, the police had dusted for fingerprints. Since Ron had a record, his prints were already stored in the criminal justice system, making him easily identifiable. No more probation. Ron, who was sixteen years old, was headed to jail. He was sentenced to serve time at the Michigan Training Unit (MTU), a youth facility in Ionia, two hours northwest of Detroit.

Far from a traditional prison atmosphere, MTU resembled more of a college campus. The objective of MTU was to return youth offenders to their communities so that they wouldn't cycle back into the criminal justice system.

The residents were never shackled; they slept in bedrooms as opposed to two-person cells (though the rooms were locked at night) and could participate in recreational activities and receive a formal education, where they could earn a high school diploma. They even had a sports program. Like Ron, the inmates were mostly poor and disproportionately African American and had been involved with drugs, theft, and truancy.

At first, Ron toed the line. When he was in class, he tried to focus, motivated by the possibility that he could position himself for a college football scholarship. But eventually, Ron reverted to his old ways; he was caught selling copies of a test that he stole from his biology teacher. The authorities sent him across the street to the reformatory.

Unlike MTU, the reformatory looked and felt more like a prison. There were no bedrooms, only jail cells. The grounds were surrounded by a security wall, and the offenders inside were not first-timers. More than a thousand young men were serving time there for serious crimes, including armed robbery and murder. They were described as "rebellious, hostile, belligerent, and suspicious of any authority figure."[13] There was even an isolation unit known as the Vault. The only difference between the reformatory Ron was sent to and a prison was the age of the inmates, who were slightly older than Ron; they were mostly seventeen or eighteen years old.

Despite the harsh environment, Ron did not mend his ways. Naturally defiant, he violated the simplest rules. He wouldn't even walk in the right direction, intentionally moving the opposite way just to antagonize the authorities. For his negative behavior, he was sent to the Vault, though the isolation didn't seem to bother him.

If he continued on this path, Ron's next stop was Jackson, home to the State Prison of Southern Michigan. What deterred him from moving in that direction was a visit from his younger brother, Gerald.

Ron was taken aback. Gerald was wearing gold jewelry and let it be known that he was a drug dealer. Feeling responsible for how his brother had turned out, Ron believed he was the only person in the world who could save him. Gerald had lost interest in school, where he once was a promising student. Georgia had tried her best but was unable to steer her youngest child away from the streets. Harry was dead, Marvin had moved out, and Ron was in jail. Even sports didn't help Gerald, who had been a star basketball player at Eastern High School, often the leading scorer in games.

When Ron saw Gerald that day in the visiting area, it was eerily similar to when Harry had lectured Ron five years earlier. Ron hadn't heeded his older brother's warnings, and now he was paying the price. He was hoping Gerald wouldn't make the same mistake. "I didn't want to be criss-crossing him in and out of prison," Ron later said.[14]

Following that visit, Ron began making better choices in the reformatory. After serving nineteen months at Ionia, he was released early for good behavior. Regrettably, it was too late to save Gerald, who was sentenced to MTU for attempted armed robbery.

In 1966, eighteen-year-old Ron moved back in with his parents, who had relocated to 5126 Iroquois Street, about a third of a mile from where they had previously resided. A single-family home, it was a step up for the LeFlores. No more dope houses on every block. The neighborhood was made up of white and Black working-class families, most of whom were employed by the auto industry. As a former neighbor recalled, "[P]arents looked after each other['s children]. Anyone of the other parents could scold you if they saw you do something wrong." Regardless of whether you rented or owned, residents took care of their property (the LeFlores rented). "Everyone kept up their yard. Lots of fruit trees . . . things were different then."

The LeFlores were friendly with the Brown family, who lived two blocks away. Their two sons, Larry and Kenny, were close in age with Ron and Gerald. Their father was a manager of a dry cleaning shop, while their mother worked at a hospital. Mr. Brown had a strong work ethic that he impressed upon his sons. He woke up at five in the morning every day to go to work and never complained.

Kenny Brown noticed immediately that the LeFlore boys took more risks than he and his brother did. They were less concerned about the consequences of their behavior. Ron, in particular, exuded a toughness, prompting Kenny to later characterize him as a "tough guy." But that did not deter Kenny from hanging out with the LeFlore brothers, whom he also remembered as "hip guys . . . dressed real nice, always got the girls."[15]

To his credit, Ron, who was on probation, tried to go straight. With his dad's help, he was hired to work at Detroit Diesel, where John was employed as a unit supervisor. Ron was placed in an entry-level position, where he worked a 3:00 to 10:00 p.m. shift on the assembly line, installing fenders and hoods onto the vehicles. It was backbreaking labor, not anything Ron had ever experienced before. It didn't take long for him to realize that he was not suited for the job. "I couldn't shower the oil smell off my body," he said. "I just couldn't get clean. I had to pick slivers of steel out of my hand, and no matter how many I picked, there were still more."[16]

The worst part was the pay. After taxes, Ron wasn't taking home much. He made more money selling drugs on the street corner in one day than in the two weeks he worked at Detroit Diesel. After an argument with his father about quitting, Ron left his parents' home.

As much as he wanted to set a good example for Gerald, the straight-and-narrow lifestyle was not for Ron. It was harder than he had thought. Performing odd jobs to survive, he remained idle and had no hope for the future. It was the summer of 1967, and tens of thousands of other young Black men in Detroit found themselves in a similar situation.

On Sunday, July 23, 1967, the rumblings began early that morning on a hot, humid day in Motor City. The Detroit Police Department's Vice Squad had conducted an ill-advised raid on a blind pig, an unsanctioned drinking establishment. As they had done time and time again, the police pulled up in their paddy wagons and waited for the call to load up Black patrons and take them to jail. It had become a routine. Those inside felt they weren't breaking the law. They were simply a group of friends, neighbors, and family members, honoring two homegrown soldiers who had made it back safely from the war in Vietnam. But the police insisted that there was illegal liquor served, and prostitution and gambling on the premises. Detroit's blue went in.

When the authorities escorted the first of their arrests from the blind pig, neighbors outside the building encircled the paddy wagons. As the tension between residents and law enforcement increased, others nearby came to see what was happening. A glass bottle was suddenly thrown in the direction of the police. More debris came, including bricks and rocks. Additional officers were summoned, but because of the early morning hour, only a few reinforcements arrived—not enough to quell the melee.

By the time Ron arrived at the scene with his friends that evening, more than two dozen square miles of central and downtown Detroit were engulfed in flames. Cocktail bombs burned down buildings. Gunfire and firecrackers erupted randomly. A newscaster described the scene as similar to what he had witnessed two and a half decades earlier in London, during the German blitzkrieg. Law and order had ceased to exist, allowing thousands—including Ron and his friends—to seize whatever they could grab and carry. At night, Ron recalled, that was "when you could loot, since you were undetected."[17]

Ron went to Stuff and Shoe Store. He climbed through the shop's broken window and stole a pair of shoes, easy to grab and run. Then he hit Cousins, an upscale clothing shop, where he took a leather jacket and a yellow and tangerine lamb fur coat.

Young, uneducated, and reckless, Ron failed to come to grips with the immorality and illegality of his actions. Nor did he recognize the risks

During the second day of the 1967 Detroit riots, police were attempting to disburse hundreds of residents where the riot was ignited. (KEYSTONE Pictures USA via Alamy)

involved. He could have been shot by a furious shopkeeper—and legally, it would have been justified. Not to mention the officers of the Detroit Police Department, 95 percent of whom were white. "To them, anyone who appeared to be involved in the melee of disorders that kept many cities in flames for days was a menace," explained Useni Eugene Perkins. And to make matters worse, "during crises like these, just being black is reason enough to be killed."[18]

Ron was fortunate that the only interaction he had with the police was a citation for violating the city's mandatory curfew. His fine was $27 (equivalent to $250 today). In the end, Detroit's civil unrest was one of 158 riots that took place that summer, yet it was the deadliest and costliest. Forty-three people perished, nearly 90 percent of whom were Black.

Ron may have escaped the worst of the riots, but his good fortune did not deter him from his life of crime. He was "hustling more than ever."[19] Ron was a heroin addict, although he denied it in his memoir. To feed his habit, he stole everything he could grab and committed robberies when theft wasn't an option. Ron was so desperate for money that he even sold one of his few possessions that Harry had given him: a participatory medal his oldest brother had earned from the 1960 Summer Olympics in Rome. The drugs had changed Ron; no longer did he fear the consequences of his actions. Now, he would walk into a store, push the clerk away from the register, and steal the money. To ensure the employee would not cooperate with law enforcement, Ron would threaten them: "If you tell the police on us, we'll burn your store down."[20]

With Detroit still reeling from the riots—there was more crime than ever and fewer police officers, many of whom left for the suburbs—Ron could get away with his criminal behavior. He was also emboldened to commit more grandiose crimes.

Technically, Ron was the ringleader. He was joined by three other conspirators: Bruce, Emmett, and Johnny, whom he used to play basketball with at his mother's church. They were bored and broke. In the winter of 1969, while most Americans were consumed by the war in Vietnam and the sudden takeover of the defunct Alcatraz prison by Native Americans, Ron and his buddies were focused on one thing: finding enough money for their next high.

"Let's go out and get some money," Ron suggested to his friends. "Let's rob some place."[21]

Ron, who was twenty-one years old now, expected them to either ignore his remark or come up with an alternative solution, something less violent. He was surprised when they agreed.* For whatever reason, Ron started having second thoughts. Something was telling him not to do it this time. He had a

---

*Based on a variety of sources, the agreed-upon robbery occurred between November 1969 and January 1970. The author was unable to determine the exact date.

bad feeling, but he couldn't back down now. He would be seen as weak—the worst type of reputation one can have on the street.

The location they agreed upon was an East Side bar on Mack Avenue called Dee's. It was across the street from the Chrysler stamping plant, where Ron had briefly worked following his stint at Detroit Diesel. He had gone to Dee's once before but didn't have a drink. He remembered a couple of things about the bar: it was packed with workers who were off from their shifts, and "there was a lot of money," since it was a check cashing business. Every Thursday, before heading home, some of the plant's workers would go straight to Dee's, hand over their paycheck in exchange for cash, and have a drink or two or more.

The plan was set. They'd hit Dee's late Thursday night, when the bar would have a lot of cash on hand but few patrons. Once inside, three guns would be pulled out. Two would be on watch. One would grab the money. The fourth would be the getaway driver.

Ron, Bruce, and Johnny went into Dee's and wasted no time when Ron pulled out a loaded .22-caliber rifle. The owners, a middle-aged couple, were behind the bar, counting the money. Ron and Johnny pointed their guns at the couple while Bruce grabbed the cash, which was stuffed in envelopes, and stuck them into a sack he was holding. During the commotion, Ron discretely stuffed some of the cash in his pocket (since it was his idea, he thought he should get extra). Emmett, who was six feet four, was in a Ford Mustang parked in a nearby alleyway.

When Ron and his crew piled into the vehicle, Emmett's knee, during the excitement, rubbed against the dashboard, accidentally hitting the switch that controlled the car's headlights. The lights were now off. Whether it was the adrenaline or their inebriation (or both), when the group took off, no one noticed that the headlights were not turned on.

Traveling on Mack Avenue, they made a quick right turn and immediately noticed a police car that was approaching from the opposite direction. Ron and his friends got quiet, thinking they were about to be caught.

"We can't let these guys take us in," Johnny yelled, cocking his pistol as if a gunfight was about to ensue.

The police car slowed as the Mustang approached. "Your lights," the officer yelled from his car with the window rolled down. "Turn your lights on."[22]

How could they have been so foolish? They had mapped out the entire robbery but made an inexcusable mistake.

They drove without another incident to Emmett's first-floor apartment. Once inside, they locked the door and opened the envelopes, where they counted the money. They were in shock.

The amount of money in their possession would have taken Georgia and John LeFlore a decade to earn. The four men had somewhere between $33,000 and $36,000 in cash (equivalent to approximately $285,000 today).

Once the initial surprise of how much they had stolen set in, that was when the arguments began. Would the money be split evenly? Ron said no way. It was his idea; he should get more. Not wanting to bring attention to themselves, someone suggested they stash it away for the night. While they argued, one of the assailants heard loud noises from the street, which was unusual at the late hour. When they peeked outside, several police cruisers had pulled up and surrounded the building.

The crew had to think fast as they heard the officers enter the building. Ron took the money and went to the top floor of the building. If there was no money found, the authorities would be unable to prove the group had done anything wrong.

Ron hid the money in a crawl space. He heard the police kick in Emmett's door. There was nowhere to go. Ron had to think of another plan.

He undressed himself down to his underwear and a T-shirt, pretending that he had been sleeping. Then he sauntered out of the crawl space and was immediately seized by the police.

"What's happening, man?" Ron asked an officer.

Bruce, Emmett, and Johnny were already handcuffed. At first, the police did not suspect Ron and told him to go back to his apartment.

"He was with me, too!" Emmett shouted.[23] His friend wasn't going to let him get away. It was Ron's idea, and he was the one who had held the gun, Emmett contended.

The police handcuffed Ron. He later learned that the same officers who had advised them to turn on the headlights had been heading to Dee's, responding to the silent burglary alarm. When the officers had made contact with Emmett's Mustang, one of them had written down the license plate number and tracked it back to the apartment.

During Ron's trial, the judge called him a "menace to society," referring to his prior arrests and brushes with the law.[24] Seen as the ringleader and given his record, Ron was looking at a sentence of no less than twenty years. But Georgia, accompanied by John, pleaded with the judge to be lenient, and he proved sympathetic. Ron pleaded guilty and was given a sentence of no less than five years and no more than fifteen.

At first, Ron was relieved, but then he heard how his friends fared. Johnny, who was armed during the robbery, received three to five years. Emmett, the getaway driver, was sentenced to five months in jail, and Bruce was placed on probation for five years. According to Ron, the other three had placed the blame on him, which resulted in shorter sentences for themselves. It's also likely that their more lenient sentences reflected their past records, none of which were comparable to Ron's.

In April 1970, Ron headed to Southern Michigan Prison, the last stop in the state's criminal justice system. Located 75 miles west of Detroit, Ron entered a world that even he—a young man who never showed fear publicly and had been hardened by a tough, traumatic upbringing—was unprepared for.

4

Jackson

"Seeing Jackson for the first time is a shock," a group of academics noted in their paper about the history of the 150-year-old State Prison of Southern Michigan (SPSM).

Forty-foot-high red brick walls surrounded the central facility that housed the majority of its 5,000 prisoners. The wall was thick, peaking at twenty-five feet at the base and sunk twelve feet underground to prevent tunneling. Dotted with sniper posts, the wall itself was built by prisoners and had taken more than a decade to complete. It made the prison resemble a medieval fortress. If officials were concerned that the wall wouldn't be enough to keep the inmates at bay, surrounding it was twenty-five-foot-high fencing topped with barbed wire. Whether it was ever officially confirmed is not known, but the prison held the "dubious honor of being the largest walled institution in the world."[1]

The fifty-six-acre prison campus was located in the town of Jackson. Seventy percent of the prisoners were Black, though African Americans were only 11 percent of Michigan's population. All of its guards, except for a small handful, were white. The prison's racial disparity contributed to a distinct undercurrent of unrest, long ignored until the appointment of a new warden, who was determined to defuse the tension.

Born in a log cabin in Alberta, Canada, in 1931, Perry Johnson began his law enforcement career as a Michigan State University police officer in nearby East Lansing. Recruited in the mid-1950s by the state to serve as a counselor

Ron spent thirty-eight months behind bars at State Prison of Southern Michigan in Jackson. (Sheryl Savas, Alamy Stock Photo)

to inmates who were about to reenter society, the personable but business-like bureaucrat rose through the ranks, rising to deputy director of correctional facilities, the number two prison official in the state, before he was appointed warden at Jackson in 1970.

Johnson not only inherited "a tense prison," as one prison researcher put it, but also a host of unprecedented problems sparked by the 1967 Detroit riots.[2] The six-day rampage in Motor City ignited a crime wave that went beyond the rioting, with new inmates entering the system at numbers that overwhelmed the state's Department of Corrections. Not only were prison staff overseeing more prisoners but also the new inmates were a different kind. They were mostly Black, younger, and outwardly defiant. They were neither deferential to older inmates nor docile around the guards. And, they were unafraid to raise their fists in solidarity in front of the prison administration—a gesture that irritated the mostly white SPSM personnel. The new African American inmates at Jackson "turned the old caste system upside down," as journalist and author Charles E. Silberman pointed out. Black prisoners used "their power of intimidation to gain the status denied to them in the free world."[3]

The situation inside the prison was exacerbated by individuals on the outside, especially the Black Panthers, who preached revolution and called out white society for its racist oppression. They had a significant number of sympathizers among the young African American prisoners—and even among radical white inmates, including John Sinclair, one of the founders of the White Panthers. According to prison officials, Sinclair and other militants inside the prison (who were estimated to comprise about 6 percent of the inmate population) "were actively organizing."[4] There were also rumors that "the Black Panthers outside were collaborating with militant allies [such as Sinclair] in the prison to stage a demonstration."[5]

The greatest threat the warden faced, however, wasn't from the inmates, but from his guards: some 900 men (and a few women), who were 98 percent white and 2 percent African American. Most of the guards resided in rural

Jackson. Their only interaction with people of color was behind the forty-foot walls. The warden's greatest fear was that the guards would overreact to a routine situation and provide inmates the fuel to launch a full-scale riot.

A committee studying the current state of the prison confirmed the warden's dilemma: "To overreact was to hand victory to the radicals. Not reacting undermined authority inside."[6] Johnson ordered his guards to take four weeks of "intensive training" with a focus on "human relations," not on physical enforcement. To those who accused him of "coddling" the inmates, Johnson explained, "We try to make their period of commitment as constructive as possible without trying to take away their dignity as men and merely consider them as numbers or treat them as non-beings."[7]

Johnson also established an honor block, which would give well-behaved inmates more freedom of mobility in a less secure area; a seventy-two-hour family furlough program; an opportunity to earn a bachelor's degree (through Wayne State University) for prisoners who completed high school; drug treatment programs; and an opportunity for inmates to voice their opinion about the prison's rule book. It got to a point where, as one convict quipped, the only way to "stir their fellow inmates to riot would be to take away their televisions and tape players."[8]

If Ron LeFlore had entered prison a few years earlier, he would have missed these opportunities. Whether he would take advantage of them was questionable. But first, he had to go through the gauntlet that every new inmate at Jackson experienced.

When Ron arrived on a prison bus on April 28, 1970, he was a scared 21-year-old high school dropout and heroin addict. He was taken to Cell Block Seven, the location of the Diagnostic Center. The purpose of the center was to determine where the prisoner should be placed and if there were additional concerns that were previously undiscovered. For example, was the prisoner suicidal? Did he suffer from mental illness? Was he suffering from a medical affliction? Was he a serious threat to others?

Ron was subjected to a contraband search first. Using gloves, the guard searched every inch of his body, including his mouth, hair, and anus, while identifying any noticeable scars, birthmarks, or tattoos. For any items that he was caught with, save drugs and stolen goods, he was asked to designate a recipient. Then there were questions about his age, religion, and whether he had served time before. After this, he took a Stanford-Binet intelligence exam (Ron scored a 132, which placed him in the top 3 percent of the outside population, genius caliber) and a personality test.

Once those were completed, Ron was given a close shave and a haircut, and handed a blanket, a pillow, a toothbrush, and a thin booklet titled *Institutional Guidebook for Inmates* (the prison's rules and protocol). His clothes were replaced with prison-issued white coveralls, and like every prisoner, he was placed under suicide watch for seventy-two hours. Finally, Ron was given his prison number: B1156143. Since Ron had previously served time in Ionia, he was given the prefix *B*, which denoted a "second timer."[9]

Arrivals typically remained in the Diagnostic Center for thirty to sixty days. During that time, the information gathered was used to determine not only which cell block each inmate would be placed in but also what type of job he would be assigned. Most were low-skilled factory jobs, such as working in the license plate plant, a shoe factory, or a textile factory, where prisoners would make pillowcases, blankets, and towels. Nonfactory jobs involved working at the prison's farm and—for those who were well-educated—as a classroom instructor.

These opportunities held little attraction for Ron. If they didn't include an athletic component, he was unwilling to participate. As he had done in the past, Ron took matters into his own hands, even if it meant breaking the law—or, in this case, violating prison policy. Managing to borrow a set of regular prison clothes from another inmate, Ron left the Diagnostic Center to play basketball in the recreation yard. His athletic skills were immediately visible on the court, and word spread about his talents. Word also spread to the authorities, who seized and reprimanded him before returning him to the center.

Once Ron transitioned to the general prison population, he realized that life as he knew it had ended abruptly. Housed in what was a warehouse, the living quarters in his cell block were five stories high, each level lined with more than a hundred 6 x 10-foot cells. Ron would never forget the ceiling's penetrating fluorescent lights and the never-ending buzzing sound of the furnace. There were no views of the outside—no blue skies, no sunsets, no stars in the sky—nothing to soothe the soul.

Along with every other cellmate, Ron woke up at 5:30 a.m., followed by the first of four head counts prison officials conducted throughout the day. There were no showers in the cell; only a toilet, a sink, a bed, and a small locker. Showering once a day was a communal experience. Breakfast was served between 6:00 and 7:00 a.m., followed by work or school. Both were considered a privilege and could easily be taken away if an inmate violated any rule—a violation that entailed staying put in your cell all day. Lunch was at 11:00 a.m., and dinner was served between 4:00 and 5:00 p.m. The twice-a-day trip to the recreation yard was what inmates looked forward to most. They could play basketball or baseball, lift weights, play cards, or walk around the yard. Prisoners were sent to their cells at 8:00 p.m. Lights were out at 9:30 p.m., and the cell door would be locked until the morning. Guards would then walk around, making sure each cell was secured and inmates were accounted for. The same routine happened the next day, and every day after that.

For the first time in his life, Ron wanted to go to school, hoping to earn his high school diploma. Prison staff rejected his request. He needed to maintain a work assignment for six months before he could attend class. Ron's first job was working in a garment factory, where uniforms were made for prison guards and inmates throughout Michigan's correctional system. Lacking skills, Ron was given the task of sewing large canvas bags that inmates used for their soiled sheets. On his first day, a civilian supervisor showed Ron how to operate a "heavy-duty" sewing machine. On the second day, Ron was admonished by his supervisor for not keeping up with the assembly line. Not one to accept a reprimand, especially if he felt it was undeserved, Ron yelled at his boss, "Look, man, I haven't done this work before and I can't do it!"[10] He then kicked the machine.

Ron was given a new assignment that was even more alien to him than working in a factory. He was sent to Dalton Farms, one of five farms owned and operated by the prison. Located outside the prison wall, the farm featured a stockyard, a greenhouse, a cannery, and a vegetable garden. Although managed by civilians, the inmates worked as farmers. Animals such as pigs, cows, and chickens were raised and slaughtered on-site. The farms were productive collectively. Annually, the five farms were responsible for producing nearly 200,000 pounds of beef and pork, as well as two million gallons of pasteurized milk. It also grew 55,000 bushels of potatoes as well as cultivating tomatoes, eggplant, carrots, corn, and peas—all of which were used to feed prisoners at Jackson and the state's other correctional facilities. The farm was viewed as a model program for the prison. It not only brought down the prison's costs but also served as a form of rehabilitation, teaching "basic work values, such as responsibility of assigned chores, ingenuity and using one's hands."[11]

Some prisoners preferred working at Dalton, since it allowed them to be on the other side of the prison wall and was less dull than working in a factory. Being a newbie (and Black, since white inmates often received these preferential assignments), Ron was given the least desired job on the farm. At any other time of year, Ron would have been assigned to the stockyards, cleaning up animal feces. However, since it was late summer (and therefore harvest season), Ron was told to pick potatoes. A potato digger machine pulled the vegetable up to the surface so that it could be gathered and placed in a crate.

After his first day on the job, Ron was "covered with black muck." When he took a shower, that muck was still on him. It reminded him of his stint at Detroit Diesel, where he couldn't remove the grease from his body. Worse, his back was sore from the constant motion of bending up and down. The next morning, at breakfast, when the bus arrived at the farm, Ron refused to leave his seat. When a guard approached, Ron told him, "You might as well write me a ticket because I can't do this work; it's too hard. Besides, I ain't no farmer. I'm not gonna pick potatoes when I leave here, so why should I pick potatoes now?"[12]

Ron was sent to solitary confinement, also known as the Hole. The bed was a metal cot without springs, a mattress, or sheets. There were only two blankets: one to cover Ron, and the other placed underneath him as a sheet. The non-flushing toilet was bolted to the floor. No shoes, underwear, pajamas, soap, or even a toothbrush were allowed. (You could only brush your teeth if you had a visitor.) Showers were weekly, and the inmate was given a small roll of toilet paper that had to last a week. There was no access to the recreation yard. No television, no reading material. The only person the inmate saw all day was known as the "hall boy," who brought the inmate food twice a day and maybe smuggled him a cigarette.[13] Otherwise, the inmate one cell over might be the only other person willing to communicate with him (and in a whisper).

With nothing but time to spare, Ron spent his days inside his head, planning his next heist. He wanted to rip off an armored truck. His score at Dee's would pale in comparison. When the truck was leaving the local market to conduct a currency exchange on Mack and Van Dyke Avenues, he visualized it would stop at a traffic light over a utility hole that led to the city's sewer system. At that moment, Ron would climb through the utility hole to the surface, quickly light a stick of dynamite, and place it on the truck's undercarriage. Boom! The truck's bottom would explode, and cash would be disbursed everywhere. Ron would then swoop in, pile the money into a duffel bag, and take off.

It all seemed crystal clear—and then Ron realized the entire idea was ridiculous. This was exactly why he was in this hellhole: always looking for the easy way out.

"You fool! You dumb, fucking fool!" he thought to himself. "You're not doing yourself any good. All you're doing is keeping the prison people in jobs."[14]

Ron felt like he was at the end of the road. Isolated and with nothing on the outside to give him hope, he cried himself to sleep some nights—the tough kid from East Detroit now sobbing for his mother. He would later refer to this period in his life as the "most frightening thing in the world."[15] All of his hustles, lies, wheeling and dealing, stealing other people's money—it had amounted to complete isolation from the world.

Teetering on the edge, Ron had to make a painful choice. He could allow himself to go crazy. He could plan the details for his next robbery. Or, he could figure out how to adjust to prison; fighting it was a lost cause.

Yet it had to be on his terms. When prison officials asked if he wanted to come back to the farm, he refused. He preferred to stay in the Hole. As winter approached, though, he needed to figure out how to pass the time while keeping warm (and mentally sane). Cold and lonely, one day Ron found himself doing push-ups in his cell. The effects of heroin and his sedentary lifestyle left this once-gifted athlete sluggish and so weak that he had trouble finding the strength in his arms to make his body rise from the floor. His initial goal was to do twenty-five push-ups in a row without pausing. He couldn't even do ten before he was out of breath.

Gradually, Ron built up his strength—there was nothing distracting him. Soon, he could do fifteen push-ups without pausing, then twenty, and eventually twenty-five. Then he did a set of twenty-five sit-ups and twenty-five jumping jacks. He'd extend his goal to two sets, then three, then four sets a day of fifty push-ups, sit-ups, and jumping jacks. Ultimately, he could do four sets of one hundred push-ups, sit-ups, and jumping jacks in a single day.

The physical effects were obvious. Ron's chest expanded. His arm muscles were more pronounced. His upper body was getting stronger. He started working the bottom half of his body. Sitting down on his cot, he moved his legs in a bicycle-riding motion, over and over until he couldn't move them anymore. Something else happened, too—his sleep improved. Falling asleep had proved difficult in the Hole, screams from other inmates, the external noise of cells opening and closing, and the discomfort of lying on a metal cot made it all but unbearable. These exercises tired Ron out to the point that he was so exhausted he could sleep through anything. He kept challenging himself. Within his cell, he maximized the minimal space he was given. "I could take three steps, turn around, take three steps in the opposite direction, and turn again. I walked like that for two or three hours every day just to pass the time," he remembered vividly.[16]

Ron's physical conditioning had a marked impact on his attitude. Once authorities recognized that he was less belligerent, Ron was released from the Hole and assigned to a cell, one that had natural light. He was also allowed to read, smoke cigarettes, have a toothbrush, and—most importantly—receive visitors. His mother Georgia would travel seventy-five miles from Detroit by Greyhound bus, which took three hours each way since there were stops along the route. From the station in Detroit, she would pick up a bus at seven o'clock in the morning. Once Georgia arrived at the prison, she would go through a security clearance and then be escorted to the waiting room. Since there were only enough seats for 100 visitors for a prison population of 5,000, it would take hours before she could see Ron. When a seat opened, Georgia would see her son for an hour before she had to depart for Detroit and get back in time for her job, where she was working as a cook at a Howard Johnson's restaurant. "She talked to me about doing right. I should not be doing these things," Ron recalled. His mother was "totally upset [and] beat up from it."[17]

Georgia visited him four or five times a month. If she didn't work on a Sunday, John and Gerald would accompany her on the visit. Not wanting her to expend her precious time or limited funds, Ron urged his mother to visit less frequently.

In a move that he would later regret, Ron had written a letter to Gus Harrison, the director of the state's Department of Corrections, while in solitary confinement. He complained about the harsh treatment that he had received (according to prison policy, inmates were supposed to be locked up for "no more than 10 days").[18] Harrison never responded. Ron wasn't sure if the letter ever made it to him; it probably didn't, since prison officials reviewed mail sent by inmates. But not long after, Harrison visited Jackson and happened to walk by Ron's cell. Seizing a rare opportunity for a face-to-face interaction with the state's top prison official, Ron asked Harrison if he had received his letter. Harrison replied in the negative. According to Ron, once Harrison left the facility, five to six prison guards charged at him in his cell. At 6 feet and 200 pounds, Ron was a formidable opponent. He reacted quickly and used his head as a battering ram into a guard's chest, which not only knocked over the lead guard but also protected Ron's head. He then started swinging his fists, trying to keep the guard's batons off him. It helped, but Ron couldn't overcome their numbers and was so severely beaten that he could barely move his body.

Charged with disobedience, Ron was dragged to what was known as the Slammer, which was worse than the Hole. When the heavy steel door to his new cell locked, Ron found himself in the most confined space the prison had on its premises. There was no light of any kind. There was not even a bed to sleep on. This cell was half the size of Ron's in the Hole. All he could do, he remembered, was "sit, hour after hour, playing with your lower lip."[19]

After some time—it's not clear how long Ron remained in the Slammer—he was moved back to the Hole, where he spent three and a half more months in solitary confinement.

In December 1970, Ron was released into the prison's general population. As he made his way around, he recognized a few of the guys from his neighborhood, whom he thought had been overseas fighting in Vietnam. He then realized that his absence back home was explained in similar terms.

As tough as Ron thought he was, solitary confinement had taken a toll on him. He grew more fearful as he mingled with his fellow convicts, not knowing if or when he would be attacked by them, many of whom had nothing to lose. "I was scared," Ron recalled.

Like at other medium- or high-security prisons, rape was rampant at SPSM. It was happening in the cells, showers, and the recreation yard, usually underneath the bleachers. Not long after his release from the Hole, an inmate wandered into Ron's cell, and he could tell where it was heading. Ron decided to play along, informing his uninvited guest to meet him at the gym area during recreation time. When the unsuspected man approached Ron in the yard, under the assumption they were going to have sex, Ron beat him severely with a baseball bat. Word spread: "Don't mess with Ron LeFlore." His plan worked.

Another lesson Ron learned in the prison culture was to never get involved in someone else's conflict. One night, after the lights were out, Ron was staying up late. He noticed an inmate walking by his cell and recognized him. The inmate stopped at a cell near Ron's and poured flammable glue on the man lying in bed. He then dropped a lit match, and flames immediately appeared. Screams could be heard throughout the five-story facility that evening. "He was burned so badly the skin was rolling off him," Ron remembered.[20] He knew who had committed this heinous crime, but fearing for his own safety, he kept his mouth shut.

Ron followed the same protocol when he witnessed another act of violence. While receiving a haircut at the prison barbershop, an inmate wearing a coat approached the chair next to his. The inmate pulled out of his coat a butcher knife with a twelve-inch blade and proceeded to stab another prisoner within an arm's distance of Ron. "I'm not going to run, I'm not going to say anything," Ron remembered his reaction. "I'm just getting my haircut. The guy cutting my hair kept cutting my hair. He [the murderer] wasn't paying attention to us. He stabbed the guy 27 times."[21]

As the one-year anniversary of his incarceration approached, Ron was determined to meet the requirements for an early release. Although he was not eligible for a parole hearing for two more years, he knew full well the need to establish the groundwork for his rehabilitation. If he failed to demonstrate that he was capable of functioning in the outside world as a law-abiding citizen, he would be required to complete his five-year minimum sentence at the very least.

Whatever job the prison officials assigned him, Ron was now willing to accept it, even if that meant working on the farm and scooping up animal waste all day. To his relief, however, Ron was sent to the textile factory, making bedsheets and pillowcases. Having been kept in solitary for so long, Ron was uncharacteristically too talkative on the job and was let go. Despite his desire to work in the kitchen, there were no openings available. He then sought to earn a high school diploma, knowing that it would reflect well during his parole hearing, but he hadn't worked long enough on any job to enter the program.

Fortunately for Ron, there was a job working at the prison's gym. The hours were long—6:30 a.m. to 9:30 p.m.—but it afforded him the opportunity to play football, baseball, and basketball. To his delight, he encountered Reggie Harding, the seven-foot Detroit playground legend, on the basketball court. An Eastern High School graduate, Harding was the first player from high school ever to go straight to the NBA. He was supposed to be the next Wilt Chamberlain. He had the height and the talent, but not the right attitude. Harding had been out of the league since 1967 and was serving time for robbery (to score drugs, he had broken into people's homes by lifting his partner to the second story). Ron played against the seven-footer, who no longer had the speed or coordination he once possessed. When Harding went up for a jump shot, Ron blocked it—and several others, earning a prison-wide reputation for his superior athleticism. Nevertheless, when an assignment in the kitchen opened up, he took it.

Thanks to his mom's efforts when he was a child, Ron enjoyed working in the kitchen. The once-defiant prisoner was now happily reporting there at 3:00 a.m., making eggs and French toast, cooking bacon, and brewing coffee. Ron had matured, but he still had a drug problem. Although he kept up his rigorous exercise routine, he continued using illicit substances. Because of its scarcity, he stopped using heroin. Instead, he took mescaline and tried psychedelic drugs like mushrooms. And, he was still scheming. When Ron was promoted to second cook from line cook, one of the privileges of the new job was having access to the pantry, where the next day's meal ingredients were located. As he recalled, "I would go to the commissary and get the supplies we needed in the kitchen—and anything else I wanted for myself."[22]

Since illegal drugs like marijuana, cocaine, or heroin were hard to obtain and costly, spud juice was the next best option. A moonshine for convicts, it was made of sugar, tomato puree, water, and yeast. Ron would make it in a six-ounce jar using the surplus of ingredients he now had access to. Although it was hardly an ideal concoction, it did what a prisoner needed it to do: "breaking up the monotony of your sentence," fellow inmate Napolun Birdsong remembered.[23] A jar would cost a cellmate five packs of cigarettes, the prison's "traditional bargaining currency."[24] Ron sold so much of it that he was earning more cigarettes than he needed. The risks were minimal; if he got caught, he would most likely receive a warning.

By the summer of 1971, Ron was finally eligible to take classes that could earn him a GED (General Educational Development), the equivlant of a high school diploma. When he earned high marks in English, history, and math, his teacher placed him in more advanced courses. Ron was also attending weekly church services. He did what he knew he needed to do in order to get released early. When he was told that playing on one of the prison's highly competitive sports teams was highly valued by the parole board, he signed up. Little did he realize that his whole life was about to change.

5

Twinkle Toes LeFlore

The odds of becoming a Major League Baseball (MLB) player are incredibly slim. Among the approximately 100,000 high school and college baseball players who were actively playing for their school in the early 1970s, no more than 0.5 percent of them would be drafted by an MLB club. Being drafted did not mean you were playing for the team on day one, either. It meant the club was betting that, someday, if at all, after you've spent years navigating the minor league ecosystem—where you travel by bus (not chartered flights), sleep in cheap motels, are paid below minimum wage, have health insurance that only applies during the season, and have zero labor protections—you might be called up one day to sit in an MLB team's dugout and wait for the manager to send you in to pinch-hit or pinch-run. Ten days later, the player you replaced because of an injury would be back in the lineup, and you'd be sent back to the minors—and waiting for your time to be called up again. Would there even be another time? The odds were not in your favor.

In 1973, there were some 1,000 MLB players who were on a team roster during the season, the vast majority of whom were not concerned about losing their spot to a bush leaguer. Instead, about 10 percent were endangered of losing their place on the team roster due to performance and another, say, 5 percent due to injury.

During that same year, there were over 5,000 minor league baseball players (not including those playing for clubs not affiliated with MLB teams), every one of them competing against their teammates for a coveted roster spot. They would normally start in the Rookie leagues and then advance to Single-A, followed by Double-A. If they showed enough potential, they would move up to Triple-A, the top level of play before the majors. It was at this level that a player had a remote possibility of entering the parent organization.*

The odds of a minor league baseball player securing a spot on an MLB team were only a shade better than the odds of the same player trying to enter the minors. Out of 100 randomly selected ballplayers who have been drafted and are actively playing for a Major League affiliate, ninety-nine of them will never make it. They'll either quit, get injured, or not be resigned. Many of these players, since they were five or six years old, have walked and breathed baseball. The sacrifices they and their families have made in terms of time and money are incalculable. And for those who do make it, a sustainable career is even more exceptional.

Ron LeFlore, who had never played catch with his father nor played on a Little League team or for his high school baseball team, achieved the unattainable. Much of the folklore behind his rapid rise to the major leagues is focused exclusively on his unmatched talents. That is partly true. Talent can only take you so far. At some point, though, it's about who you know. For Ron, it was a fellow inmate named Jimmy Karalla, a Mafia enforcer and friend of a bar owner who happened to be close with the manager of the Detroit Tigers.

James "Jimmy" Karalla Jr. was born in 1935 at Detroit's St. John Hospital and raised in the East Side of the city. His father, James Sr.—known in the neighborhood as Cokey—had deep ties to organized crime, dating back to the 1920s during the Prohibition era. When Jimmy was three, Cokey was behind bars, serving time on a federal drug charge at Leavenworth Prison in Kansas.

---

*The figures are based on the twenty-four MLB teams (with forty-man rosters) in 1974 while accounting for extra players who were brought up from the minor leagues during the season. Regarding the minors, according to baseballreference.com, there were 131 teams affiliated with an MLB club in 1973. This excludes the independent leagues, who also fielded approximately forty players on each team's roster.

A decade later, after being released, Cokey was charged as an accessory to murder. Involved in a racketeering scheme, he had tipped off Mafia loan sharks about a gambler who was in debt to them. The killers fired five shots into the victim, a 35-year-old male who had a wife and two children. The victim owed $140. Not only was Cokey a poor role model for his son but he also left him fatherless.

Although Jimmy Karalla never went to juvenile hall, he was already "partying" at thirteen years old. If there was any hope of escaping the Mafia lifestyle, sports would be his ticket. He was a "tremendous athlete," his son James Karalla III recalled, but his grades prevented him from becoming a star.[1] Karalla attended Catholic Central for only two years before dropping out because of his academic performance. Public high school offered even less structure, and in the absence of parental guidance, it was only a matter of time before he followed in his father's footsteps.

Karalla would spend the next two decades running with Detroit's notorious Giacalone Mafia family, led by brothers Anthony and Vito (the same family Ron had tried to rip off by attempting to open the brothers' safe). Karalla was involved in a lot of "shady dealings." "He was out to make a buck and didn't care about the laws," recalled Mel Butsicaris Jr., who knew of the mobster.[2] Even if Karalla wanted to escape the underworld, his son later noted, he couldn't: "Once you're in, you're never really out."[3]

Throughout the 1950s and 1960s, the Giacalone brothers had managed to avoid jail even though they had been arrested and charged multiple times; they were never convicted. But that would change. In 1963, during congressional testimony before a senate committee, it was revealed by the US Department of Justice that the brothers were, in fact, Detroit's "Mafia chiefs."[4] Five years later, in 1968, a federal, state, and local law enforcement task force had caught and finally convicted the Giacalone brothers. Anthony and Vito, along with Karalla and two other defendants, were charged with "corrupting, intimidating, and destroying witnesses" and "conspiring to extort with threats and violence."[5] A sixth defendant never made it to the courtroom. His body was discovered in a car trunk parked at the Atlanta airport. He had been shot in the head.

Working hand in hand with the Department of Justice, Michigan law enforcement charged the five men for their involvement in a "juice loan," a loan made with inordinate interest.[6] Although the principal loan amount was $1,500, the victim had paid $5,000 interest and still owed the Giacalone brothers. For his involvement, Karalla was sentenced to serve four to twenty years at SPSM.

Karalla's son, James III, was never close with his father. He was nine years old when his dad was sent to Jackson. His mother had kicked him out of their home years earlier. They visited him in prison, though, and Karalla kept in touch with his son through monthly letters. In one of those letters, Karalla told James III about "a kid here, who is a phenomenal athlete. . . . Watch out for this guy. If he's going to make it, he's going to make it big."[7]

At first, sports at SPSM was another scam for Ron. Having spent a year in prison, he was learning how the system worked. He realized that athletes had privileges that other inmates didn't. If you played for a varsity team, it would often result in you moving to the Honor Block, created by Perry Johnson when he was a deputy warden and established as a reward for positive behavior. Honor Block residents had access to better jobs, a television in their cell, a washer and dryer, hot water, and the capability to freely move around more frequently throughout the day. It also better positioned Ron for something else: his freedom. "Playing sports helped them [himself included] meet the right people, the warden, the important staff people, the people you needed if you were looking for a parole recommendation," Ron pointed out.[8]

Within the fifty-three acres of SPSM, there was a large recreation yard with green grass, pedestrian pathways, a swimming pool, and playing fields. During the day, there could be as many as 1,000 men in that yard, walking, congregating, talking, and playing cards. It was almost as if, one observer recalled, you were in a "city park on a busy afternoon, except that the park is rather seedy and there are no women or children to be seen."[9] Among the sports amenities were a football field, handball courts, weights, a jogging track, two softball fields, and a baseball diamond—enough opportunities to afford inmates their sport of choice.

Ron took up softball. He tried out and made the prison's varsity team. He noticed right away that there was tension between the manager and his players. After a while, Ron was tired of "standing there and listening to these guys arguing all the time."[10] The team was losing a lot more than winning. But the worst part was being groped by a teammate. "The son of a bitch," Ron recalled, "was always grabbing guys by the pants, trying to feel them up."[11]

Softball was out. Ron channeled his focus on football, the only sport that he had previous experience with as part of an organized team (though short-lived).

"Ron was, by far, my most talented player," prison athletic director Kermit Smith said.[12] It was Smith who brought organized football to Jackson that year. A former running back and linebacker at Michigan State University, Smith tapped into the resources of his alma mater. He contacted his former coach and a teammate to see if they could contribute their surplus sports equipment, which they did.

On the prison's football team, Ron played running back, punter, kickoff returner, and cornerback. He shared the backfield with two other men, both talented in their own right and both sentenced for murder. There were multiple football teams at Jackson, and they were racially segregated. One team, the Vikings, was all white; the rest were all Black. The games were highly competitive, causing players to leave the field with broken bones in addition to the expected aches and pains. But there was a far more ominous consequence of the competition. A player on the Vikings complained that when his team was on the field, it felt more like "small race wars."[13] During the playoffs, a player pulled a knife on an opponent in response to being hit too hard. After that, prison officials decided to terminate tackle football and change it to flag football.

Whoever was watching or playing in the game always noticed "Twinkle Toes LeFlore."[14] Richard Herr, a former player on the Vikings, recalled, "Make no mistake about it, he was fast, and damn near impossible to catch once he got the ball and had a little bit of running room."[15] Players would have to double-team Ron in order to prevent him from scoring. He was so fast and proficient that when his team's quarterback was in trouble, Ron instructed him to "throw the ball in the air as far as you can, and I'll run under it" and catch it—which he did, more than once.[16]

When the prison formed an All-Star team made up of the best players and competed against visiting teams like Hillsdale College, Grand Rapids Junior College (now Grand Rapids Community College), or even a semipro team, it was clear to athletic director Smith that "Ron was good enough to play in the NFL."[17] In fact, Smith contacted his former coach, Duffy Daugherty, who had retired from Michigan State and was being interviewed for a coaching job with the Buffalo Bills. The coach promised to give Ron a tryout if he got the job. He didn't. When the football coach from Hillsdale saw Ron score against his team, he told Ron (unaware that he was a high school dropout) that he would offer him a football scholarship once he was paroled.

There wasn't a specific reason why Ron started playing baseball. He might have been attracted to the sport because baseball players received more practice time than other athletes and had more food choices. Or, maybe he was simply looking for another activity to suppress his boredom. It certainly wasn't for his previous experience. He had "never hit a hardball with a real baseball bat" prior to trying out for the prison team.[18]

It was the summer of 1971. Ron had already served eighteen months of his sentence. Since leaving the Hole, he had worked a series of jobs, attended school, and become involved with prison athletics, positioning himself for an early release. Baseball, football, softball—they were simply viewed by Ron as a means to exit Jackson. He did not want to end up as one of the "guys with [prison] numbers that dated back" to a previous decade. "What kind of life can that be?"[19]

When it came to baseball, there was probably no other activity that brought the inmates and guards together like America's national pastime. Like his football teammates, those playing baseball were in prison for various offenses. Some had been sentenced to ten to twenty years for armed robbery, the pitcher was doing ten to twenty for rape, and a second baseman and infielder were both serving life sentences for murder.

As talented as Ron was athletically, his limitations in baseball were noticeable. He could run the bases well and had the strength to hit the ball deep into the outfield and beyond, but he didn't have the proper techniques when it came to sliding into a base or strategically tracking down a fly ball when playing the outfield. He also didn't have the instinctual knowledge of which base to throw to when two men were on and there was only one out. And, he wasn't familiar with hand signals. Having not grown up participating or even watching the sport, Ron was unfamiliar with the intricacies of baseball. It would take him years to learn it. Despite his deficiencies, however, Ron's performance on the diamond was nothing short of mesmerizing.

"I could see he had natural abilities," observed athletic director Smith, who had also been a former high school baseball All-Star.[20] Prisoner Napolun Birdsong, who was serving a ten-year sentence for breaking and entering, was both a reporter for the prison's newspaper, *The Spectator*, and the announcer for the baseball games. Birdsong always injected humor when he was broadcasting games, hoping to keep his audience engaged. "[Ron] started stealing bases when he started stealing cars," he would joke. Or, if someone hit a towering home run, he would say, "There goes another ball out on parole."[21] Whenever Ron played, he noticed his "exceptional athletic ability."[22] "He had great hand-eye coordination like Henry Aaron," Birdsong still remembered five decades after seeing Ron first play in the prison yard. He had great speed and power—so much so that he'd "snapped the ball over the wall" with little effort.[23]

With an enormous learning curve ahead of him, Ron practiced every afternoon. He was so raw in the early days, but his performance was noticeably better with each passing day. The entire team was helping him improve: "I'd go to the field we had, and guys would hit me balls. . . . I'd take grounders, I'd catch flies. . . . I started loving baseball a lot."[24] Ron was learning the game's fundamentals, such as timing a fly ball in the outfield, hitting pitches besides fastballs, and monitoring the pitcher before stealing a base.

Since they were locked up, there were no away games. Visiting squads—semipro teams, local colleges, or intramural-level players—would see how fast Ron was on the basepaths. A pitcher from Lansing once recalled how Ron had "what appeared to be a single"; however, when the pitcher turned around to see where the runner was, he found Ron standing on third base.[25] After the game, managers would come up to Ron, curious about where he had played prior to prison. They "couldn't believe" he had never played the sport until he'd arrived at Jackson.[26] Neither could the team's manager, Jimmy Karalla.

Ron wasn't someone who developed close relationships, but Karalla was an exception. Athletic, tough, and knowledgeable about the game, Karalla, Ron believed, had his best interests at heart and could truly help him as a player. When Jimmy wasn't hitting grounders to Ron, teaching him how to slide properly to avoid future injuries, or clocking his speed, they'd chat about what it took to play in the majors. "The more he talked about it, the more I thought about it. I began believing that maybe I could play professional ball when I got out of prison, so I began watching games on TV, trying to learn as much as possible."[27] And it paid off.

Ron became the most dominant player in the prison league. During his first season, he was voted Rookie of the Year. The following season, he won a batting championship and earned the Most Valuable Player Award. While playing at Jackson, he was hitting anywhere between .409 and .569 during the forty-game season. Essentially, he was getting a hit every other time he was at bat, unprecedented for any new player.

And it wasn't just Ron's teammates and manager who were supporting him. *The Spectator* consistently mentioned Ron's supremacy. "Twinkle Toes Bosco Homers Again," one headline ran in the Sports section.[28] Ron, who had put on nearly thirty pounds in prison before playing baseball (but would ultimately slim down), was given the nickname "Bosco" because of his hefty stature, reminiscent of the Bosco bear in the 1960s chocolate milk commercials. "Twinkle Toes" was in reference to Ron's speed. Eventually, someone put the two names together, and with some help from *The Spectator*, it stuck.

Visiting teams had heard in advance about the standout player. When a semipro team from Muskegon visited the prison, its manager contacted the Milwaukee Brewers, whom he scouted for, inquiring whether they might be interested in Ron. The Brewers declined.

Encouraged by the praise he had received, Ron contacted Detroit Tigers general manager Jim Campbell by mail, requesting a tryout. A month later, he received the standard rejection letter. According to Ron, a team representative explained that tryouts were for invited players only. Understandably, teams were hesitant to take on an ex-convict. Not only would they take on the risky behavior of a former inmate, posing a threat to teammates or themselves, but the club would also be responsible for parole conditions and held liable if they were violated. Yet, there was precedent for former inmates to succeed as professional athletes.

Two decades before Ron set foot in SPSM, eighteen-year-old Arkansas native Sonny Liston was serving five years for armed robbery at Missouri State Penitentiary in Jefferson City. A prison chaplain, who was also the institution's athletic director, observed Liston's exceptional toughness when he beat up three white gang leaders, who were lying "unconscious" on the concrete floor.[29] The chaplain encouraged him to channel his aggression in the prison's boxing program. Liston was a natural in the ring. When word had spread to the outside world, a local heavyweight boxer got wind of Liston and challenged him to a fight. In the fourth round, Liston's opponent told the referee to stop the fight: "He's going to kill me."[30] The prison chaplain knew boxing was Liston's only chance to turn his life around once he was released. He spoke with the parole board, and after two years behind bars, Liston was released and would go on to become the heavyweight champion of the world.

Liston was not the only ex-convict to achieve athletic prominence. After serving time in the penal system, Detroit's native sons, boxer Alvin "Blue" Lewis and football's Jess Phillips, also had notable careers in their chosen fields.

Lewis was seventeen years old when he was sentenced to Jackson for twenty to thirty-five years for a fatal mugging. While in prison, he grew six inches to six feet four, making him a menacing figure in the boxing ring. After winning his fifth championship bout at Jackson, a local promoter watched him fight and secured him an early release. Lewis later fought in the heavyweight division, experiencing moderate success. His claim to fame was twofold: as Muhammad Ali's one-time opponent (he was knocked out in the eleventh round) and as Ali's sparring partner.

Phillips was attending Michigan State University when he was caught forging a check and sentenced to eighteen months to four years at Jackson. The fleet-footed running back served four months before he was paroled. He was drafted by the Cincinnati Bengals in the fourth round and went on to a decade-long NFL career.

America's national pastime probably had the longest and most fruitful relationship with those who were behind bars. During the first half of the twentieth century, prison baseball teams were often a rural town's sole source of entertainment. Since there was no television, games were open to the public (under tight security), and fans would watch barnstorming semipro and professional teams take on the talented but locked-up men in prison garb. Among the players, a few were worthy of a tryout, including Edwin "Alabama" Pitts.

In 1929, nineteen-year-old Pitts held up a grocery store in New York City and stole seventy-five dollars (equivalent to over $1,000 today) before getting caught. Sentenced to New York's notorious Sing Sing Correctional Facility, he played for the prison's baseball team. When Pitts arrived, Sing Sing had fielded a formidable baseball team, occasionally attracting as its opponent the New York Yankees, who featured future Hall of Famers Babe Ruth and Lou Gehrig. Upon his release, Pitts was offered a contract by the Albany Senators, a minor league baseball team affiliated with the Cincinnati Reds and the Pittsburgh Pirates. News of the ex-convict's signing was frowned upon by the league, and Pitts was ruled ineligible. Following public backlash, however, he was reinstated and played a few seasons, but he never made it to the major leagues.

Twenty-two-year-old Jim Rivera was in the army in 1944 when he was arrested for rape and sent to Atlanta Federal Penitentiary. A boxer and a baseball player, Rivera played on the prison's baseball team and caught the attention of the local minor league club, the Atlanta Crackers, whose management worked with officials to have him paroled after serving five years. Rivera made his Major League debut in 1952 and played for eight seasons, including a World Series appearance and a stolen base title.

And then there was William James "Gates" Brown of the Detroit Tigers. Brown was born in 1939 in Crestline, Ohio, ninety miles southwest of Cleveland. A standout athlete in high school, Brown gravitated toward football. He likely would have played at the college level if he had stayed out of trouble. When he was eighteen, Brown was arrested for breaking and entering. He was sentenced to prison and served twenty-two months at the Ohio State Reformatory in Mansfield.

While behind bars, the five-foot, eleven-inch, 225-pound athlete swapped his football spikes for a bat and glove. The coach was a prison guard and was in "awe of his [Brown's] raw ability with the bat."[31] While Brown honed his skills on the diamond, the coach contacted several MLB clubs, hoping to secure a tryout for his star player. The Tigers, who were in the middle of the

GATES BROWN

William James "Gates" Brown, the veteran Tiger pinch-hitter, also was incarcerated prior to becoming a professional baseball player. (Rucker Archive, Society for American Baseball Research)

standings by the late 1950s and had only one African American on their roster (Larry Doby), responded, sending scout Pat Mullin to see him. Brown was signed, though he had nine more months to serve on his sentence. The Tigers' organization met with the parole board, who agreed to release Brown early. Spending four seasons in the minors, Brown was called up in June 1963. He played for the Tigers for more than a decade, including on the 1968 World Series championship team. He's regarded as one of the game's best pinch hitters.

If Ron LeFlore was to follow a trajectory similar to Brown's, then he was going to need more help than talent alone.

Rising to the occasion, Jimmy Karalla contacted his well-connected friend and bar owner, Jimmy Butsicaris. "I'm writing this letter in respect to the information given you earlier about a black ball player in here, the kid really has a lot of potential Jim, or believe me I wouldn't bother you with it," wrote Karalla.[32] Receiving no written response, Karalla used the phone and "kept calling, kept calling" Butsicaris at his bar, known as the Lindell AC. "I got a ballplayer here that's pretty good. Come take a look at him," he'd tell his friend.[33]

Throughout 1972 and 1973, Karalla called and wrote to Butsicaris obsessively, hoping he would do him the favor of contacting Detroit Tigers manager Billy Martin. Martin was a close friend of Butsicaris, who served as the best man at Martin's second wedding (he was married four times). He was also a frequent patron at the Lindell.

Jimmy Butsicaris and his brother, Johnny, were born in the early 1920s and raised in Detroit's Lower East Side by Greek immigrant parents. Following the Japanese attack on Pearl Harbor on December 7, 1941, the brothers enlisted in the army. When they returned from the war, Johnny, a decorated pilot, enrolled in college, studying aeronautical engineering, while Jimmy was "bumming around from one job to another," to the chagrin of his father, Meleti.

"Whattya doing?" Meleti asked once. "You still got a few bucks left [from his card winnings on the ship back to the states], why you give it to me and we'll go downtown and find some joint!"[34]

In 1949, with the help of Meleti, Jimmy, "a gregarious, fun-loving and a self-professed street fighter," convinced his introverted and bookish brother to join him in leasing the ground-floor bar in the seedy, four-story Lindell Hotel in downtown Detroit on Cass Avenue and Bagley Street. Since all of their money was tied up in the bar's operations, there wasn't anything left for a new sign. Thus, the brothers decided to use the hotel's name, the Lindell.

Only blocks away from Briggs Stadium (home to the Tigers and the NFL's Detroit Lions) and Olympia Stadium, where the Detroit Red Wings hockey team played, the bar had two sets of crowds. There was the lunchtime gang, made up of the city's automobile executives who downed martinis for their midday meal. That was Johnny's shift. Jimmy worked nights, when the bar was livelier, attracting a more diverse clientele that often included players in town from the opposing sports teams. Since the unspoken rule for visiting teams was that players didn't drink in the same bars as their coaches (who drank at the fashionable hotels), the players needed somewhere to go. They discovered the Lindell, which was nearby, off the beaten path, and dimly lit, making it the ideal night spot for professional athletes wanting to let their guard down and kick back a few drinks.

Within a few years of opening, the Lindell became a haven for visiting teams from all sports, attracting such notables as Mickey Mantle and Wilt Chamberlain as well as entertainers such as comedian Milton Berle and singer Dean Martin. Politicians (including Mayor Jerry Cavanagh), gamblers, writers, and even members of Detroit's infamous Mafia were also known to patronize the joint.

By the end of the 1950s, the neighborhood where the Lindell was located, on the edge of the downtown's Skid Row, was getting worse for business. The building was slated to be razed in 1962, a result of urban renewal. The Butsicaris brothers had to move quickly if they wanted to keep their bar humming along. Fortunately, with financial assistance from Alex Karras, a defensive tackle for the Detroit Lions and one of their regulars, they moved the Lindell to Michigan and Cass Avenues, which was even closer to where the Tigers played (now called Tiger Stadium).

Even though the bar was no longer part of the Lindell Hotel, the brothers kept the name but added the letters "AC." According to local folklore, *Detroit*

News sports columnist Doc Greene, a frequent patron, was spending so much time at the Lindell (since it was where all of his sources were at the end of the day) that he once told his bosses that he was at the Lindell AC. There was only one other AC in town: the exclusive Detroit Athletic Club, an urban country club for automobile executives and the city's political elite. It became an inside joke among bar regulars. So when the brothers changed the bar's location, they added the "AC" to the business's name as an ode to Doc.

Even with a new name, the bar didn't miss a beat, serving as *the* spot for Detroit fans on game day and a refuge for professional athletes and other celebrities. On October 10, 1968, the night the Tigers became World Series champions for the first time in twenty-five years, beating the Yankees at home, the Lindell AC was (not surprisingly) where the after-party occurred. The team took over the bar and poured free booze for patrons all night long. Johnny Butsicaris said it was akin to the celebration of "New Year's Eve on Times Square."[35]

But it was Billy Martin who made sure the Lindell AC would become America's most famous sports bar. When Martin told Jimmy that the bar needed something to spark it up—his exact words were, "Why don't you decorate this dump!"—he suggested replicating a small sports bar in New York City that put "bats and balls and photographs . . . on display."[36] Jimmy liked the idea, especially since Martin offered to help procure the items. It was a hit among the patrons and even became a mark of distinction to have your photograph on the wall of the bar. The Lindell AC was now a bar *and* a museum, becoming the "most popular sport celebrity hang out in the country."[37]

To Jimmy Butsicaris's annoyance, Karalla wasn't giving up. This was his best (and probably his only) connection to the MLB. He continued to write the bar owner letters and call him collect, enough that "his phone bill was getting him very upset."[38] Even the mail carrier was growing suspicious of all the letters being sent from SPSM. It was time for Butsicaris to talk to his friend, Billy Martin.

As a player, the five-foot, ten-inch, 165-pound "rail-thin" Billy Martin, a native of Berkeley, California, was never going to hit like his Yankee teammate and drinking buddy Mickey Mantle. Being part of a winning dynasty—the Pinstripes won five World Series titles while he was on the team—had its own perks, and Billy was fine with that. If only he could stay out of trouble. The team's general manager had warned him: "No fighting, no trouble," or else. But Billy was a "battler who never backed away."[39] He couldn't control his temper. After seven seasons with the Yankees, following a dustup at New York City's famous Copacabana nightclub, Martin was traded to the Kansas City Athletics. The trade triggered a downward spiral for Martin, who spent his final five years in the majors playing for six different teams.

For most players, that would be the end of the line. Perhaps a coaching gig here and there, and a slot at the Yankees' old-timers game. But for Billy Martin, baseball was in his blood. If he couldn't continue as a player, he'd find another way to stay engaged.

When he arrived in Detroit in 1971, he had one season of managerial experience, which was with the 1969 Minnesota Twins. He took a small-market, struggling club to the playoffs in a single season, but his gruffness didn't sit well with the owner. Maybe he should have avoided getting into a highly publicized fistfight with his pitcher at the Lindell AC. Or, maybe he should have allowed Hubert Humphrey, former vice president of the United States (and former mayor of Minneapolis), to come down to the locker room and visit with the players following a loss. But Martin didn't care who it was; it was his team, and his rules prevailed. No celebrations after a loss. That move didn't sit well with his boss.

After one season with the Twins, Billy Martin was out of baseball for the first time since his career had begun in 1946. Having spent the 1970 season adrift, Martin jumped at his next job offer with the lowly Detroit Tigers.

Although it had only been two years since the Tigers were champions, the team quickly went into decline. Their star pitcher Denny McLain, baseball's last thirty-game winner, was caught up in a gambling scandal and was no longer with the club. The team's heavy hitters and gate attractions, Al Kaline (destined for the Hall of Fame) and Norm Cash, were in their mid-thirties by then, and their bodies were showing it. There were no up-and-comers in the farm system to offer immediate relief, and life in the city had only gotten worse following the deadly riots.

"Most of baseball had given up on the Tigers, and most of the country had given up on Detroit," wrote Bill Pennington, a *New York Times* reporter and Billy Martin biographer. "The city's baseball team was seen as representative of the city itself—scarred and withering."[40] The riot hastened white flight, which further disrupted essential services, leaving Detroit's once-bustling streets void of economic activity, further crushing Motor City and those left behind, especially its African American residents. One out of four Black residents living in Detroit were unemployed, nearly twice as many as white residents. Conditions would only get worse. And so would the Tigers, if not for their new manager.

In the lead-up to the 1971 season, Billy Martin went out of his way to get to know his players. During a trip to Dallas, he not only saw his former teammate Mickey Mantle but also connected with first baseman Norm Cash, who spent the offseason serving as a vice president of a local bank in Fort Worth. Martin also played a role in the acquisition of the Spanish-speaking Aurelio Rodríguez, who would become one of the franchise's best defensive third basemen.

In his first season as manager, Martin took the 1971 Tigers, who had ended up fourth in the American League East division (out of six teams) the previous season, to a second-place finish. The following season, he pushed his team even harder. The Tigers captured the division title, beating the "invincible" Orioles.[41] They made it to the postseason for the first time since 1968. Unlike that year, where they had gone on to win the World Series, Martin's team was an older version of that championship squad. The '72 Tigers lost in the playoffs to the Oakland Athletics, who would win it all that season.

"The success of that season did not come without a cost," Tigers historian Todd Masters observed. "The feeling by many at the time was that Martin had squeezed everything out of the club and a rebuilding job needed to be started before the team got too old."[42]

In baseball, getting old meant two things: a lack of speed, and players who were more prone to injury. Both of these realities afflicted the 1973 Tigers. To score runs, for example, the team was dependent on hitting home runs, since base hits would rarely be stretched for a double. When players got on base, opposing pitchers weren't concerned about anyone stealing; they'd be caught before starting their slide. They were, without exception, the slowest team in the major leagues. They were desperate for speed, but how far would they go to find it?

6

The Tryout

Ernie Harwell wanted to do something for Detroit's underserved community. The Tigers' beloved play-by-play radio broadcaster was a lifelong baseball fan who knew at an early age that the only way he would ever make it to the major leagues was through a notepad or a microphone. A native of Atlanta, Harwell, who would have the distinction of being the only broadcaster ever traded for a baseball player, came up with the idea for the Tigers to develop a goodwill tour. Politicians had done it. Other sports teams had done it. Why couldn't the Tigers?

It was 1972, and Motor City was still healing from the 1967 riots that had sent it into a downward spiral. The team needed to reingratiate themselves to Detroiters, in particular its non-white fanbase, who seemed to be the only ones left in Detroit proper; most white households had moved to the suburbs. Although the team had participated in inner-city school visits in the past, Harwell wanted to do something different. He recruited Lew Matlin, the Tigers' director of community affairs, and they came up with the idea of a team visit to the state prison.* They immediately thought of bringing along

---

*In Ron's memoir, *Breakout* (1978), co-written with Jim Hawkins of the *Detroit Free Press*, the sports reporter claims that the idea stemmed from the prison's athletic director. In Ernie Harwell's autobiography, *Tuned to Baseball* (1985), Harwell takes credit for coming up with the goodwill tour, including the team visit to the state prison.

pinch hitter Gates Brown, who had been incarcerated prior to becoming a professional ballplayer. "We felt that the prisoners could relate to Gates and would enjoy hearing him," Harwell recalled.[1]

There was one obstacle, the same obstacle that was omnipresent whenever an idea was proposed that involved any aspect of the Tigers' day-to-day operations: General Manager Jim Campbell. They knew it would not be an easy sell to Campbell, whose politics and business style were on the conservative side. They wanted to show that the Tiger organization *really* cared about the entire Detroit community, especially Black and Brown fans whom they wanted to feel welcome at the stadium on Michigan Avenue and Trumbull, historically something neither group had ever felt. And with three-quarters of the inmates at Jackson being African American and many hailing from Detroit, a trip to the prison could have that effect. Campbell gave it the green light.

It would take months before the Tigers and prison officials could settle on a mutual visiting date, which was scheduled for May 23, 1973. With Gates Brown on board, Harwell and Matlin recruited other players: Mexican American third baseman Aurelio Rodríguez; African American left fielder and Detroit native Willie Horton; and designated hitter Frank Howard. There's no doubt that these men were strategically handpicked by Harwell and Matlin. Rodríguez, the club's lone Hispanic, and Horton, one of three Black players on the team who played regularly, would be the most relatable players (save for Gates Brown) to the non-white inmates. The six-foot, seven-inch, 255-pound Howard, known as the Capital Punisher when he had played for the Washington Senators and Big Daddy to his teammates, was the muscle in case anything got out of control.

Everything seemed to be falling into place until a few days before the visit. Brown hurt his leg and was unable to go. Horton and Rodriguez "backed out" for unknown reasons. No other players volunteered to participate. Harwell was disappointed, since he knew the inmates would not be interested in seeing the team's radio announcer, PR man, and the veteran Howard, a white giant past his prime. Alas, it would have to be.

On the evening before the trip to Jackson, the Tigers suffered a heartbreaking home loss against their division rival, the New York Yankees. After the game, Harwell was in the team manager's office, sharing his predicament about the next day's trip to Jackson.

"Hey I'll go with you," said Billy Martin, the Tigers' skipper and ex-Yankee. "I'll get Jimmy Butsicaris to take me. We'll meet you there."[2]

Harwell was taken aback. Billy Martin wanted to tag along? They had just lost to Martin's former team an hour earlier and were playing them again the following night. Harwell thought he was being put on by Martin, whom he assumed was on his way to drain his sorrows at the Lindell. There was no way, Harwell thought, that the team's volatile manager would get up early enough the next morning to make the trip to Jackson with a night game scheduled later that evening. He couldn't even make it to the game on time! But if Martin tagged along, the inmates would be excited to see him. He might not have been Black or Hispanic, but Billy Martin was no doubt a fan favorite.

Despite inmate Jimmy Karalla's letter-writing campaign and collect phone calls to the Lindell AC, owner Jimmy Butsicaris was reluctant to bother Billy Martin about the talented "kid" at Jackson. Martin was on the road often, and when he did stop by the bar, he didn't want to be bothered about yet another prospect, no less a convict. During the hour-long drive to Jackson, Butsicaris finally brought it up to Martin, who apparently shook his head and moved onto the next topic.

It was a cold, overcast, rainy May day when Butsicaris, Harwell, Howard, Martin, Matlin, and team traveling secretary Vince Desmond arrived at SPSM. They were escorted by guards and given a tour of the complex. The plan was for the correctional staff to have the Tiger contingent watch the inmates play in a baseball game at the recreation yard, but the inclement weather prevented it. The group, nonetheless, continued with the tour. When they made their way into the yard, they were greeted by the prison's assistant athletic director, Bob Sudberry, and anywhere from a dozen to two dozen inmates (accounts vary) who were the players on the baseball team. Shaking hands with the visitors, the players focused mainly on the Tigers' manager.

"Billy," a Black inmate shouted. "I hear there's a lot of dissension on the Tigers between the white guys and the blacks. How 'bout it?"

"Listen," Martin responded, "nothing to it. Willie Horton and Frank Howard are roommates on the road. How do you like to try and break into that room?"

"Why don't you give LeFlore a trial?" another inmate yelled. "Why don't you give him a chance. Look at him, look at him, he can play."[3]

Before the manager could respond, a third inmate—who happened to be Jimmy Karalla—shouted, "Hey, Martin, why doncha give the kid LeFlore a chance?"

"Yeah, sure," Billy said. "When he gets out [we'll] have him come to Tiger Stadium for a tryout."[4]

Whether Martin truly meant it, under the circumstances he had no choice but to respond accordingly. As Ernie Harwell observed, "[Billy] is a quick guy with his fists, but this wasn't one of the times he could fight his way out of a jam."[5]

Among the players swarming the Tiger contingent was Ron LeFlore, six feet tall with muscles bulging out of his prison uniform. He was standing face-to-face with Billy Martin.

All that work—hitting drills, catching flyballs, running exercises, endless advice from Jimmy—came to a head. This was the opportunity that Ron and Karalla had been waiting for. And yet, because of the weather conditions, Ron was unable to show off his skills. Fortunately, Ron and the Tigers' manager were able to have a tête-à-tête.

"Mr. Martin," Ron said. "I'd like a chance with the Tigers. I know some of the guys have told you about me."[6]

"[I] talked to the kid," Billy remembered. "I discovered that he was really a nice kid. He told me he was in for armed robbery, told me all about it, and how sorry he was about what happened, and after talking to him I became convinced that he was really a good person."[7]

Most importantly, Billy consented to a tryout. "Sure, sure. We'll arrange for you to come up to Detroit and work out with us."[8]

Would Martin, known for his mercurial temperament, really keep his word? As soon as he returned to Detroit, would Ron become an afterthought? After all, Martin had a game to prepare for.

Three weeks later, Martin was sitting at his desk in his wood-paneled office, getting ready for his team's upcoming evening game against the Chicago White Sox. Sporting five World Series rings, he was sitting in his white undershirt (his gameday jersey hung up on a hanger behind him), his pipe and tobacco at arm's length and the team's 1973 schedule tacked on a wall, when suddenly the phone rang.

"Huh," was his initial response.

State Prison of Southern Michigan? A canceled tryout? The feisty manager had no idea what the caller was talking about. Billy didn't have time for shenanigans.

It wasn't a shenanigan, the caller assured him. Fortunately for the person on the other end of the line, Lew Matlin was in Martin's office.

"Who's Ron LeFlore?" Martin whispered to the team's PR man, cupping the rotary telephone receiver so the caller wouldn't overhear.

"That's that kid you met up in prison, when you went there last month," Matlin said.

"When are you coming down, Ron?" the manager asked, trying to sound nonchalant.[9]

The next day, Ron was granted a forty-eight-hour furlough pass, a program that Warden Perry Johnson promoted to certain inmates in exchange for their cooperation—once, of course, they had proven they could be trusted. For

Ron's father, John LeFlore, Jr. (Ron LeFlore's personal collection)

the first time in three years, Ron LeFlore had the freedom to leave Jackson temporarily, which he gladly did. His father had picked him up on Friday, June 15. Since the tryout was scheduled the next day, John drove them to the LeFlore home, where Ron could rest before the big day, and then head back to prison on Sunday, June 17.

Meanwhile, the Tigers were beginning a three-game home stand against the Minnesota Twins. Although there was a game scheduled the afternoon of the tryout, Ron was invited to participate in the team's morning workout. Given the short notice, Martin's only other option was to back out, which he refused to do. The Tigers' manager viewed the tryout as a gesture of kindness. When he had first met Ron, he "was very impressed." As Martin later put it, Ron "admitted his mistakes. He was very honest."[10]

Determined to give the kid a break, Martin went well beyond the normal protocol. Typically, team tryouts were scheduled months in advance, were not hosted at Tiger Stadium, and were by invitation only.

On the morning of the workout, Ron was scheduled to meet Jimmy Butsicaris at the Lindell AC at 9:30 a.m. Since it was Ron's twenty-fifth birthday, he celebrated with a beer. It was the first time he had consumed "real alcohol" since he had been arrested.[11] From there, Butsicaris drove Ron and his father to the stadium to meet with Martin.

When they arrived, Butsicaris led Ron to the manager's office, where Martin warmly greeted him. Martin took Ron to the locker room and got him a glove from pitching coach (and Billy's confidante) Art Fowler, then introduced him to veteran players Al Kaline, Norm Cash, and Willie Horton.

At this point, Ron was in disbelief. Twenty-four hours ago, he had been sitting in his prison cell. Now, he was shaking hands with the Tigers' most popular players. "I was kind of in a fog," he remembered.[12]

When Ron stepped out of the tunnel that led to the field, he found himself in the team dugout. Compared to what he was used to at Jackson, Ron was awestruck with the Tigers' dugout and the well-maintained, pothole-free, manicured grass field. To him, it looked like heaven.

The team was warming up. Fowler was throwing batting practice. Frank Howard, the team's designated hitter, was in the batting cage. Non-everyday players Ike Brown (one of the only three active major league players who had played in the Negro League) and Tony Taylor were working on their hitting. Howard handed Ron a bat—"the longest bat" he had ever seen.[13]

"Relax," the 36-year-old veteran told him, sensing the young man's nerves. "Let your athletic ability take over."[14]

Martin directed Ron to take some swings in the cage.

With the exception of Martin and Howard, it is unlikely that anyone else on the field that morning knew about Ron's criminal background. There was no reason to tell the others, since the chances of Ron getting signed were one in a million. Why make it awkward? To the players, coaches, ground crew members, and front office personnel, several of whom were sitting in the stands, Ron was just another long-shot talent, hoping to impress the organization's higher-ups and fulfill his lifelong dream of becoming a professional baseball player.

For Ron, even to be at Tiger Stadium that morning was a fluke. How many times did the Tigers allow a prospect to join the team during a workout? On top of that, this was a player they had never seen perform and were inclined to do so because of the opinion of a convicted felon (Jimmy Karalla) with close ties to the Mafia. If Martin wasn't a frequent patron of the Lindell, or if Ernie Harwell hadn't helped organize the goodwill tour, this tryout would not have occurred. Maybe it was his mom's prayers being answered. Whatever the reason, Ron LeFlore had his rendezvous with destiny.

When Ron stepped into the cage, he at least looked the part of a ballplayer. The coaches and players could tell he was in shape, slightly puffy but muscle-bound. Third base coach Dick Tracewski thought he looked like a "brickhouse."[15] When Howard had met Ron briefly at Jackson, he had failed to appreciate the size of the young man. Now, he could see that this was no pint-size kid. Ron had a "tremendous athletic body."[16]

Tough-looking on the outside, Ron was feeling uneasy in the batting cage. The bat felt different. He had never been closely scrutinized at the plate. He was used to playing with amateurs. It was also the first time he was surrounded by so many white people. Aside from Horton, Brown, and Taylor, there were no other Black players on the field or in the stands that morning. But Ron was able to set aside his jitters, as he explained years later. "I didn't have the capacity to be nervous, having come from Jackson prison. That [the tryout] was easy."

On the first pitch, Ron, who wasn't wearing batting gloves, held the bat harder than he had ever before. He swung and whiffed, missing the ball completely.

He took a deep breath and then recalled what Frank Howard had told him earlier: *Relax. Let your athletic ability take over.*

The next pitch was thrown right over the plate.

Bam! Hit to right field.

Bam! Hit to left field.

Bam! Bam! Bam! Ron was hitting balls to the upper deck in left field.

Bam! Bam! And on and on.

Ron was a hitting machine. He might have bloodied his hands because he was swinging so hard, but he was oblivious to the pain: "I just threw some dirt on it and kept swinging."[17] Fowler kept throwing pitches, and Ron kept hitting them. He had never taken so many swings before.

Bill Lajoie, head of scouting for the Tigers, was working out in the team's weight room when he was summoned by Coach Tracewski to see this kid at the plate. Over the past decade, Lajoie had watched hundreds of would-be professional ballplayers, hoping to find that one diamond in the rough. The way Tracewski described Ron, this kid could possibly be that jewel every scout was seeking.

Lajoie "rushed . . . to the field to see what the buzz was about." First, he was struck by Ron's physical build. "[He was] chiseled with muscle. His legs were thick and sculpted and he was well developed in his torso and arms." He swung a "fast bat and [had] plenty of raw power."[18] Martin was excited, too, but he knew that this was just a tryout. "Whether he can hit or not on a regular basis," that was one of Martin's concerns.[19]

And what about Ron's speed? Martin told him to run to first base the next time he made contact with the ball. They were going to time him. According to Lajoie, the average time that it took a professional ballplayer to get to first base was 4.2 seconds. "[A] good runner gets to first in 3.9 to 4.1" seconds; 3.8 seconds or less was "outstanding."[20]

Bam! Ron hit the ball and took off. He ran to first base in 3.8 seconds.

"They didn't tell me about his speed," Martin said, then added in his inimitable way, "They should have signed the cop who caught him."[21]

"He could run like the wind," Tracewski excitedly declared.[22]

One player told Martin, "My goodness, Billy, he's sensational."[23]

For a team that had lacked a running threat for many seasons, it was refreshing for the coaching staff.

Bill Lajoie was also amazed by what he saw. But always the realist, he knew Ron would need time to fine-tune his mechanics, especially fielding, which became apparent when he was placed in the outfield with Gold Glove center fielder Mickey Stanley.

There was no question, however, that Ron had potential to play at the major league level.

Frank Howard, the fifteen-year veteran who had been coached by the game's greatest hitter, Ted Williams, was convinced that Ron had potential for greatness. "That kind of athletic skill comes along every fifteen, twenty, twenty-five years," Howard maintained. "He had all the tools you look for.... He could fly.... You knew he was destined to be, with that foot speed and arm strength, a very fine center fielder. Had big league power."[24]

Al Kaline, the team's most popular player and a future Hall of Famer, could not have agreed more. "[He] was better than anybody the Tigers had at Toledo," he said, referring to the club's Triple-A minor league team at the time.[25]

Among those present in the stands was *Detroit Free Press* sports reporter Jim Hawkins, who "always got to the ballpark early," hoping to beat his rivals to a story.[26] He watched Ron that morning and, like everyone else, was duly impressed. Nevertheless, he was of the opinion, without explaining why, that "ninety-nine times out of a hundred, cases like that don't ever pan out."

Also seated in the stadium was 63-year-old Ed Katalinas, Lajoie's predecessor. If Lajoie had scouted hundreds of amateur players, Katalinas had likely seen thousands. Now in the twilight of his career, the portly Katalinas was best known as the scout who had discovered Kaline. After watching Ron in the cage, he stood up, waddled in between the stadium rows, went up the stairs, and down the hall to the elevator that led to Jim Campbell's office.

"Boss, you gotta come down and see this," Katalinas said, red in the face and huffing, trying to catch his breath.

Campbell looked at him questionably.

"I'm telling you, you gotta come down and see this. You won't believe it," exclaimed Katalinas.[27]

After the tryout, the Tigers played against the Twins and were shut out, five to nothing. After the game, reporters were milling about in the locker room, doing what they always did: talking with the players, trying to get a quote and maybe some gossip for the next day's paper. *Detroit News* sportswriter Jerry Green was in Billy Martin's office. Wanting to avoid talking about the team's loss, Martin mentioned a tryout the team held earlier that day for a talented young athlete who happened to be a convict. This kid could turn the club around, Martin insisted, almost with a sense of giddiness. But there was one problem: Jim Campbell. Martin knew he would have to convince his boss to sign the kid. Like many reporters, Green always enjoyed speaking with Martin. He had no filter and always provided colorful quotes that he could use for his articles.

But this time, Martin's words struck him as mere hyperbole, and Green made no mention of them in his column. Years later, he realized that the kid Martin was referring to was Ron LeFlore.

To no one's surprise, Campbell was resistant to signing Ron. It was one thing to give him a tryout—and quite another to enter into a contract with a convicted felon who was still serving time behind bars.

"If you saw him on the sandlots, you'd give him a hundred thousand right now," Martin told Campbell.

"He's a jailbird," Campbell responded.

"Where did you get Gates Brown, out of Sunday School?"[28]

That season, Tigers' management had "looked at hundreds of free agents."[29] Although the team had a 30–29 win–loss record and was only four games behind the division-leading Milwaukee Brewers, the team was getting older and slower, and as Martin pointed out, it was only a matter of time before the Tigers would end up in the cellar. Martin kept at it, hoping to wear down his boss. Deep down, Campbell knew Martin's assessment was accurate. The Tigers were getting "desperate" for new talent, but for some reason, Campbell refused to admit it—to the annoyance of *Detroit Free Press* reporter Jim Hawkins. It had been four years since the team had won the World Series. That same victorious squad was still the main corps of the team, five years older.

"They rode too long with the '68 team [who won the World Series]," Hawkins argued. "They were on their last legs in '72. By this time [1973], everybody was aging. They didn't have enough good, young players in the farm system."[30]

The suit-and-tie Campbell, who lived and breathed his job, finally acquiesced and gave Lajoie permission to pursue Ron.

The timing of Ron's tryout could not have been better. The following week, the Tigers had an invite-only tryout for the area's top amateur players, mostly high school and college athletes. The team asked Ron to attend the event, which would be held at Butzel Field in Detroit. It was great news for Ron, but he knew that he wasn't eligible for another temporary release, since he'd just had one. With pressure from the Tiger organization, prison officials agreed to let Ron attend, though they would only allow him to be released for sixteen hours, which meant that he would need to leave and return the same day.

Ron's father volunteered to drive him to the workout, which began at 10:00 a.m. At around 9:15 a.m., on their way to Tiger Stadium, the car conked out on Interstate 94. They pulled over and tested the engine, but nothing was happening. Ron felt "sick. . . . the whole thing was going to fall through."[31]

Standing on the shoulder of the road, Ron was frustrated with his father, whom he thought hadn't helped him much in his life. And now, here was an opportunity, and he had blown it. As far as Ron was concerned, Big John couldn't do anything right.

There was no gas station or pay phone within sight. Ron knew if he missed the workout, he was through with the Tigers. They weren't going to give him a second chance, regardless of the show he had put on the previous week. The team was already hesitant about signing an ex-convict; no need to give them an excuse to back out.

So Ron did what anyone would have done if stranded on the road in 1973: hitchhike. But would two large Black men on the side of the road attract a Good Samaritan? Luckily, a middle-aged African American factory worker was heading home after his graveyard shift and offered them a ride. He asked where they were headed, and Ron told him the story, astonishing the driver that his passenger "was going to work out with the Tigers."[32]

When Ron finally arrived at Butzel Field, he was wearing blue jeans, sneakers, and a T-shirt. He immediately stood out from the others, who were all wearing baseball athletic attire. Other than Bill Lajoie and Ed Katalinas, no one else knew Ron was currently serving a prison sentence. To all the other players, he was just another guy trying to pursue his dream. Given his clothing, they likely assumed (correctly) that he was a poor kid from the East Side.

In batting practice, Ron hit the ball hard and far; however, he had his fair share of pop-ups. During the game, he hit a double and scored a run. Overall, Ron held his own. When it was time to clock the players' speed, it was then that Ron separated himself from the pack. With cones set up in the outfield, Lajoie had each player run a standard sixty-yard dash, which is 180 feet, the equivalent of hitting a triple. They would be timed.

Anyone who could run it in 6.7 seconds or less was considered fast. Most amateur players ran in the high sixes. When Ron took off, he blazed through somewhere between 6.2 and 6.4 seconds. To have run sixty yards that fast on grass and in street clothes was astounding. If you were to adjust for surface and attire, it was possible that Ron could have tied the time set by the best runner in the world, 1968 Olympic bronze-medal sprinter John Carlos, who ran sixty yards in six seconds flat with track spikes on an all-weather track.

"The fastest players in Major League Baseball at the time would have eaten his dust," Lajoie declared.[33]

Word of Ron's talents began to circulate in and out of the majors. The Oakland A's, for example, had gotten wind about Ron and expressed interest. Given Ron's physique, he was also being courted by football teams. Richard "Night Train" Lane, the ex-NFL star cornerback (and husband of the late singer Dinah Washington), was coaching at Central State University in Wilberforce, Ohio, and would have liked Ron to play for Central once he was eligible for parole.

Lajoie became so paranoid about losing Ron to another team or sport that he believed spies had prowled Butzel Field that day. "I wanted him back in prison where he would be safe from scouts until we could arrange for a parole and arrange to sign him," he confided to another team official.[34]

While Ron waited to hear from Tigers' management, he continued to keep on the straight and narrow. Whether he fully realized it, prison had changed him for the better. For the first time in his life, he was reading for pleasure (Iceberg Slim and Donald Goines were his favorite authors). He was taking care of his body. Most importantly, he was becoming more empathetic. As a volunteer in the prison's psychiatric clinic, he had observed that the patients had few recreational options. Successfully lobbying prison administration, he secured sports equipment and consequently organized a football team, serving as its coach. Surprisingly, in its first season of play, the team finished in first place and lost by only one point in the playoff championships. Afterward, Ron used money from his prison account to host a banquet for the team, complete with food, drinks, and trophies. One of the participants said Ron spent $200; in prison, that was a lot of money. The inmate later wrote a kind letter to the Tigers' organization, mentioning how it was a "wonderful thing for this man [Ron] to do, especially in here, when one is always facing perplexing problems."[†][35]

[†] The man whom Ron thinks wrote the letter was John Norman Collins, a notorious serial killer who had been convicted of murdering an eighteen-year-old woman in Ann Arbor. He was also suspected of killing several other women, which he was never convicted of. He was known as the "Co-ed Killer."

Ron also achieved academic success, completing his GED. Rewarded for his improved conduct, he was now living in the prison's Honor Block, where he had access to more amenities and could come and go as he pleased within the prison. At the same time, the Tigers were hastily working behind the scenes to secure his early release.

All of this would never have transpired if not for Warden Perry Johnson's reform program at SPSM—a program that was short-lived. By the mid-1970s, federal and state budget cuts resulted in less funding for social services, including rehabilitation programs for a growing inmate population. Ron had his share of bad breaks, but the timing of his imprisonment was not one of them. In the very month he became inmate #B1156143, Johnson had taken an oath to serve as warden of the prison. During the first few years of his tenure, he implemented his reform plan without serious opposition. Among the scores of inmates who were beneficiaries of that vision was Ron LeFlore. If Johnson had been thwarted at the time—as he would be in later years—it's likely that Ron would have continued on his path of self-destruction, not to mention that baseball fans around the country would have lost out on watching the improbable career of one of the sport's most captivating players.

7

Freedom

It was a win–win situation for all the parties involved. The Tigers had found their next marquee player—and for a great price. For SPSM, the prison could tout Ron LeFlore as a positive example of an inmate gone straight, a result of Warden Perry Johnson's new policies. And Ron got his freedom back.

Over the past twelve months, Ron had positioned himself to become eligible for an early release. Part of the reentry process included a prisoner assessment made by the correctional staff. When the guards were asked to share their impressions of Ron, they marked the following categories:

- Follows orders
- Good inmate
- Clean
- Keeps to himself
- No trouble

Nothing was checked for "agitator," "loud and noisy," "looks for trouble," or "dangerous."[1]

Following Ron's successful back-to-back tryouts, the Detroit Tigers worked with prison officials to "orchestrate an early release" sometime in the summer of 1973, eighteen months less than Ron's minimum five-year sentence.[2] Anxious to alleviate the overcrowded conditions, prison officials were more than amenable to accommodate the Tigers. The fact that Ron had also demonstrated he was not a threat to society and had a well-paying job waiting for him upon his release further justified his sooner-than-expected parole.

Although the Tigers were effective in lobbying correctional officials, Bowie Kuhn, the commissioner of Major League Baseball, was not as easily convinced. To expedite Ron's entry into the league, the Tigers dispatched Ed Katalinas to convince Kuhn's aides that their newest recruit was not an embarrassment to the league. On the contrary, Katalinas pointed out, Ron could serve as a boon for the sport. In 1973, baseball was still America's favorite pastime, but its status was under siege by professional football and basketball. Ron's incredible rags-to-riches story and his unmatched talent had the potential to lure a younger, more diverse audience to the ballpark. The league consented.

On July 2, 1973, at eight o'clock in the morning, Ron LeFlore stepped outside the world's largest walled prison. He was a free man.

Met by his father, Ron was driven—without a problem this time—straight to Tiger Stadium, not even stopping first at the LeFlores' house.

Anxious to sign Ron, the Tigers were still concerned that other professional organizations might preempt them. The Detroit Wheels, a team that recently joined the newly formed World Football League, which was looking to compete against the NFL, were ready to enter into a "bidding war" for Ron's services.[3] Instead of using this as a negotiating tactic, Ron accepted what the Tigers offered: the league minimum for a player starting at Single-A (the lower level of the minor leagues), $500 a month plus a one-time signing bonus of $5,000 (equivalent to $36,000 today). A parole officer was present to oversee the proceedings. Upon signing, Ron was told to report on July 5 to Clinton, Iowa, home of the team's entry-level Clinton Pilots. Scouting director Bill Lajoie would drive him.

The next stop was the LeFlore household, where Ron was greeted with a warm hug from his mother, Georgia. Ron offered his bonus to his parents, which they used to purchase a pre-owned Buick LeSabre sedan. Wasting no time, Ron headed downtown and went on a shopping spree for new clothes. "I didn't know enough to go to the cheaper stores," he commented in later years, managing to spend an excessive amount of money that day.[4]

That very night, Ron went out for drinks with his old neighborhood friends. But for someone who had spent the last three and a half years with a ten o'clock lights-out curfew, Ron cut the evening short, unable to stay awake.

Fortunately, for Ron, in a day or so, he was scheduled to report for minor league play in Iowa. Whatever misgivings he might have felt about leaving his hometown, Detroit had little, if anything, to offer him.

Still grappling with the effects of the 1967 riots, Detroit was in far worse condition now than when Ron was sent to prison. The new mayor—Coleman Young, the first African American to hold the position—provided residents with a sense of civic pride and hope; however, the socioeconomic problems he and Detroiters faced were profound. Only a decade earlier, Detroit had been hailed as the nation's model city. No more. The riots had expedited white flight, which further diminished the tax base, significantly impacting schools and other critical city services such as police, fire, and transportation. The once-proud city had been abandoned, now left with "rotting hulks of factory buildings . . . surrounded by blocks of boarded-up stores and restaurants . . . [and neighborhoods] pockmarked with the shells of burned-out and empty buildings, lying among rubbish-strewn vacant lots."[5]

Normally, the signing of a low-level baseball recruit received scant mention in the press. At best, one would expect a brief paragraph in the player's hometown paper and their name listed in the sports section's daily transactions. But Ron's story was anything but routine.

"Tigers Fulfill His 'Dream'—Sign ex-Jackson Prisoner" was the headline splashed across the front page of the *Detroit Free Press*'s sports section. It was also accompanied by a photograph of a leaner Ron (no more Bosco chubbiness) sporting a combed Afro.

"It was really beyond my wildest dreams," Ron said to the *Free Press*'s Curt Sylvester on the day of his signing. "I never had any idea I'd be looked at as a professional ballplayer."[6]

From the *New York Times* to the *Sporting News*, Ron's life story became known across the country, helped by the efforts of the team's PR rep, Lew Matlin. Ron was happy to be on board. He was not only a natural on the field but he was also at ease and personable with the media, who were eager to share his unbelievable tale with readers, especially hometown fans, who viewed Ron as a symbol of hope for their dying city.

The articles also marked the first of many inaccuracies concerning Ron's age. When Ron was released from prison, he had just turned twenty-five years old, which was not within the preferred 17- to 22-year-old age range that scouts sought (and still seek) when signing a player. "After 22 years of age, a scout will hesitate because a player must require certain professional skills," according to scout Dick Groch.[7] If it took two or three years to get promoted from the minors and the player was starting his baseball career at twenty-five, his playing window was diminished. And so was the team's investment.

According to the Tigers, Ron's date of birth was June 16, 1952, which made him twenty-one years old upon his signing.

It's nearly impossible to determine whether Ron or the Tigers intentionally misled the public. On the one hand, Ron had more of an incentive to lie about his age than the Tigers had; on the other, there is more than a possibility that the organization may have played a role in the matter.

While Ed Katalinas served as the team's liaison to the commissioner's office concerning Ron, Bill Lajoie was Ron's direct contact with the Tigers' organization. Lajoie was scheduled to drive Ron to Decatur, Illinois, where the Clinton Pilots were taking on the Decatur Commodores. Someone else could have driven Ron, but Lajoie wanted that time to learn more about the team's new recruit. It was highly unusual for any prospect to have one high-ranking front office staff, let alone two, working on his behalf.

Despite the team's efforts, there were no guarantees this experiment would work. It was one thing for Ron to excel in a couple of tryouts and put on a show. But would he have the discipline and endurance to make it to the major leagues?

"You never know what a kid will do once he gets on a professional ball field," Lajoie noted, a view similar to what *Detroit Free Press* sports reporter Jim Hawkins had expressed when observing Ron's first tryout.[8]

Since the Pilots were based outside of Michigan and would travel to other states for games, Lajoie was required to notify Ron's probation officer. "I guess you could say he was in my custody," Lajoie recalled before jokingly adding, "I don't know what I would have done if he tried to run away."[9]

And what would these two Detroit natives with French surnames talk about during a six-hour car ride? Baseball, naturally. It was all Lajoie cared about.

Born in 1934 in Detroit, William Richard Lajoie, from the moment he was a young boy, was a baseball fanatic. A southpaw, he had trouble finding left-handed baseball gloves to play with and was forced to use a right hander's. It didn't affect his desire to master the intricacies of the game. When he wasn't practicing, Lajoie avidly followed his favorite team, the Tigers, on the radio and in person at Briggs Stadium (before it was called Tiger Stadium). The five-foot, eleven-inch Lajoie played center field for his high school and earned a spot on the Western Michigan University baseball team, where he would become an all-American.

In 1955, at the age of twenty-one, Lajoie signed a major league contract with the Baltimore Orioles. For the next six years, he bounced around the minors and would go no further as a player. He was never the quickest or strongest player among his peers. However, while he was playing for the Amarillo Gold Sox, the team manager noticed how Lajoie watched each game attentively from the bench. Short on help, the manager asked Lajoie if he was interested in preparing scouting reports of the opposing team. Lajoie leaped at the opportunity. When he submitted his report, the manager told him, "[Your] future would be in scouting, not playing."[10]

Lajoie was encouraged, but during that time he had gotten married and needed to make a living. He returned to Detroit and became a teacher at Northern High School, where he was also the baseball team's assistant coach. The head coach happened to be a part-time scout for the Cincinnati Reds and, knowing Lajoie's background, asked his new assistant if he was interested in joining him, driving around town to hunt for talent. Lajoie immersed himself in the assignment, attending hundreds of amateur games that year, writing letters to high school and college coaches throughout the state, introducing himself and letting them know to contact him if they had a player that should be evaluated.

Whenever Lajoie found a player who piqued his interest, he observed that player closely—and not just what he did on the field. Lajoie would "watch him stretch before the game, towel off his forehead, interact with his teammates, talk to his parents, play catch on the side . . . everything the player did would tell you something."[11] How competitive was the kid? How often did he practice? Lajoie was partial to players who participated in other sports because he wanted to see how the athlete acted when he wasn't the best player on the court or on the field. He believed that becoming a major leaguer was as much about physical ability as it was about mental acumen. Yet, the player had to be focused on baseball and nothing else. If there were negative distractions, no matter the athlete's size and talent, the recruit would not survive "the rigors of minor league baseball."[12]

The Reds took notice of Lajoie, and in the mid-1960s, they hired him full-time, even though he was already working those hours (he just wasn't getting paid for it yet). He quit teaching and went on the road. Unfortunately, he came into conflict with the Reds' management when he questioned the team's unspoken rule about not allowing Black and white players to room together. Lajoie wouldn't go along with team policy and was fired.

The Reds' loss was the Tigers' gain, however. His hometown team hired him in 1968, the same year they would win the World Series. It was an ideal setting for Lajoie, who had already established connections throughout Michigan, giving him an advantage over other scouts. A natural competitor, when he spotted a player he wanted, he would go to his game, and when the prospect was at bat, he would intentionally distract other scouts from watching. Lajoie moved up in the Tigers' organization, eventually working directly for Katalinas. By 1972, Katalinas was in his twilight years and was reassigned to a less grueling position. Lajoie took his spot, becoming the Tigers' head scout.

Ron didn't exactly fit Lajoie's ideal candidate. He didn't have the track record of playing year-round baseball under a regimented schedule. He hadn't demonstrated he could withstand the grind of playing a nine-inning game in the stifling heat and then hopping onto a bus for an overnight trip to play a doubleheader the following afternoon. Doing it, day after day, for months, not knowing if it would ever amount to anything, could take a mental and physical toll.

On the other hand, as Ron reminded Lajoie, being in prison was no picnic. "In prison, you have to be mentally sharp, especially in trying to avoid certain situations," Ron explained. "If you do anything wrong, you are going to be sent to the Hole." Or worse. "You see people [commit] murder. Nobody can understand what prison conditions are like if they haven't done time." Ron went on and on, likely giving Lajoie second thoughts about the decision to sign him.

During their drive along Interstate 94, Lajoie prepared Ron for what to expect in Clinton. It was rural, white, and conservative. Black people were treated less fairly than white people, he told him. Dating white women, for example, was forbidden.

"Ron, you got to keep your cool," Lajoie warned him while driving and puffing away on a Marlboro cigarette. "You can't let people get underneath your skin. They are going to say things about where you came from. They are going to call you names," such as "nigger" and "jailbird."[13]

"We talked all the way there," Ron remembered. "He wanted to feel me out and see how I would react to certain things." Ron reassured Lajoie that he could handle it.[14]

In some ways, the situation was similar to the advice that Branch Rickey, general manager of the Brooklyn Dodgers, gave to Jackie Robinson when he signed with the team more than a quarter century before. You were not just another ballplayer, Rickey told Robinson, who was the first African American to play in Major League Baseball and for years would experience racist taunts in a white-dominated game. Ron's situation was different from Robinson's, but since he was a Black ex-convict on a predominantly white team, he would inevitably encounter problems. Lajoie reminded Ron that there was one thing he and his fellow players had in common: to make it to the majors. Hopefully, that goal would help to neutralize any petty, vindictive behavior toward him.

On a far more practical level, Lajoie was concerned about Ron's hitting. Fielding would take longer to develop, which was common among younger players who did not have time to specialize in one position. But if Ron couldn't hit a curveball, which he had rarely seen in prison, he wouldn't last six weeks in Clinton. The number one reason most hitters failed to make it to the pros was their incapability to time big-league pitching.

As they drew closer to their destination, Ron was beginning to wonder whether he was in over his head.

After dropping off Ron at the team's motel in Decatur, Lajoie met with Jim Leyland, the Clinton Pilots' 29-year-old manager. Sensing Leyland's unease about Ron, Lajoie was quick to say, "Just treat him like one of the guys."[15]

But Ron was not just one of the guys. Leyland didn't know what to expect. In the first place, he was now responsible for maintaining contact with Ron's parole officer. And how closely should he monitor Ron's behavior? "Do I have to keep him out of bars and pool halls?" he asked himself. "What happens if a brawl breaks out on the field and he piles in?"[16]

Lajoie didn't have all the answers, but Leyland had enormous respect for him. The two chain-smokers had spent time together as roommates during spring training at TigerTown in Lakeland, Florida. They often stayed up late talking about baseball. According to Leyland, Lajoie "really knew the game" and did most of the talking, while Leyland, with pen in hand, took copious notes.[17]

A former catcher in the Tigers' farm system, Leyland, like Lajoie, was never going to make it as a professional baseball player. Starting in 1963, at the age of nineteen, Leyland had begun a six-year career in the minors. Throughout that time, no matter how discouraging it may have been for him to see others rise in the organization, he was always willing to help out the team. No task was too small—"warming up pitchers, driving the bus, coaching base runners."[18] He also was a keen observer, taking away vital lessons from each of his team managers.

In 1971, 26-year-old Leyland had been hired as the head coach of the Rookie League-level Bristol (Virginia) Tigers. The following year, he was promoted to lead the Single-A Clinton Pilots. Leyland was known to have a "fiery" temper and often took it out on locker-room furniture. On one occasion, he threw a chair through a glass window, shattering the window and sending shards of glass flying. One piece of glass landed right next to a player's foot, nearly causing a major injury. Leyland was a relentless competitor and a dedicated instructor, willing to work with anyone to improve their fundamentals. One of his players accurately forecasted, "This guy's going to be a big-league manager."[19]

When Ron met with his new manager, the first thing Leyland did was review the team rules. Foremost among them: be on time for games and practices, and no facial hair. (Ron was forced to shave his mustache.) Since it was already public knowledge, Leyland had decided to inform the team about Ron's background prior to his arrival. Leyland had hoped the players would avoid bombarding their new teammate with questions about prison. Destined to encounter queries from the media and the public, he didn't need to hear them in the locker room, too.

When Ron was introduced to the Pilots at the motel, the team was leaving for their night game against the Commodores. Immediately, Ron noticed that they had steered clear of him. "Everybody seemed skeptical of me, like they didn't know quite how to take me," he recalled.[20] That initial reaction, however, foreshadowed the fact that the "ex-con" label would live with him wherever he went.

There were high expectations for the 1973 Clinton Pilots. They were projected to have a "stronger team" this season, one that would contend for the Midwest League title.[21] Of the twenty-five players on the roster, only five had played on the previous season's team, which, in the minor leagues, was (and still is) common. Rosters were constantly in flux, with players being promoted, demoted, injured, or simply leaving.

When Ron joined the team, the Pilots were in first place in the Northern Division, while the Commodores were in third place in the Southern Division. Ron suited up but was told in advance that he wouldn't be playing that evening. Leyland was aware Ron hadn't played at night because all the games at Jackson happened during the day. "They had other uses for the floodlights," Ron cleverly remarked.[22]

The Pilots lost 6–3. Ron sat in the dugout, watching his first professional baseball game from start to finish. After the game, he joined his teammates for a nightcap at a local bar. They played pool. They drank beer. They took shots. They did what other minor leaguers would do while on the road. Having just served three and a half years in prison, as much as he wanted to fit in, Ron wasn't sure how to win over his teammates.

Unlike the others, Ron wasn't used to drinking anything but homemade alcohol. After a few beers mixed in with a couple of shots, he was drunk—or so it seemed. Around 1:00 a.m., the players headed back to the team motel. Along the way, they walked by a clothing store, where there were leather and fur coats displayed in the window.

"If we were in Detroit," Ron yelled, "I would throw a brick through this window" and steal the merchandise.

The players froze. Was he serious?

Ron gave the impression that he was serious, checking to see if anyone was around. "What do you guys think?" he asked.

There was an uneasy silence.

Ron smiled. He was just putting them on, he told them. "I just got out of prison," and he had no intention of returning.[23]

His teammates laughed. They returned to the motel, stayed up late, drank more beer, and smoked cigarettes. Ron was now one of the guys, but for the next game, he was still riding the bench.

After two nights in Decatur, the Pilots headed home to Clinton. The following day, they had a pregame practice at Riverview Stadium, the team's home ballpark. It would be the first opportunity for the coaches and teammates to see Ron in action.

Leyland was throwing batting practice to the team when Ron stepped up to the plate. He smacked the ball toward Leyland, tearing through the protective net on the mound and hitting him in the abdomen, leaving a "big welt" near his kidney. After catching his breath, Leyland asked Ron to run to first base after making contact.

Bam! Ron took off.

"I couldn't believe what I saw," Leyland remembered. "He was special, and I knew he could make it."[24]

That evening, on July 7, 1973, Ron LeFlore made his professional debut. It was the bottom of the eighth inning, and the Pilots had a healthy lead over the Cedar Rapids Astros. With close to 900 fans in attendance, Ron stepped up to the plate to pinch-hit for his roommate Ray Gimenez, who had gone three for four with two runs batted in (RBIs). The Astros had played pitifully, having already committed six errors in the game.

When Ron's name was announced, he received a polite applause. Some of the fans were likely familiar with his backstory, since an article and photograph of him had just run a few days earlier in the local paper's sports section. As he walked from the dugout to home plate, Ron was more nervous than he had expected to be. It was his first night game and the largest crowd he had ever played in front of.

The first pitch was delivered and Ron swung at it, making contact. It was a hopper that headed toward third base. Not waiting a moment to watch where the hit went, he took off, lunging along the first baseline. The third baseman fielded the ball, making the mistake of doing so too casually. When he threw it to the first baseman, not knowing how fast the hitter was, Ron had already touched the bag. Safe! Ron LeFlore had his first hit.

"It was a cheap hit," he acknowledged, but it was a relief.[25] And the crowd acknowledged it, responding with a "lusty round of applause."[26]

Ron's meager hit made its way to Detroit, where the *Free Press*'s tongue-in-cheek headline read, "LeFlore Batting 1.000."[27]

Gerald Tyler, one of Ron's roommates in Clinton, was the winning pitcher that night. The lanky, six-foot-tall African American pitcher had been apprehensive about living with Ron: "Everybody was talking about this tough ex-con when he walked in." Noticing his roommate's nervousness, Ron had not minced his words: "Yes, I've been in prison. I messed up. When I was sitting in solitary confinement for three months the first time, I thought maybe I'd go back to crime and drugs. But now I've got a chance in baseball. I've served my time." Tyler appreciated Ron's candidness.[28]

Ron's other roommate, Ray Gimenez, the player he had pinch-hit for in his first at bat, was born in Havana, but at age ten had fled Cuba with his family to escape the Castro regime and settled in the Bronx. He, too, was also a bit out of his comfort zone living in Iowa. But since he had been in the minors for two seasons and given his similar urban background to Ron's (and the fact that Gimenez had a reputation for being "Mr. Nice Guy"), Leyland thought Gimenez was the right person to live with Ron.[29]

Playing baseball professionally was one thing. Living in rural Iowa, however, was a culture shock. In Clinton, life revolved around the harvest, including minor league baseball. At night, when farmers had their crops sprayed for mosquitos by plane, they did not work around the Pilots' home games. The players had to adjust, sometimes wearing goggles on the field because the ball was harder to see amid the fumes. It was not uncommon for players to leave the ballpark with baked pies made for them by residents. It was the Iowan way. For fans, winning a new vacuum cleaner or a certificate for a free night out at the bowling alley was part of the minor league game experience at most venues. In Iowa, a ticketholder could also expect to walk away with a free hog.

It was also in Iowa where Ron experienced what it was like to live in a white world. In 1970, the Hawkeye State was approximately 98 percent white. Being single, heterosexual, and twenty-something, it was inevitable that Ron would encounter white women, which was a first for him. Having already been warned by the Tigers' organization to stay away, Ron refused to follow the policy.

Three of Ron's teammates—left-handed pitcher Ed Glynn; Gerald Tyler, Ron's roommate; and speedy outfielder Art James—were selected to play in the annual mid-season All-Star Game, with Leyland chosen as the North Division's manager. By the time the All-Star break began, Clinton was in first place by one-and-a-half games. The Pilots continued their tear through the Midwest League, led by James, the team's leadoff hitter. Known by teammates as Spider, James led the league in stolen bases. The Pilots had the hottest bats in the Midwest League, though it did not trickle down to Ron's. Following the All-Star Game, Ron went zero for four in back-to-back games while playing all three outfield positions. After three weeks in a Pilot uniform, Ron had the second-lowest batting average in the entire league, hitting a paltry .125 with one RBI. In twenty-four at bats, he had accumulated only three hits.

Part of the problem was the expectations that were imposed upon Ron. "I felt the crowds were expecting more out of me, because of all the write ups. I started over trying," he later maintained.[30] In fact, his problem was twofold: a lack of experience and a hostile fan base. Heckled for his past criminal behavior, he was also subjected to death threats.

"I went through hell in Clinton," he remembered.

As Lajoie had predicted, people yelled at him from the stands and called him "nigger." Some fans publicly questioned why he was given an opportunity to play professionally. One disgruntled father even shouted that his son had "never been in any trouble. So why are they giving you a chance?"[31]

While that was unnerving in itself, Ron also had to master the basic fundamentals of the game—including how to hit a curveball. "In prison I saw curve balls only once in a great while, but in the minor leagues I saw hundreds of them," Ron later remarked.[32] When a ball is thrown at you at eighty miles per hour, the natural reaction is to move out of the way. When, at the last possible moment, it moves away from the batter, that is known as a "good curveball."[33] Ron had trouble timing this type of pitch and asked Leyland for help, who offered to throw him batting practice before the rest of the team arrived. No matter whether they were, home or away, teacher and student met at the ballpark at 9:00 a.m. and Leyland would throw to Ron. "He put in a lot of extra time with me," Ron fondly reminisced. "[Leyland] really cared about me as a player and as a person."[34]

The manager also worked with Ron on his fielding. It is inaccurate to assume outfielders have it easy compared to other positions. Most of the time, it seems they just wait until the ball gets hit to them, and when it does, they run to the ball, catch it, and throw it back to the infield. But appearances are deceiving. Being an outfielder is "the toughest position in baseball to play," according to former Major League Baseball manager (and outfielder) Bill Virdon.[35] When there are 120–130 pitches being thrown in a given game and you're only involved in seven or eight of them, it requires a player to maintain absolute alertness. "An outfielder does more than just catch fly balls," scout Dick Groch pointed out. He must "know the hitters, possess the speed to chase down long fly balls, have an arm capable of throwing out an advance runner, and have the knowledge to know how to back up the play in which he is not directly involved."[36]

While in Jackson, Ron had never been properly shown how to catch a ball when playing outfield. He had done what had felt natural: run to where he felt the ball was going to land. In reality, a player should position himself a few steps behind where he thinks the ball will land "in order to gain some momentum for the throwback to the infield." That's not easy to predict in the heat of the moment. It is a skill that takes time to develop, and Ron knew he didn't have unlimited time. He had to show progress, or else his playing career would be short-lived.

By the end of July, Clinton was in first place, four games ahead in the division standings. At 19–13, the team was tied for the best record in the league. The Pilots' All-Star outfielder Art James was arguably Ron's biggest barrier to playing regularly. Meanwhile, Ron no longer possessed the second-worst batting average in the Midwest League. In his past six at bats, he had collected three hits, including an RBI and a run scored, demonstrating that the extra effort had panned out. He was now hitting .167, the league's sixth-lowest batting average. It was an improvement, but Ron had a long way to go before replacing James in the outfield.

Not only did Ron have to be diligent on the field, but he also had to keep a close eye on his obligations as a released convict. Twice a month, Ron was required to meet with his parole officer (and would do so for the next two

Ron was signed out of prison to play for the Clinton (Iowa) Pilots on July 2, 1973. (Rucker Archive, Society for American Baseball Research)

years). Mr. St. Claire (Ron never knew his first name) had a "no-nonsense approach" toward his parolee. An infraction, he reminded Ron, could land him back behind bars. And once released, St. Claire showed him what would happen if he was back on the streets: "This will be you!"[37] He handed Ron a graphic photo of the body of a deceased former acquaintance, who was a drug dealer. His arms were cut off at the shoulders. His torso was sliced off at the waist. "It scared the shit out of me," Ron later admitted.[38]

Even if Ron tried to move beyond his past, the local media was there to remind him about it, peppering him with questions about what life was like behind bars. Instead of shying away from the questions, he answered them dutifully, revealing, on one occasion, how tentative he felt about his freedom.

"It's still spooky to me," he told one reporter. "I keep thinking I'm going to wake up and it'll be gone."[39]

By early August, the Clinton Pilots were still in first place. Ron had raised his batting average to .189, now the fourteenth lowest in the league. Despite his dismal performance, Ron was featured in the national media. *Time* ran a piece titled, "A Batter from the Pen." He was also profiled by Dan Even of the Associated Press. His article, which covered Ron's first month in the minors, was syndicated in newspapers throughout the country. He even did a thorough job of interviewing team personnel to determine how Ron was faring one month out of prison.

"He's paid his price to society and we are just happy to have him here," Fritz Colschen, the Pilots' business manager, said. "He's been nothing but a real gentleman since he came to the club." Manager Jim Leyland viewed Ron as just "another ball player," trying to make it to the majors. When asked about his minimal playing time, Leyland pointed out that Ron was a "victim of circumstance," noting, "We have one outfielder hitting about .320 (Ray Gimenez), another around .300 (Billy Baldwin) and the third has stolen 40 bases (Art James).... I hate to break up a winning combination."

By mid-August, with only two weeks left in the season, the Pilots remained in first place, two and a half games ahead of the second-place Waterloo Royals. In the meantime, Ron had hit his first home run, stolen his first base, and boosted his batting average to .250. Still, he played infrequently, often in a pitch hitter's role. As the playoffs neared and it was clear the Pilots would be playing in the postseason, attendance at Riverfront Stadium soared, more than doubling from 1,000 fans to 2,500 for one of the final regular-season games against the team's interstate rival, the Quad City Angels.

Unfortunately for Ron, he made only three plate appearances in the final two weeks of the season. Although he struggled at the plate at times and played inconsistently, he stayed optimistic, showed determination, and finished the season with a respectable .277 batting average. His improved performance at the plate made him a fan favorite, at least in the town of Clinton. Whenever he got a hit, "the fans cheered as if he hit a grand slammer."[40]

The Pilots, who were at the top of the league standings throughout the season, came up short in the playoffs, losing in the North Division finals to the Wisconsin Rapids Twins. But there were some bright spots. Jim Leyland was rewarded with a promotion to the Tigers' Double-A team, the Montgomery (Alabama) Rebels in the Southern League. It would not be his final stop. He would later move up again to the team's Triple-A club, the Evansville Triplets, and ultimately be promoted to the major leagues, where he and Ron would cross paths again a decade later. The 1973 Pilots would produce seven future major leaguers: Ron, Billy Baldwin, Ed Glynn, Art James, Bob Kaiser, Phil Mankowski, and Mark Wagner. Considering that only 3 percent of all players at the Single-A level make it to the majors, it's an impressive number for any ball club at that level to produce so many future professionals.

While the Pilots ended its season short of a championship, its parent club was struggling. After a successful 1972 season, when the Detroit Tigers had made it to the playoffs but lost to the Oakland A's, who would win the World Series title (the first of three in a row), there had been optimism for the following season.

Billy Martin had exceeded expectations and taken an aging team that most experts considered past its prime to a winning season. But the good times would not last. It was an ongoing pattern throughout Martin's career as a manager. He would take over a team in decline, turn it around, and then sabotage his own success. He just couldn't control his explosive personality or his addiction to alcohol.

While Martin's frequent temper tantrums and demands for better, younger players did not cease, the 1973 Tigers surprisingly remained in playoff contention throughout most of the season, staying only four games behind the mighty Baltimore Orioles, who were led by future Hall of Famer Brooks Robinson. By August, however, the unpredictable and irrational behavior of Billy Martin was becoming too frequent for general manager Jim Campbell to defend or deal with. Martin argued incessantly with baseball personnel and fans and was constantly late to practices and games. His drinking also led him to make poor decisions. From propositioning players' wives to flipping over the team's buffet table in the locker room following a loss (and yelling at his team, "Go ahead and stuff your faces, you fucking bunch of losers!"), Martin was making it difficult for Campbell to retain him, even as the team continued to win games and stay in the playoff hunt.[41]

The final straw for Campbell came during Labor Day weekend, when the Tigers played against the Cleveland Indians. Martin had mistakenly bragged to reporters how he "ordered" his pitchers to use "saliva and Vaseline" on the ball to give them an edge because he thought the Indians were doing it against his team.[42] When it was reported in the press, Martin was suspended by the American League. It was during the suspension—a month before the season's end—that, in a highly unusual move, Campbell fired his manager.

"[H]e was an individualist, not an organization man," Campbell told reporters, "and he became a threat to the efficiency of our organization."[43]

True, but Martin had taken a "dying ballclub" two years earlier and turned it into a playoff contender.[44]

For Ron LeFlore, Billy Martin's dismissal was disappointing news. If it hadn't been for Martin, Ron likely would never have had the chance to showcase his talents. Yet Ron wasn't the sentimental type. He had worked too hard to get caught up in other people's business. For now, his focus was on the offseason. What was he going to do? Go back to Detroit? That was the last place he wanted to be. Luckily, the Tigers had a plan.

8

A Story From Day One

In the fall of 1973, the Detroit Tigers sent Ron LeFlore to Dunedin, Florida, located in the Tampa Bay area and about sixty miles east of the Tigers' spring training facility in Lakeland. The organization wanted to keep Ron focused on baseball (and out of trouble). This noncompetitive, offseason facility at Dunedin offered Ron opportunities to receive one-on-one assistance, which was exactly what he needed. In addition, he would be exposed to players who were already at the major league level, some of whom were there to enhance their baseball acumen or recover from an injury. And Ron would have his first opportunity to hit against major league pitching. Fellow Clinton Pilots outfielder and Detroiter Art James was also at the facility and would share a room with Ron.

Back home, life hadn't gotten any better. Ron's mother called to tell him that one of his accomplices in the armed robbery he had been involved in three and half years earlier had attempted to rob a jewelry store and was shot and killed. Across town, Tigers' general manager Jim Campbell and his front office were facing the grim reality of the post-Billy Martin years. *Sports Illustrated* highlighted the Tigers' woes in an article titled "Anyone Finding Fountain of Youth, Call Detroit."[1] Al Kaline (age thirty-eight) and Norm Cash (thirty-nine), once gods of Detroit, were embarking on their final season with the club. Aside from third baseman Aurelio Rodríguez, the overwhelming majority of the Tigers' everyday players, such as outfielder Jim Northrup (thirty-four), catcher

Bill Freehan (thirty-two), and pitcher Mickey Lolich (thirty-three), were in the thirty-plus age category, well past their prime. On top of that, the team would have a new manager soon. In contrast to the irascible Billy Martin, Campbell hired the older, more reliable Ralph Houk, a longtime Yankee manager who, during his first three years with the Bronx Bombers, led the team to three consecutive American League pennants and two World Series championships.

The *Sports Illustrated* article, which focused on the aging Tigers team, was not all doom and gloom. It also highlighted an up-and-coming prospect, Danny Meyer. The 21-year-old sandy-haired, hot-hitting minor league infielder was being groomed as the club's future franchise player, a possible heir apparent to the great Al Kaline. What readers weren't aware of was that Ron was supposed to be featured as well. Yet there was no mention of him. The reporter who interviewed Ron had assured him that he, too, would be included in the piece. Whether it was an editorial decision or the team had second thoughts about Ron and contacted the magazine not to include him as another viable prospect is still unknown.

Since he had contacted family and friends about the forthcoming article, Ron was sorely disappointed. Nevertheless, he remained focused on his mission: "I made up my mind I was going to have to do something to let people know I could play, too."[2]

When choosing where they hosted spring training every year, most ball clubs in Florida selected cities by the water. The Yankees played in Fort Lauderdale, the Baltimore Orioles were in Miami, and the St. Louis Cardinals were based in St. Petersburg. The Detroit Tigers, on the other hand, chose Lakeland, a town that was nowhere near the coast. More than an hour's drive from the beach, Lakeland was not the picturesque Florida town that fans thought of when they visited the Grapefruit League every March. It was known for its "cheap hotels and cheap eats"—ideal for the frugal Campbell, who hated to spend more of his boss's money than was needed.[3]

In February 1974, with half a season under his belt, Ron was invited to work out at TigerTown, the name of the campus in Lakeland that housed the Tigers and their staff every spring. TigerTown was previously used as an air force base and had been home to the Ludwig School of Aeronautics, where American and British pilots had trained during the Second World War. Since the team had taken it over, it had been transformed into a "sprawling complex," complete with training facilities, a dormitory, and Joker Marchant Stadium, where the Tigers and its local minor league club, the Lakeland Tigers, played home games.[4] More than 200 players would be on hand that spring, the majority of whom were minor leaguers competing for a coveted roster spot on the team.

Far from glamorous, TigerTown was still an ideal setting for spring training. The military barracks, renamed John Fetzer Hall after the team's owner, were converted into sleeping quarters for players and coaches. Although the air force was long gone, Campbell ran his team similar to how the military operated its base: rigid, with no room for error. When players arrived, they would check in and be handed a welcome pamphlet, explaining the dos and don'ts (mostly don'ts). "[W]e are expecting a complete cooperation in compliance," the Tigers' organization clearly stated. Curfew was at 11:30 p.m., and "[l]ights out at 12:00 midnight and all radios, televisions, stereos, etc. must be off. . . . There will be periodic bed checks with automatic fines for missing bed check."

Alcohol was not allowed in the dormitory. Gambling was banned. Profanity was discouraged. Smoking was allowed, but not in the room. Dress code requirements were enforced both inside and outside TigerTown. "Bermuda shorts in the area and in the city are allowed," however, no "cut off football jerseys, T-shirts, and other sloppy attire [in public]. . . . We expect all of you to keep yourself neat and properly groomed."[5] When eating in the cafeteria, players were allowed to take only "one juice, salad, beverage, and dessert"—at least until everyone had eaten, and then "you may have as much of the main course as you want."[6] The restrictions that the team imposed help to explain why many of the older players opted not to stay in the dormitory.

When not at practice or on the road playing another squad, some players explored Lakeland. Many preferred to stay in TigerTown, however, since there was little to do in town. Whatever free time players had, they played cards, wrote letters home, watched television, or rested. The team trained all day, doing calisthenics, working on mechanics, and studying their opponents in the film room. Older teammates would tutor younger ones. Catchers would work with pitchers. Training was not only to get into physical shape but it was also meant to bring the team together, creating a cohesive atmosphere that would ultimately percolate to Detroit once the season was underway.

If Ron had arrived in Florida a decade earlier, he would have had a far different experience. As an African American, he would have been separated from his white teammates once play ended for the day and players returned to the team compound.

"The only time we were with the Caucasian guys was when we were on the field," said Jake Wood, a former Tigers second baseman who played with the team from 1961 to 1966.[7]

During spring training throughout the late 1950s and early 1960s (the Tigers were one of the last teams in the league to integrate when they promoted Ozzie Virgil in 1958), Black and Brown players, when not on the field, were forced to stay in the segregated part of town. The Jim Crow-enforced segregation extended to every aspect of life in Lakeland except on the diamond. From restaurants and hotels to restrooms and dormitories, Black players who grew up in the North, like Wood, experienced a "culture shock."

"These men, and many others, went through some awful things," Al Kaline recalled.[8] When Willie Horton had arrived for spring training, he had to walk seven miles from the bus station to TigerTown, since no taxi would pick him up. Once he had arrived at the team's spring training facility, he and other players of color had to eat on separate sides of the cafeteria and could not stay in the same dormitory as their white teammates. The building they slept in lacked air conditioning, which in Florida was insufferable. Horton once told a reporter "you could lose 10 pounds staying in those barracks on a hot night."[9]

The situation was worse when the team had an away game, and the travel secretary had to make last-minute reservations with Black homeowners to host the non-white players, since the hotels refused to take them in. Sometimes the conditions were sufficient, but often the players were in tight quarters, hardly conducive for optimal performance on game day.

By 1963, most professional ball clubs that hosted spring training in Florida had begun or had already implemented the desegregation of their spring training facilities. The Tigers' organization was one of the last holdouts. When the Major League Baseball Players Association sent letters to every ball club that held spring training in Florida prior to the 1963 spring training, inquiring about each team's status when it came to player housing, an unnamed Tigers representative (likely Jim Campbell) claimed that the team had "made every effort to house all of their players under one roof in Lakeland."[10] The representative added that local officials had not accepted their proposals and that they would need to maintain the status quo. Whereas some clubs went so far as to move their spring training and tourism dollars to another municipality within Florida (such as the New York Yankees, who left St. Petersburg for Fort Lauderdale) or purchase a hotel outright so as not to be beholden to local customs (the St. Louis Cardinals took such action), the Tigers stayed put. After the 1963 season, the Tigers finally moved to their current facility and could allow integrated housing.

Instead of continuing to play for the Clinton Pilots in Iowa, Ron was assigned to the Lakeland Tigers, the team's other Single-A ball club, which competed in the Florida State League.

The only person whom Ron knew on the team was Dick Tracewski. A former Tigers infielder, Tracewski was later hired as a coach for the Lakeland team and had met Ron the previous June during his tryout at Tiger Stadium.

Dick Tracewski was a former shortstop with Detroit before he became a coach with the club. He was a daily presence when Ron became a Tiger. (Perkins-Phillips Collection, Lakeland (FL) Public Library)

Like everyone else who had been present that day, he had been impressed with Ron's speed. What Tracewski (or Trixie, as he was known by the players) also remembered was that Ron was heavier than he should have been and had sported a giant Afro.

Since then, Ron had cut the Afro, dropped the excess weight, and developed a trim, muscular body of 180 pounds. When he spotted Tracewski and approached him, acting as if they knew each other, the coach had a quizzical look on his face. Realizing that Tracewski didn't recognize him, Ron said, "I'm Ron LeFlore."

Tracewski couldn't believe it. His jaw dropped. Was this the same guy from the tryout?

"Wow, you look great," Tracewski unabashedly told Ron.

The coach was even more delighted to learn that Ron, who "looked like steel covered in rawhide"—Tracewski's words—was joining the Lakeland Tigers.[11]

Ron's new manager was Frank "Stubby" Overmire, a former pitcher with Detroit who had played for ten seasons in the major leagues during the 1940s and 1950s before becoming a manager in the minors. Having previously managed Lakeland before in the late 1960s, it was Overmire's second stint with the club.

Frank "Stubby" Overmire, a former pitcher with Detroit during the 1940s, managed Ron when he played for the Lakeland Tigers. He was a convincing voice to elevate Ron to the Majors when Tiger outfielder Mickey Stanley was injured and a spot opened in centerfield. (Perkins-Phillips Collection, Lakeland (FL) Public Library)

For the 1974 season, the Lakeland Tigers were strong defensively and had the potential to hit consistently, but pitching was questionable. The expectations for Ron were minimal. He was not on anyone's radar, given his mediocre performance in Clinton. He wasn't even assured a starting position, since there were four outfielders who would be competing for three spots. Overmire planned to shuffle them around to see what combination worked best.[12]

At the home opener against the Winter Haven Red Sox, the Tigers were hoping for a sellout crowd of 3,500. Although less than half that many fans passed through the gate, the team came up big in the win column, beating the Red Sox 12–0. Among the seventeen hits the Tigers belted out, three of them came from Ron's bat, including one that was almost a home run but fell short of the left field wall.

The team continued to win big, defeating North Division rivals the Tampa Tarpons and the St. Petersburg Cardinals. Within five games into the season, Lakeland was already leading the division by 1.5 games. On April 23, with less than 200 people in the stands, the visiting Tigers tore through the Tarpons 19–0 on twenty-two hits. "The small crowd," a sports reporter for the *Tampa Times* wrote, "cheered sarcastically the few times the team [Tarpons] managed to do anything right."[13] Ron was among three Tigers who hit a home run. He went four for five with four hits (including a double), four RBIs, and two runs scored.

Ron's hitting did not let up. By the end of April, the Tigers were 8–1 and leading the North Division by four games. When the team traveled to the southern tip of the Sunshine State, they played against the Key West Conchs and the Miami Orioles, who were led by future Hall of Fame first baseman Eddie Murray. The Tigers were brought down to earth, splitting their wins and losses evenly, returning home with a 13–6 record but still leading the North Division comfortably by five games. Ron's bat remained hot. By the end of May, he was hitting a staggering .382 for the first-place Tigers. He led the league in runs, hits, and batting average and swiped twenty-three stolen bases, likely becoming the leader in that category, too. His accomplishments did not go unnoticed, as he was recognized as the league's Topps (Baseball Cards) Chewing Gum Player of the Month for the month of May.

Recognizing they might have a star in the making, the Lakeland Tigers gave Ron a raise. He went from making $500 a month to $750 (equivalent to $5,500 today).

Known for always having "traces of tobacco juice on his uniform," Overmire was helpful in Ron's development, offering him advice where he saw it was necessary.[14] But the biggest influence on Ron while he was in the minors was not the team manager. It was the team's director of player development (in actuality, CEO of Detroit's minor league operation), Hoot Evers.

Walter Arthur "Hoot" Evers began his career with the Detroit Tigers when he was signed out of the University of Illinois in 1941. After serving in the army during the Second World War, he returned to baseball. Plagued by injuries, the outfielder would be better known for his post-playing career, where he held a series of positions in the front office of the Cleveland Indians before leaving in 1970 for the Tigers, working under Ed Katalinas, followed by Bill Lajoie.

Within the Tigers' farm system, Evers welded all the power. Referred to as the "Masterful Magician of the Minor Leagues," in consultation with Jim Campbell—everything went through the GM—Evers decided who would get promoted and released. As one player put it, "[W]ith one swift stroke of his pen, he [Evers] can sign your unconditional release and instantly transform a professional ballplayer back into a common, ordinary civilian." Suffice to say, when the rugged Evers showed up to your game or practice, "everybody starts to bear down just a little harder."[15] Unlike some imperious bosses, Evers knew what he was talking about, and the players respected him for his knowledge of baseball.

"I would pay attention to whatever he told me," Ron recollected. "If he said I was wrong, I would change and do it the way he told me to do."[16] Evers often had a mean scowl, which intimidated the players—except Ron, who had met his share of tough guys on the streets of Detroit and in prison. As far as he was concerned, Evers was more of a mentor than an authoritarian figure to be feared.

Evers recognized Ron's potential on the field, but he was deeply concerned about his naivete when it came to social norms in the South. Blunt as usual, Evers firmly admonished his star pupil, "Don't mess with white girls down in Florida."[17]

Since the fall of 1973, when he was playing in Dunedin, Ron had been dating a girl named Laura, who was white. After he was sent to Lakeland for the season, she got a job there with the intention that they would live together. Since Ron was on the road, Laura found them a place to live, a two-bedroom unit in an apartment complex near Marchant Stadium. Anxious to secure it, Laura lied to the property manager, informing him that she and Ron were married. The apartment was theirs.

When Ron showed up the next day to help with the move, the manager, who was white, suddenly changed his mind, claiming that the unit had already been rented. Ron held him to task. Apparently, his impressive size was enough to convince the manager to hand over the keys to his new tenant. Ron's menacing posture could have caused him serious problems. Even in the mid-1970s, Lakeland had an active Ku Klux Klan, which had made national headlines years earlier for protesting the integration of public schools and unionizing Black workers. More recently, the Klan chapter had held a rally at a nearby plaza, at which time Ron and other African American players were instructed, "Watch yourself. Don't go outside."[18]

In June, Ron's playing showed no signs of abatement, helping the Lakeland Tigers to remain in first place. But the Tampa Bay Tarpons had turned the corner and were now only two games behind them. At the start of July, which was already past the halfway mark of the season, Ron continued his dazzling hitting display. He led the league in batting average (.350) and hits and was second in runs scored—a performance that made him the talk of the town.

"The fans down there all love to watch him," said Dave Miller, Evers's assistant. "He gets on base and all of a sudden—boom, he steals."[19] The media was just as ecstatic, though it never lost sight of Ron's criminal past, usually referring to it in a benign manner. *Tampa Tribune* sports columnist Jim Selman noted, for example, "LeFlore's life seems to be heading for a storybook finish." Former-catcher-turned-broadcaster Joe Garagiola interviewed LeFlore in an NBC pregame interview, asking viewers, "[H]ow could this splendid athlete . . . have gotten mixed up in such a thing?"[20] When *The Sporting News* ran a feature about Ron, calling him "one of the brightest young prospects in the Detroit farm system," his backstory was never far behind: "You might think LeFlore was probably a top draft choice by the Tigers out of high school or college, got himself a nice bonus and started his way up to the minor-league chain to what appears to be certain success. Not so."[21]

Ron's life story was already legendary, and he hadn't even made it to the majors.

The Lakeland Tigers, in particular, benefited from Ron's unique background and sensational performance on the field. In 1973, the team attracted 19,189 fans to Marchant Stadium for the entire season. By July 8, 1974, the Tigers had already exceeded that number, and the team still had a month more to play. The increased attendance could be attributed to the team's first-place standing, but few could deny Ron's contribution to those numbers. Overmire compared him to Lou Brock, baseball's top (and soon-to-be all-time) stolen base king. The manager gave Ron the green light to run at will, something rarely done given Ron's limited experience.

Ron was performing at such a higher level than his teammates that there was concern among the staff at Lakeland that Detroit might promote Ron to Montgomery (Double-A) or Evansville (Triple-A)—or even the majors, to help the fifth-place Tigers. Team officials allayed those concerns, declaring that they had "no plans to move any players up in the system from Lakeland unless injuries forced the move." They added, "Outfielder Ron LeFlore will remain at Lakeland for the summer."

When a Lakeland-based business group was visiting Detroit on July 11, Ron's name was mentioned during a meeting with Ed Katalinas. The business owners were concerned that if Ron left Lakeland, it could impact the local economy. "Why move him up?" Katalinas responded. "Let him have a good solid year and then next year he can go as far as his talent warrants."[22] Katalinas's remarks provided further peace of mind for the Lakeland team and the town's hotels, restaurants, and other businesses.

This collective sigh of relief was short-lived. Eleven days later, the Tigers office did a 180-degree turn. Whether it had intentionally misled the public or not, the organization announced that Ron would leave Lakeland and move up to Evansville, Indiana, to play for the Triplets, Detroit's Triple-A club, bypassing the Double-A Montgomery Rebels. Evansville was the final stop before the majors.

Although Ron didn't finish the season in the Sunshine State, he was voted the 1974 Florida State League Player of the Year. The Lakeland Tigers, however, failed to maintain its first-place standing once Ron departed with his league-leading .339 batting average and forty-two stolen bases. The team ended the season in second place behind its division rival, the Tampa Tarpons.

Evansville, Indiana, was 850 miles and a time zone away from Lakeland. Located near the border of Kentucky and geographically closer to Louisville than Indianapolis, the city was more Southern than Midwestern. The Triplets were the most popular sports team in the region, partly because it was a Triple-A club. The club had been in the Milwaukee Brewers' farm system until 1973, when it was announced that the Tigers would take it over—to the delight of fans and the Triplets' management. Detroit was a bigger market, with bigger names, all of which would attract more ticket buyers in Evansville. The Triplets played in the American Association league, requiring more traveling than a Single-A or Double-A ball club. While the Lakeland Tigers never ventured outside of Florida and the Clinton Pilots ventured no more than 300 miles for a game, the Triplets often traveled over 1,000 miles to play a team in Colorado or Kansas.

The team was led by new manager Fred Hatfield. A former infielder who had bounced around the majors in the 1950s, including a stop in Detroit, Hatfield had been recently promoted from Montgomery to serve as the franchise's inaugural manager in Evansville. When Ron arrived on July 22, the team was four games under .500 and 8.5 games out of first place. That evening, at Bosse Field (the Triplets' home ballpark), the team was hosting the Indianapolis Indians, a Cincinnati Reds affiliate. It was Goodwill Night, when the Triplets

Fred Hatfield, a former Tiger infielder in the 1950s, was Ron's coach when he played for the Evansville Triplets. (Perkins-Phillips Collection, Lakeland (FL) Public Library)

gave away free tickets (which normally went for $2.50) in exchange for a bag of clothing that would be donated to a local Goodwill Industries store. Members of the press hadn't been notified until gametime that Ron had been added to the roster. As soon as it was known that Ron would play, *Evansville Press* reporter Tom Tuley prophetically remarked, "he was a story from day one."[23]

Triplets pitcher (and future Tiger) Vern Ruhle was on the mound that evening. He remembered Ron when he was attending Olivet College in Michigan, playing second base for the school's team. In an exhibition game against SPSM, Ron was at bat and had hit the ball to Ruhle. "I fielded it sharply, turned to throw, and he was already at first," Ruhle said. "I couldn't believe it."[24]

Ron would hit leadoff in his first game as a Triplet. He struggled in his debut, striking out twice and bouncing out once. He managed, however, to get a hit—a line drive single to right field, at which time most runners would stay put. The outfielder took his time fielding the ball. When Ron noticed it, he flew past first base and slid into second base. Safe!

Although Ron did not advance as the inning came to an end, Tuley and his fellow reporters in the press box took notice: "All of us... looked at each other and said to ourselves, 'what the hell just happened there?'"[25]

But the night belonged to Ruhle, whose parents were in the stadium, watching along with 1,482 other fans as the pitcher threw a three-hit shutout. The Triplets won 3–0.

After the game, Tuley interviewed Ron for a profile piece to appear in the next day's *Evansville Press* sports section. The 600-word article, "Ex-Convict Flying Free with Triplets," included a photograph of Ron wearing a Detroit Tigers cap—perhaps a prescient message.

"Ron LeFlore was a long way from the walls of Jackson, Michigan," wrote Tuley. "It's a living story of a man who lifted himself up by the bootstraps."

During the interview, Ron shared how he originally preferred football over baseball, how he got connected with baseball through a friend in prison, how the Tigers' organization discovered him, and how all this went beyond his "wildest dreams."[26] Over the years, it was a tale Ron would deliver word for word.

In the next two games, Ron's output was unimpressive. He was zero for six with a walk, a stolen base, and a run scored, although his manager claimed the umpire had taken two hits away from him "because they can't believe anybody can make it down to first that fast." While Ron struggled at the plate, his team remained unbeaten, winning three games in a row. Ron finally broke his hitless streak in his fourth game with the Triplets, where he went three for five against the Oklahoma 89ers, helping the Triplets extend their winning streak to four games since joining them.

Tuley's *Evansville Press* colleague, columnist Pete Swanson, was just as mesmerized by Ron's "flying feet."[27] Even when the opposing catcher called for a pitchout (where a pitcher intentionally throws out of the strike zone to keep the runner at bay) during one game, Ron still managed to safely steal second base, prompting Swanson to conclude that Ron ran "faster than any other right handed hitter that these eyes have ever seen."[28] In another display of his blazing speed, Ron was on first base when one of his teammates hit the ball to the shortstop. Normally a routine double play, Ron swiftly headed to second, slid into the base, and beat the tag.

Whenever Ron was on base, Triplet fans chanted "Go, go!" hoping he would attempt a steal. Ron's electrifying performance on the bases was more than a rare display of athleticism, observed Tuley. It had enormous entertainment value. A player like Ron had the showmanship, Tuley believed, to rescue baseball from "becoming our national bore."[29]

In his fifth game with the Triplets, playing against the 89ers again and with Hall of Fame pitcher Bob Feller in the audience, Ron put on his biggest hitting display to date. After being moved to fourth in the lineup (known as the cleanup spot), Ron went three for five, including a two-run home run that traveled 400 feet and a game-tying RBI single in the ninth.

Despite a rare loss against the Tulsa Oilers (led by future St. Louis Cardinals first baseman Keith Hernandez), the Triplets continued piling up victories. In eight games with Ron in the lineup, the Triplets were 7–1, climbing above .500 for the first time that season with a record of 51–50. The team that had started the season with three wins and eleven losses had found its stride. Inevitably, the buzz about the Triplets' success had reached Detroit.

For the past week, Hoot Evers had been scouting the Triplets at Bosse Field to see who was ready for a "major league promotion."[30] There was trouble in Motor City. The Tigers were three games below .500 and five games out of first place. Having lost fourteen of their last seventeen games, they were no longer in playoff contention. Subpar pitching and a recent spell of injuries had taken their toll. Catcher Bill Freehan had a groin injury. Left fielder Wille Horton, the heart and soul of the Detroit franchise, had just gotten off the disabled list while recovering from a problem with his leg and was put back on for an undisclosed amount of time. But there was also the undeniable issue that the team was aging. Over the past half decade, general manager Jim Campbell had stubbornly refused to overhaul the team, and he was now paying the price.

Following a Tigers loss, *Detroit Free Press* sports columnist Joe Falls wrote, "The worst possible thing is now happening to the Tigers. People are laughing at them. Their own true-blue fans. Laughing." He went even further, singling out the team's serious-minded GM. "Maybe Campbell didn't hear it from behind the protection of that glass, enclosed booth hanging from the upper deck out in right field. Or maybe he didn't want to hear it."[31] Even more humiliating, when the Texas Rangers visited Tiger Stadium, their new manager, Billy Martin, received loud cheers from the stands.

The worst was yet to come.

Center fielder Mickey Stanley was in his eleventh season with the Tigers. The 32-year-old native of Grand Rapids, Michigan was a four-time Gold Glove winner, a vital contributor to the 1968 World Series Championship squad, well-respected by his teammates, and adored by fans. He was a hard-charging player who would never become a superstar, but he was an integral cog within the organization. With Stanley, you always got superb defense and decent hitting. In fact, he was becoming more productive at the plate as of late, leading the 1973 squad in hits, runs, sacrifice flies, and at bats. But it was his capability to cover the outfield that drew comparisons to Joe DiMaggio and Mickey Mantle.

A week after Ron's promotion to Evansville, on July 30, at Fenway Park in Boston, Stanley was at bat during the fourth inning of the Red Sox–Tigers game when he was clipped on his right hand by pitcher Reggie Cleveland. He took first base, thinking that his hand was just bruised and he'd be all right. But once the inning concluded, it had swelled and Stanley was taken to a local hospital. The x-ray revealed that there was a bone fracture, and he would miss at least five weeks. With Stanley out, that left only one starter in the outfield, Jim Northrup, who was thirty-four years old. With Northrup in right and newly acquired Tiger Ben Oglivie in left, benchwarmers Marv Lane, Dick Sharon, and Jim Nettles—who were brought up from Evansville earlier in the season—were rotating in center field. This was not the outfield the Tigers had envisioned in April that would carry them to the playoffs. The team was breaking down and needed to find a fix—quickly.

Speculation among the Tigers' press corps was that the team would bring up Triplet All-Star outfielder Leon Roberts or up-and-comer Danny Meyer. The 23-year-old Roberts was two years older than Meyer; had more experience in the minors, having played on each of Detroit's three farm clubs; and was a solid hitter, with a .278 batting average, collecting 102 hits, fifty-four runs, and fifty-nine RBIs. Most importantly, the outfield was Roberts's dedicated position. He was the most logical replacement for Stanley.

Meyer, on the other hand, was initially recruited as a first baseman who didn't play outfield until he became a Triplet. Meyer's secret weapon was his hitting, which was superior to Roberts. He had a higher batting percentage

(.298), got on base more, and had more hits and runs scored. "Danny is ready to hit at any level," said the Triplets' manager Fred Hatfield.[32]

Either one of these prospects would give the Tigers a needed boost to carry them through the end of the season. Both players had positive reputations on the field as well as in the clubhouse.

While Roberts and Meyer joined three other teammates for the league's annual All-Star Game, Ron LeFlore was enjoying his day off in a hotel room at the Executive Inn in Evansville when he received a phone call.*

"Pack your bags," a team official said to Ron. "You're going to Detroit."

Ron was shocked. Was this a prank? This was something he didn't expect would happen for another couple of years. He wasn't the only one caught off guard.

Tuley of *The Evansville Press* thought that Ron needed "further minor-league experience."[33] His colleague, Pete Swanson, felt Leon Roberts was "more polished" than Ron.[34] According to Tuley, the entire "press box was surprised he went up that quickly."[35]

For that matter, Ron himself believed that either Roberts or Meyer "were better players" than he was, not to mention "with more experience."[36]

Ron's statistics for the 1974 season were anemic compared to those of Roberts and Meyer. Most of Ron's plate appearances were at the Single-A level, which was less competitive than Triple-A. At the Triple-A level, he had only had thirty-eight at bats, one home run, three RBIs, and three stolen bases; and his batting average was a paltry .235. In his first four games, he had gone one for thirteen. In his final three games, he was one for eleven. His defensive skills were also questionable.

Why was Ron chosen?

---

*In Ron's memoir, *One in a Million*, he said that he was in his "apartment" when he was notified about his promotion by a Triplet administrator. However, in an interview with *The Evansville Press* and during an interview with the author, Ron said he received a phone call at the Executive Inn, which was where he was living when he was promoted to Evansville.

Detroit Free Press reporter Jim Hawkins believed it was for the simplest of reasons: "They needed a body for center field. He was the best option they had."[37] Triplets manager Fred Hatfield arrived at a more plausible explanation when he stated that the Tigers "wanted somebody up there who can excite the people a little bit, kind of a showcase, and LeFlore can do that with his speed."[38]

Ron's initial take was that the Tigers were going "nowhere [in the standings] and they were looking for somebody to help put fans in the seats. And I had a better story to tell them than Leon Roberts or Danny Meyer."[39] Larry Paladino of the Associated Press, who was also a Tigers beat reporter, thought race might have played a role: "And [Ron] being a Detroiter, and being that Willie Horton [the team's most popular Black player] was at the tail end of his career," Ron was the obvious successor.[40]

During the 1970s, the majority of a professional sports club's revenue came from ticket and concession sales; broadcasting rights were also a source of income, but nowhere near as lucrative as they are today. To financially break even in 1974, the Tigers needed to sell 1.3 million tickets. They had been averaging about 18,500 fans per home game; if that held up through the end of the season, they would have passed the breakeven point. However, fans didn't pay to see their hometown team lose, even if a native Detroiter with a captivating story was in uniform. After Ron's promotion, attendance actually decreased, and the team failed to break even, having sold short that season approximately 65,000 tickets.[41]

So why did the Tigers promote Ron instead of Roberts or Meyer?

Having covered Triple-A-level play night after night, Tuley acknowledged it was "difficult... to understand why some guys went up and some didn't. There were some players who you thought were major league-bound but never got there and players that came through that you thought were borderline and the next thing you knew they were in Detroit."[42]

In fact, the actual decision to bring Ron to Detroit was less random and far more strategic than Tuley might have thought.

The day after Mickey Stanley's season-ending injury (which would also end his days as the team's regular center fielder), Jim Campbell, Hoot Evers, Ralph Houk, and Ron's minor league managers, Stubby Overmire (Lakeland) and Fred Hatfield (Evansville), held a "lengthy" five-way conference phone call.[43] Hatfield "favored" Leon Roberts, who had been excelling all year at the Triple-A level. He had proven he was ready for the job. Evers concurred.

Overmire advocated for Ron. The Lakeland Tigers manager was the only one on the call who had watched Ron play regularly over a period of time, albeit in Single-A-level competition. He saw Ron's potential for greatness. He could hit for power, his speed was undeniable, and he was an "intelligent" player who would compensate for his "glaring lack of experience."[44] And one couldn't dismiss the personal adversity Ron had overcome. Through his first thirteen months of professional baseball, Ron had gone from a recently released parolee, riding the bench in Iowa, to earning most valuable player (MVP) honors in the Florida State League, to playing Triple-A ball. Despite his struggles in Evansville, there was a brief period where, over two games, he went six for ten, culminating with a 400-foot home run and a game-tying single that led to him scoring the winning run. Although it was a small sample of play, it demonstrated Ron's capability to turn games around single-handedly against stiffer competition.

Houk and Campbell, neither of whom had much exposure to the players, closely listened to what the two minor league managers and Evers had to say.

There was no doubt that Leon Roberts checked all the essential boxes when evaluating a player's capabilities. He would, someday, make a fine, everyday player. But if there was a moment to take a "gamble" on someone, this was it.[45] The Tigers' top brass needed to think about the future. It was Al Kaline's final season. Who would be the next Mr. Tiger? The organization needed a player it could build a team around. Ron had that capability. Plus, he could run.

In the era of Maury Wills of the Los Angeles Dodgers and Lou Brock of the St. Louis Cardinals, who had both transformed baseball over the past decade with their unprecedented base-stealing capabilities and showed how it could alter the direction of a game, speed had a new premium. This was where the game was heading; it would be won on the basepaths. Because the Tigers hadn't replenished the old-timers from the 1968 championship team, quickness had eluded them. It was no secret. In 1971, Ed Katalinas, the team's previous top scout, had been quoted in *The Sporting News* as saying, "Our club is always looking for speed."[46] The Tigers hadn't had anyone fleet-footed since the days of Ty Cobb, who had played more than a half century ago. With Ron, they could *finally* fill that void.

"[T]he reports on LeFlore's speed, combined with his hitting," persuaded Campbell and Houk to join Overmire, edging out Hatfield and Evers.[47] It was three against two. LeFlore would get the call.

"When you've got that kind of speed, it makes up for a lot of other things," Houk later said.[48]

Evers still wasn't convinced: "I thought we were insane bringing him up to the big leagues so quickly."[49]

But to Houk and Campbell, who had more riding on this decision than anyone, Ron was the Tigers' last hope to save a franchise from becoming a permanent fixture in the cellar.

9

Becoming a Tiger

It was a cool summer evening on Thursday, August 1, 1974, in Milwaukee, Wisconsin. The Brewers were hosting the Tigers. Gametime was set for 8:30 p.m. It was the first of a two-game series at Milwaukee County Stadium, and both clubs came into the game with losing records, fighting to avoid last place in the American League East Division. Currently, the Tigers occupied that position. If they were fortunate enough to win both games, it would catapult them out of the cellar and compel the Brewers and the Yankees to share last place.

Unlike Fenway Park in Boston or Wrigley Field in Chicago, County Stadium did not have a rich baseball history, having opened only two decades earlier when Hank Aaron was the star of the Milwaukee Braves. Once the Braves left for Atlanta, the expansion Brewers took over the 46,000-seat venue in 1970. Since their inaugural season, the team struggled to avoid being at the bottom of their competitive division. The fans showed their displeasure by doing what fans of losing teams do in any sport: they stayed away. On the evening of Ron LeFlore's Major League Baseball (MLB) debut, a crowd of only 9,010 passed through the gate, leaving 80 percent of the stadium vacant. To Ron, it must have felt like he was still in the minors.

When Ron arrived in Milwaukee, he was told to take a cab downtown and check in at the historic, high-end Pfister Hotel, where the Tigers were staying. He had just signed a contract for $15,000 (equivalent to $100,000 today)—the major league minimum, though it was an enormous increase compared to his minor league salary. He was then taken to his room, where he met his teammate, fellow Detroit native and backup outfielder Marv Lane, who was competing for a regular roster spot. Ron had barely put his luggage down when Lane told him to see Tiger manager Ralph Houk in his hotel room.

"You're starting tonight," Houk told Ron after shaking his hand.[1] It was the first time the two men met.

Houk got right to the point: "I know you don't have a lot of experience; you're gonna have to learn by playing. So I'm gonna put you out there in centerfield every day. Don't worry about anything. Just do your best."[2]

Don't worry? Ron had barely been in Triple-A-level ball for a week when he had gotten the call to come to Detroit. Thinking that he'd ease into the lineup like he had with the Clinton Pilots, he was immediately overwhelmed. When he returned to his room, Lane dropped another surprise.

You know you're leading off, his roommate shared. Since the Tigers were the visiting team, that meant Ron would be the first hitter of the game, which was just a few hours away. To heighten Ron's nerves even more, Lane told him about the Brewers' starting pitcher, Jim Slaton.

"He's got a helluva curve ball," he said.[3]

Curveball? Ron knew it was inevitable that he would confront his old bugaboo, but not on his first day in a Tiger uniform—and as the game's leadoff batter to boot. He was so nervous that his knees shook uncontrollably all the way to the ballpark.

At the stadium, Ron and his teammates went to the visitor's locker room, where they got dressed. *Detroit Free Press* reporter Jim Hawkins, who had published a story about Ron on the front page of the sports section of that morning's paper, was also there. He noticed how "several of the veteran stars" went over and shook Ron's hand, welcoming him to the team. As the leading Tiger beat reporter noted, it was "something you seldom see when a rookie arrives."[4] But with Ron, it was different. He hadn't even taken an at bat yet, and his name and photograph had already been published in nearly every small, mid-size, and major metropolitan newspaper in the country that morning.

Given the extensive publicity about Ron's criminal background, Houk had called a team meeting prior to his arrival. The Tigers' manager had wanted to make certain that Ron was treated like he "was part of the team," and he advised his players to "make him feel comfortable; give him a second chance."[5]

But not all of Ron's teammates welcomed the newbie with open arms. Reporter Jerry Green of the *Detroit News*, the *Free Press*'s crosstown rival daily newspaper, heard "grumblings" from some Tigers who were concerned about leaving their personal belongings in the locker room. "This guy is an ex-offender," one player told Green, expressing his concern that he might disrupt the team chemistry.[6] Dennis Clotworthy, a Tiger batboy, overheard a conversation in which first baseman Norm Cash informed a fellow player to "Make sure you don't leave any cash in your locker. I heard he stole money from his teammates down in the minors."[7] Although Ron had been out of prison for a year, managed to stay out of trouble, and met consistently with his probation officer, it was not going to be easy to shake off the "ex-convict" label.

At the conclusion of the national anthem that night, Ron warmed up in the on-deck circle, stretching his muscular body. His bulging biceps almost tore through the team jersey that had the word "Detroit" marked across it. Waiting for his name to be called over the loudspeaker, Ron was about to reach a milestone few men his age ever experienced. He was forty feet away from achieving what he had spent every day over the past three years working toward. No one in that stadium had any idea what he had gone through to get there—nor did they care.

"Go back to jail, jailbird!" fans yelled from the stands.

As Ron walked to home plate and set himself up in the batter's box, his knees were still shaking—so much so that he thought he would topple over. When Slaton threw his first pitch, Ron jumped out of the way.

Strike one!

It was a "goddamn curve!" Ron thought to himself.[8]

He had never seen a ball curve that late and be called for a strike. Before he could settle his nerves, his first at bat in the majors went quickly, and he struck out.

Ron had the misfortune of making his debut in the midst of a pitcher's duel between Slaton and the Tigers' Woodie Fryman. Neither team that evening could mount much of an offense.

Ron struck out in his first three plate appearances: once looking and twice swinging. At the top of the eighth inning, with the Tigers leading 1–0, Ron finally made contact with the ball. He hit a grounder to Don Money, the Brewers' third baseman, who fielded it and threw it safely to first base. Ron was clearly out, but it gave the public a glimpse of his speed. Designated hitter (DH) Al Kaline, in the final season of his twenty-two-year career, all with the Tigers, was watching from the dugout and was astonished. Even though Ron was out, Kaline had "never seen anyone faster to first base."[9]

Having held the Brewers to two hits and up 2–0 in the bottom of the ninth, Houk could have taken out Ron and put in someone with better defensive capabilities to maintain the lead. He knew the Brewers would attempt to take advantage of the rookie center fielder, hoping he'd bobble the ball or make an ill-advised throw that could swing the game in their favor. Joining Ron in the outfield was his new roommate, Marv Lane, who relieved Ben Oglivie. The first batter was Money, who hit it hard to center field, hoping the new guy would screw it up. Ron got under it and caught it safely. One out.

The next batter, catcher Charlie Moore, struck out. It was Fryman's tenth of the evening. Two outs. Fryman, who had a no-hitter going into the seventh, was an out away from a shutout.

The third batter was first baseman George Scott, who was hitting .310 for the season but had struck out twice that night. Scott had the power to go the distance and prolong this game. Fryman threw the ball hard, right over the plate at Scott's knees—"where he likes it." Scott swatted it toward center field. Ron, still suffering from shaky knees, focused on where the ball would land and got under it. He caught it.

Game over. The Tigers had won!

Although the night belonged to the 34-year-old Fryman, the hero of the evening made sure to credit his young outfielder for closing the one-hour-forty-seven-minute game. "The kid made a good play," Fryman said about Ron's catch for the game's final out.[10]

When the team returned to the Pfister Hotel after eleven that night, some of the players headed to the hotel's bar for a nightcap, breaking the well-established tradition that players didn't drink in the hotel; that was reserved for the manager and his coaches. In view of the fact that the Tigers were an older group and had a reputation for not "causing problems," the unspoken rule did not apply to them. Ron joined his teammates.[11]

When he found an empty stool, he was hoping to drink the night away and forget about his poor performance at the plate.

"Ronnie, come on, sit down, I've been waiting for you."[12]

When Ron turned around to see who was calling his name, he was stunned. It was Kaline, known to fans and teammates as Mr. Tiger. Ron walked over and sat down with one of the few Tigers he remembered as a youth. Kaline ordered him a drink.

The son of a broommaker, Albert William Kaline shared some similarities with the rookie. He, too, had grown up in a poor family. Although he hadn't been a gang member, Kaline had had his own problems to overcome. As a child, he had developed a chronic bone disease in his left foot that, following a medical procedure, left his foot partially deformed and Kaline feeling ashamed. But that did not negatively impact his personality. Unlike other superstars such as Mickey Mantle or Joe DiMaggio, Kaline had a reputation for being polite, easy to get along with, and mild-mannered. He wasn't intimated by Ron's past. In fact, he wanted to help him.

Over a drink, Kaline told Ron about the different pitchers around the league and what to expect. He also explained how the 162-game season was like running in a marathon; you had to pace yourself, or you'd burn yourself out. Overcoming mistakes, he pointed out, is part of the game. The conversation put Ron at ease, who was tipsy.

Eventually, Kaline excused himself. Other teammates came over to join Ron, including third baseman Aurelio Rodríguez, left fielder Jim Northrup, and Gates Brown, who was splitting time at the DH with Kaline. They welcomed Ron to the team by getting him even more drunk.

Once the bar closed, the players carried Ron to his room, left him on the floor, put a flower on his chest, and crossed his hands over each other as if he were lying in a casket. Welcome to the major leagues.

Nursing a hangover, Ron had a few hours to relax before the team headed to a pregame workout at Milwaukee County Stadium for his second game in a Tiger uniform. The number of fans attending Friday increased threefold that evening to see Brewers pitcher Clyde Wright on the mound against the Tigers' rookie right-hander Dave Lemanczyk, who was starting his first game ever after pitching in the relief spot. Ron was hoping he'd collect his first hit against Wright, who had been struggling all season, with a record of 8–14.

As leadoff hitter again, in his first at bat, Ron made contact and hit the ball to the shortstop. He raced along the baseline and was safe, but it wasn't a hit. The shortstop committed an error. Still, Ron was touching a bag for the first time in the major leagues.

Unfortunately, the Tigers' bats went dormant. The aging Kaline hit into a double play, and veteran catcher Bill Freehan, who was back from an earlier injury, hit a ground out to end the inning. At Ron's next at bat in the top of the third, and with the game scoreless, he grounded out.

Later, after an hour-long rain delay in the fifth inning, the game resumed. With the Tigers up 1–0, Ron once again hit the ball to the shortstop in a forced-out situation. The shortstop wisely went after the runner on second instead of challenging Ron. With two outs, second baseman Gary Sutherland was at bat. Ron got the green light to steal and took off from first.

Safe! It was Ron's first stolen base in the major leagues.

Now, with Ron in scoring position, the hot-hitting Sutherland drilled a single, sending the rookie around third base and straight to home. His first run scored in the majors. The score was now 2–0.

This was an example of Ron proving his value to the team. If he hadn't stolen second base to put himself in scoring position, he would have been left on base, since Kaline, who followed Sutherland, grounded out to end the inning.

In the top of the seventh, with the Tigers now leading 3–0, Ron yet again hit a ground ball to the shortstop, who forced out the runner on second. With Sutherland up, Ron put the pressure on the pitcher, who was now obliged to pay attention to both the batter (Sutherland) *and* the runner (Ron). As soon as Wright released the ball, Ron took off for second. Safe! It was his second stolen base of the game.

Unfortunately, neither Sutherland nor Kaline could advance Ron, and the inning was over.

By the ninth inning, it looked as if Ron would have to wait for another game to break his zero-for-eight hitless streak. There were two outs when catcher (and the ninth man on the roster) Gene Lamont came to the plate. He knocked in a single, his fourth hit of the evening to keep the inning alive. With the Tigers up 3–1, another run would pad the Tigers' lead and give them a sweep of the Brewers before heading back to Detroit later that evening. It was back to the top of the order.

With a man on first and two out at the top of the ninth, Ron stepped up to the plate against Wright, who was still hanging in there despite having given up three runs and twelve hits.

Pop!

Ron hit a single to center field, his first major league hit. Lamont advanced to second. With Sutherland up, there were runners on first (Ron) and second (Lamont). Sutherland knocked in a single, scoring Lamont. Ron raced past second and into third safely, a preview of how quickly he could charge around the bases. The team hadn't seen anything like this in recent memory, which was what Campbell and Houk had hoped for when they had selected Ron over more experienced players.

Unfortunately, the man who had given Ron a pep talk the night before might have needed one himself. Kaline, who had been hitless all night, lined out to right field, and the inning was over. Nonetheless, the Tigers won the game.

The team flew out of Milwaukee immediately after sweeping the Brewers and were now heading home in fourth place. It was the first time in more than two weeks that the Tigers were no longer at the bottom of their division, which the Brewers and the Yankees now occupied. In his first year as the Tigers' skipper, Ralph Houk had to endure constant comparisons to his predecessor (Billy Martin) as his team struggled with injuries, mounting losses, poor pitching, and an identity crisis. Perhaps Ron's presence was the spark they needed to turn the season around. Houk had a lot riding on Ron. It was his first significant personnel decision that he had made as the Tigers' manager. But for those who knew the former army major, making tough decisions was something he had been doing for a long time.

Born in 1919 in Lawrence, Kansas, Ralph was eleven years old when he was introduced to the game of baseball by his uncles, who played for a semipro team. He was a natural on the diamond, and after graduating from high school, he signed with the New York Yankees in 1939. After three years in the minors, soon after the United States entered the Second World War, he and his brother Harold joined the army. Houk was sent to a specialized training center in Kentucky, where he would be commissioned as a second lieutenant before shipping out to Europe in July 1944. After landing on Omaha Beach during the invasion of Normandy, he was nearly killed when a bullet pierced through his helmet and missed his head by an inch. Months later in Luxembourg, he and his squadron were occupying foxholes when the Battle of the Bulge began. During the ensuing combat, Houk demonstrated extraordinary valor, saving the lives of members of his squadron and leading a counterassault against the Nazis. Awarded the Silver Star, the third-highest military combat decoration in the US Armed Forces, he rose to the rank of major.

When Houk returned to the States, he resumed his playing career. However, it would be uneventful. Backing up Yogi Berra, one of the greatest catchers playing in one of baseball's greatest dynasties (the 1950s New York Yankees), Houk would spend the majority of his time warming up pitchers in the bullpen. During those eight years backing up Berra, Houk played in only ninety-one games. His days on the field were over, but his managerial career was just beginning.

At the age of thirty-five, Houk was tapped by the Yankees' farm director to become a manager of their minor league club in Denver. He then returned to the Yankees as one of manager Casey Stengel's coaches and, in 1961, took over and became the only manager in MLB history to win two World Series in his first two seasons (1961 and 1962). It helped that he had Berra, Mantle, Roger Maris, and Whitey Ford on the same team. After three years as the team's skipper, Houk was promoted to general manager of the Yankees, but he was not as successful in the front office. He returned as team manager until a new owner, shipping magnate George Steinbrenner, purchased the club in 1973. Houk resigned at the end of that season.

Two weeks later, Jim Campbell hired him to lead the Tigers. It was a welcome break for Houk. After nearly thirty years in the Big Apple, the Tigers represented a new challenge. He was taking over a club that was in its twilight years. A *Sports Illustrated* reporter deemed the 1974 Tigers "so old that one cannot help but think of going out and getting them hot tea and shawls as they sit in the dugout."[13]

Fortunately, Houk possessed a quality that was an asset when managing a team in transition: patience. In many ways, he was the antithesis of his predecessor, Billy Martin, which explains why Campbell was attracted to him. (The other was his connection to the Yankees' organization at the time, considered the gold standard in professional sports.) Houk, for example, would never bash a player publicly the way Martin did. "I don't think you can humiliate a player and expect him to perform," he once said.[14]

Houk's reputation as a no-nonsense manager reassured Campbell that he wouldn't have to worry about receiving a phone call in the middle of the night. On the road, Houk "was a loner," recalled radio broadcaster Ernie Harwell, who traveled with the Tigers. "He was one of the few managers who almost never went out with his coaches or the media for an evening meal. Most of the time he would stay in his room, alone." What did Houk do in his room? "He works on the lineup," Harwell was told.[15]

On the other hand, there were some concerns about the new manager. Like Martin, Houk tended to get angry easily. But it was not simply a short fuse, according to *Detroit Free Press* sports columnist Joe Falls, who was of the opinion that Houk had the "most violent temper of any man I have ever known."[16]

His track record as a manager was troubling, too. Campbell was hoping Houk could take a struggling team and quickly turn it into a winner. When Houk had resumed his duties in 1966 as skipper of the Yankees, he had a less talented lineup to work with. Over the next seven years, the Yankees never finished higher than second, and that was only once; during the majority of those years, the team finished closer to the bottom of the standings.

For Ron, however, Houk was the ideal manager. His war experience prepared him well to deal with overbearing general managers and prima donna players. As he put it, "Having men under me in combat helps me to understand personal problems in a stressful situation. . . . You have to treat each individual differently. Some you have to kick a little, and some you have to pat a little."[17] With Ron, he would do both—sometimes at the same time.

RALPH HOUK

Detroit Tiger Manager Ralph Houk was Ron's first MLB manager and the most influential. (Rucker Archive, Society for American Baseball Research)

When the Tigers returned to Detroit after picking up two wins against the Brewers, they began a five-game, three-day series (including two doubleheaders) against the Baltimore Orioles, the division leader and favorite to win it all that year. It would be Ron's hometown debut. In center field, where he played, homemade signs hung over the railing that read "LeFlore's East

Side Legion" and "Good Luck LeFlore."[18] Among the fans in the center field bleachers was his younger brother, Gerald.

When Ron arrived in the Tigers' locker room, the locker he was assigned to was in between Willie Horton and Gates Brown, the team's two African American veterans. Was it a coincidence? Unlikely. Campbell's position, common among other GMs when it came to race relations, was to keep the Black players together. Sure, he wanted Ron to feel comfortable and be surrounded by positive influences, but there were several other teammates who could have provided the same support as Brown and Horton. In Campbell's defense, though, Brown was the only other player who had served time in prison. In fact, Brown provided mentorship to Ron, reminding him to "keep his nose to the grindstone," that he was getting a second chance and shouldn't blow it.[19]

Like all of the other teams in the American League during the first half of the century, the Tigers were resistant to integration. When the team had been owned by automotive manufacturer icon Walter Briggs (from 1919 to 1952), he had been more than willing to lease the stadium to all-Black teams like the Detroit Stars to play their home games. Nevertheless, integration of the Tigers was not going to happen under his watch. Briggs never considered signing a non-white player to play for his beloved Tigers, even after Jackie Robinson of the Brooklyn Dodgers integrated MLB in 1947. While other clubs were scooping up future Hall of Famers like Willie Mays, Ernie Banks, and Hank Aaron, whom the Braves recruited for the "rock bottom price of $3,500," Briggs would rather lose than add a player of color to his roster.[20]

It would take Briggs's passing for Black players to be welcomed into the Tigers' organization. In 1958, eleven years after Jackie Robinson's debut, the Tigers finally promoted a non-white player to Detroit: infielder Ozzie Virgil, a 26-year-old native of the Dominican Republic. The club was the second to last to integrate its squad (the Boston Red Sox was last). It would take another year and countless protests from local Black Detroiters, who had been picketing since 1948 for the team to integrate, before an African American (outfielder Larry Doby) was signed.

Within two years of signing Doby, the team had made significant progress adding non-white players to its roster, including starting outfielder Bill Bruton, shortstop Chico Fernández, second baseman Jake Wood, and backup outfielder Bubba Morton. By 1961, three of the nine Tiger starters (Bruton, Fernández, and Wood) were players of color, unprecedented for any team in the American League.

In 1963, when Willie Horton and Gates Brown joined the club, the club regressed just as the percentage of Detroit residents was increasingly African American, nearly doubling its size by 1970. While Detroit's Black population rose, the Tigers were moving in the opposite direction. By 1969, aside from Horton and Brown, there were only two other non-white players on the forty-man roster: pitcher Earl Wilson and pinch hitter Ron Woods. Horton became so resentful of management for not promoting more Black and Hispanic players that he went AWOL for four days in May of that year.

Jake Wood, the Detroit Tiger second baseman, was one of the first African Americans to play for the team. (Perkins-Phillips Collection, Lakeland (FL) Public Library)

Willie Horton, played most of his career in Detroit, was a fan favorite and got along well with management. Horton attempted to provide guidance to Ron, but he was not receptive to the veteran's advice. (Perkins-Phillips Collection, Lakeland (FL) Public Library)

While the public was under the impression that Horton's absence was because of his hitting slump, behind the scenes he was communicating his frustration to Campbell, who knew he couldn't afford to have an unhappy Horton, who was a graduate of Detroit's Northwestern High School and a fan favorite. The big man got his message across. Personnel changes were made immediately. By the end of the season, the Tigers had added second baseman Ike Brown, pitcher Norm McRae, infielder César Gutiérrez, and outfielder Wayne Redmond. By 1974, when Ron arrived, more than 20 percent of the Tigers' roster was non-white. It might not have been as much of a percentage as the Pittsburgh Pirates (33 percent), who fielded the first all-Black starting lineup in 1971, but it was progress.

If Ron's hometown fans were expecting a win in his Tiger Stadium debut, they left disappointed. The division-leading Orioles rocked the Tigers in the first inning with home runs by Don Baylor and Tommy Davis. The Tigers fell behind 4–0 before they had even gotten an at bat. Down 6–1 in the eighth inning, Ron, who had been zero for three with infield groundouts, roped a single. With Al Kaline at bat, Ron, who was ready to take off, distracted the pitcher, Ross Grimsley, who threw a wild pitch. Ron easily advanced to second, putting him in scoring position. Kaline then hit a single to left, and Ron glided home.

Unfortunately, the team did not produce anything else and lost the game 6–2. But once again, Ron's speed demonstrated how he could impact a play or game, or even improve his teammate's performance. Second baseman Gary Sutherland, the hitter who batted behind Ron, saw his batting average increase twenty points in Ron's first eleven games. It would have been even higher if Ron could get on base more.

Ron's hitting remained erratic. In his first five games with the Tigers, he went two for nineteen. He was, however, fortunate to have an unassigned mentor that season.

"You're late," Kaline told Ron, who had just arrived at the ballpark prior to a game.

"What do you mean?" Ron asked.

"We're here two and a half hours before the game so we can shag [catch fly balls as part of batting practice] for the other guys. They shag for us and we should shag for them. Ralph [Houk] doesn't have many rules, but we are to follow the ones he gives us."

While Campbell thought Ron would naturally gravitate toward Gates Brown or Willie Horton, it was Kaline who had the greatest impact on him during the 1974 season. Ron needed to continue to put in the work if he was to have a long, productive career like Mr. Tiger. Kaline and his pupil conferred all the time before games, with Ron gaining insights that would give him an advantage on the field.

"You remember what I told you about [Oakland A's pitcher Ken] Holtzman?" Kaline asked Ron one time. "He'll give you that head fake every time, but he'll never throw over to first. Go every chance you get."

They would also discuss how to conduct one's life off the field. Kaline warned Ron about hangers-on and how people were going to try to take advantage of him: "They'll come to you with all kinds of deals, but don't sign anything.... Even if it's your relatives, don't sign. Get a lawyer. Call Jim Campbell or even call me at home."[21]

When Ron did get on base, it was one of the few bright spots for Tigers fans that season. Fans chanted "Go, go!" every time he was in a position to steal.[22] Even reporters were caught up in the excitement. While he was typing a column in the press box, *Free Press* sports columnist Joe Falls told a reporter from the *Toledo Blade* to get him when "LeFlore came up."

"I can't think of the last player who took this kind of hold on the fans," Falls wrote in that very column.[23]

On August 12, Ron hit his first home run in the majors against the Kansas City Royals at home. It was a two-run blast in the bottom of the third inning that helped the Tigers defeat the surging Royals. Ron shared the spotlight with two teammates that day. Pitcher Mickey Lolich moved up to ninth place on the all-time MLB strikeout record, and Al Kaline moved up to sixth place in total games played. Despite these accomplishments, the Tigers had a dismal record.

When the team took on Billy Martin and his Texas Rangers, the former Tigers manager gloated as the Rangers won five out of six games, having outscored the Tigers thirty-four to nineteen. Among the wins was a come-from-behind-victory where, after the game, Martin told the press, "I won't have to eat dinner tonight. I'll be tasting this win all night."[24]

With the Tigers out of playoff contention, the season's focus turned to Al Kaline's pursuit of 3,000 hits, an exclusive club that only eleven other players in history were members of (including, most recently, the late Roberto Clemente in 1972). It was the only reason 39-year-old Kaline opted to play in 1974. On September 24, with his parents in the stands at Memorial Stadium in Baltimore (Kaline's birthplace), Mr. Tiger, who came into the game with 2,999 hits, whacked a double in the fourth inning. A week later, Kaline finished his career with 3,007 hits.

If there was anyone in the organization who had the potential to become the next Mr. Tiger, it was Ron LeFlore. Even though he had played MLB for only two months, he was developing a reputation for being a baserunning threat—something no Tiger had done since the days of Ty Cobb. When the team took on the Yankees on September 7, Ron led off the game with a single. When he stole second, Thurman Munson, the Yankees All-Star catcher, attempted to throw Ron out, but his throw was off the mark (likely because he knew Ron would be a tough out and released the ball too quickly). It landed in center field, enabling Ron to advance to third base. First base coach Dick Tracewski began the ritual of educating umpires before every game to make sure they were "aware of this kid's speed"[25] so they weren't caught off guard when he took off. Even Houk, who played and coached the great Mickey Mantle, who had the rare combination of power and speed, had never "seen anybody any faster than" Ron.[26] In his eight weeks with Detroit, Ron stole more bases than any Tiger had in a single season since Jake Wood in 1962.

As the 1975 season approached, every sportswriter agreed. From the national sports magazines to the local papers, the Detroit Tigers would finish last—again. The pundits argued that the team was even in worse shape than in 1974. Mr. Tiger himself, Al Kaline, had retired, as did Norm Cash, one of the team's all-time best home run hitters. Outfielder Jim Northrup, the only full-time starter in the outfield when Ron had made his debut last August, and pitcher Woodie Fryman, the starting pitcher in Ron's first game, had been traded to the Montreal Expos. Aside from 32-year-old and injury-prone Willie Horton (who would take over the DH spot previously occupied by Kaline), pitcher John Hiller, and catcher Bill Freehan, the few remaining veterans from the 1968 club—pitcher Mickey Lolich, outfielder and Ron's predecessor Mickey Stanley, and pinch hitter Gates Brown had little left in the tank to make any meaningful impact.

If the Tigers finished at the bottom of their division again, this would be only the third time in their seventy-four-year team history—a devastating blow for this once-proud franchise. Yet it seemed likely that it might happen, given their competition in the American League East Division. This included the Yankees, the Red Sox, and the Orioles—all of whom, according to Tigers beat writer Jim Hawkins, were stronger than they had been last year.

Even before the season had started, the team's supporters were registering their discontent. At spring training, one fan shouted, "Come on, Houk, do something." Another bellowed, "Give Al Kaline another year." One loyalist expressed the frustration of many when he yelled, "Let Jim Campbell do the pitching."[27]

The fans were being asked to "adopt a whole host of new heroes" as they perused the spring roster.[28] There was hardly a recognizable name in the program: infielder and former San Diego Padre Nate Colbert, catcher Terry Humphrey, and pitcher Tom Walker. And then there were the rookies, unknown and untested.

The 1975 season was supposed to be a celebration of the franchise's seventy-five-year history. Instead, it would be a reminder of how far the Tigers had fallen since their World Series championship in 1968. The only major change from the previous season was how they went from being the oldest club in the major leagues to the youngest.

That spring, the buzzword frequently associated with the Tigers was "rebuild." It was used by the team, reporters, and fans alike to justify the expected mounting losses while they planned for the future.

There was a sliver of hope for the Tigers, though. All eyes would be on the Black kid from the East Side of Detroit.

"I really think he could be a super star," Jim Campbell said at the start of spring training. "[He's] one of the most exciting young players to come on the scene here since Al Kaline."*[29]

---

*Both Danny Meyer and Leon Roberts were also compared to Al Kaline during the 1975 preseason. The Tigers' yearbook called Meyer the "Tigers' best hitting prospect since Al Kaline," while Jim Hawkins in the *Free Press* speculated that Roberts was the "heir apparent to Al Kaline in right field." In the end, LeFlore, Meyer, and Roberts never came close to replicating Kaline's stellar career.

Even early in his Tiger career, well before he became an All-Star, Ron was "a story from day one." (Rucker Archive, Society for American Baseball Research)

In its annual baseball preview issue, *Sports Illustrated* noted that Ron LeFlore, despite his brief two-month tenure in the majors, was "the talk of the division."[30] During the offseason, Ron had been voted by the Detroit Sports Broadcasters as the team's Rookie of the Year. Featured in *People, Time, The*

Sporting News, Popular Sports, Baseball Bulletin, and *Sports Today* (which used snappy headlines such as "From Prison Cage to Batting Cage"), Ron even graced the cover of the Tigers' official 1975 yearbook.

Before the start of spring training, Campbell kept a "close eye" on Ron, fearful that he might do something to jeopardize his probation.[31] The slightest infraction could endanger not only Ron's future but also the Detroit Tigers' franchise. The 26-year-old kept a low profile, living with his parents and attending the Instructional League in Dunedin, Florida, to improve his mechanics. Just before spring training got underway, Ron received good news: he was no longer on parole—a relief to both himself and the team.

When the players reported to TigerTown in Lakeland, Florida, the city's civic organizations, youth clubs, and business roundtables had requested Ron—in prior years, it was always Al Kaline—to be the featured speaker at their luncheons. To the team's delight, Ron thrived in the public spotlight. Charming and well-spoken, he was becoming the most sought-after Tiger that spring. His audiences wanted to hear the same story: how he overcame his adversities to become a professional athlete. To younger crowds, however, he was careful to point out that there was nothing glamorous about his past. He didn't "want them to think they could go out and get in trouble and then play baseball. It just doesn't work out that way."[32]

Ron also had a devoted following among Detroit's journalists. "He is the one irresistible player on this team—the one player you can never take your eyes off," wrote Joe Falls, the veteran *Free Press* sports columnist and "elder statesman of Detroit sports writing."[33]

Ron didn't always live up to the hype. Inconsistent as a player, he had trouble hitting a curveball and going a week without committing an error. During a spring training game against the Cardinals, a fly ball was hit to him in the outfield. Having put on his sunglasses too late, Ron lost the ball in the sun, and it hit the edge of his glove before dropping to the ground. Later in that same game, with the Tigers at bat and the bases loaded, Ron, among the base runners, wasn't paying attention and got picked off. He was still learning the fundamentals.

On the other hand, Ron demonstrated how he could take over a game. When the Tigers played against the Philadelphia Phillies in another spring outing, Ron hit a two-run home run. A week later, against the Expos, he tripled in the ninth inning to win the game for his team.

As the Tigers headed into the 1975 season, there were plenty of changes happening around the majors. The biggest news during the offseason was All-Star pitcher Jim "Catfish" Hunter leaving the mighty Oakland A's, whom he had helped lead to three straight World Series championships. Hunter signed with the New York Yankees, becoming baseball's first true free agent. A year later, following an arbitration hearing, free agency became official and would forever change the game and professional sports, unleashing an "explosion" of player salaries.[34]

The other major news that offseason was Frank Robinson, who became MLB's first African American manager when he took the helm of the Cleveland Indians. Since Jackie Robinson's debut in 1947, there had not been any progress made when it came to hiring people of color in management positions. Throughout that time, several Black players had dominated the game, yet not a single one was offered a managerial job. For example, New York Yankees catcher and 1963 MVP Elston Howard was in the running to become the first African American to hold such a position when Houk left the Yankees in 1973. He was already on the coaching staff and was popular among the players. Yet, Howard was passed over.

A year earlier, during the second game of the World Series, 53-year-old Jackie Robinson, who was in poor health and suffering from diabetes, was honored with throwing out the first pitch. Before the game started, he was asked to make a speech. He seized the opportunity to express his frustration with the league: "I am extremely proud and pleased to be here this afternoon, but I must admit that I am going to be tremendously more pleased and more proud when I look at that third-base coaching line one day and see a Black face managing in baseball."[35]

Nine days later, Jackie Robinson passed away.

The Tigers' season opened as expected. They were beaten badly at home by the Baltimore Orioles by a score of 10–0. Any optimism that had permeated Tiger Stadium that afternoon dissipated. The Orioles' future Hall of Fame pitcher, Jim Palmer, allowed only three hits. The next day, the Tigers left for the Bronx to play against the Yankees. Ron, who went hitless against Baltimore, continued to struggle at the plate. In fact, Ron went zero for twelve in his first three games of the season.

For the fourth game, Houk had had enough with his star player and took Ron out of the lineup in the first game of a doubleheader, replacing him with Art James, Ron's former teammate in Clinton. In the second game of the doubleheader, Houk put LeFlore in for James, who also struggled at the plate. That decision paid off. In the first inning, on the fourth pitch of the game, Ron stroked a home run, his first hit of the season. He went two for five that afternoon and four for thirteen over the remaining games in the series against the Yankees.

Ron continued hitting the ball well, breaking up a perfect game against Boston Red Sox ace Luis Tiant, who hadn't allowed a base runner in six innings. During another outing against the Orioles, Ron hit a home run in the tenth inning, clinching an important win on the road. His spark rubbed off on his teammates.

By the end of April, the Tigers were 10–6, and to everyone's astonishment, including their own, the team was in first place in their division. Willie Horton, who many had assumed was past his prime, had a team-leading four home runs by month's end. And following his season-opening slump, Ron was now hitting a respectable .284, leading the Tigers in runs scored and stolen bases.

He also displayed his capacity to hit for power, having smacked two home runs in one week. He was just getting started.

Over the course of nine games, starting on April 30, Ron put on a magnificent hitting performance. He went nineteen for thirty-seven, increasing his batting average by more than seventy points (to .344). He rang up two triples (which would have been doubles for most other players), six RBIs, and four stolen bases during that period. Ron no longer worried about anyone taking over his starting role.[†]

Beyond statistics, Ron showed how he could deliver in clutch moments. With the bases loaded against the Milwaukee Brewers, he knocked in a decisive single that allowed the Tigers to take over the lead and win the game. He displayed his Olympic-caliber speed on the basepaths when, following Willie Horton's single along the third base line, he flew from first base and ran through Tigers' third base coach Joe Schultz's stop sign to score. It wouldn't be the last time he'd do that to Schultz.

On May 27, at Tiger Stadium, the Minnesota Twins' intimidating Bert Blyleven was on the mound. He had already given up four runs when he faced Ron at the top of the fifth. Blyleven came into the game with a 5–1 record and a 2.99 earned run average (ERA). If he could settle the Tigers down, he'd probably get into his groove and sail through. The count was two balls and two strikes when he threw a high, inside pitch that brushed by Ron, catching him off-balance. Unshaken, Ron got back into the batter's box and ripped the ball deep into center field, over the Twins' outfielder's head, hitting the 440-foot fence marker before bouncing back onto the field. The ball was still in play. Realizing it wasn't an automatic home run, Ron raced to second and headed toward third. It was a sure, uncontested triple. Schultz flashed the sign for Ron to hold up at third, but Ron ignored it and continued at full speed, bypassing

---

[†] Art James, a once-promising minor league prospect who had started eight of the team's first fourteen games in the outfield, would only play as a professional in three more games that season. It would be his only season in the majors.

third and Schultz and racing toward home plate. Safe! It was the Tigers' first inside-the-park home run since Willie Horton had done it in 1971.

With the score 5–0, it seemed the Tigers were sure to win it. Momentum was on their side. They were mistaken. The Twins came back and won the game 6–5. This would be the frustrating pattern throughout the season. After occupying first place briefly, the Tigers returned to reality by the end of May and were fighting to stay in third place, with a 19–21 record. And then when June came, the bottom fell out.

Entering June, Ron was ranked among the league leaders in runs scored and hits, which were vital stats for any leadoff hitter. Whereas in May he had batted an impressive .313, in June his average dropped to a lowly .231. He was also striking out frequently, averaging one for every four at bats, which was high, even for a rookie.‡

Ron wasn't the only one struggling on the Tigers. In June, the team showed why they were picked by every sports media outlet to finish last. Against the Red Sox, they were annihilated 15–1, with rookie Fred Lynn doing most of the damage by slugging three home runs with ten RBIs. Two days later, against the Yankees, the Tigers blew a 7–0 lead to lose 10–9. During a span of eleven games in mid-to-late June, the Tigers lost ten times, falling deeper into the division cellar. In a post-game interview in the locker room, Houk, when asked what type of new strategy he planned to impose, couldn't muster much of anything profound except that he was going home to "think of something," anything to get his team to win.[36]

Whatever time Houk spent mulling over those losses, it did nothing to change the team's course. The Tigers lost twenty-four out of thirty-two games in June. They went from third place and still in playoff contention, to last place and fourteen games back from first place.

---

‡For example, one of Ron's counterparts, first-year Oakland A's outfielder Claudell Washington, was averaging one strikeout for every ten at bats. Even players who were strikeout-prone, such as Yankees veteran outfielder Bobby Bonds, were averaging less than one in five at bats.

It got so bad that, on one late June day, Houk took out his frustration on Phil Hersh, a 28-year-old *Baltimore Evening Sun* journalist. Hersh had referred to the Tigers as "hopeless" in that day's *Evening Sun*'s paper.[37] The 54-year-old, cigar-chewing, former combat veteran grabbed the reporter, who was nearly half his age, and "dragged" him by the back of his neck into the Tigers' clubhouse, yelling, "You can't call my team lousy!"[38] Tigers veteran Mickey Stanley came to Hersh's aid and convinced Houk to stop. Hersh filed a police report, and an arrest warrant was issued the next day for the Tigers' manager. Houk was photographed and fingerprinted, then released on his own recognizance.

According to *Free Press* reporter Jim Hawkins, it was all a performance. Houk's team was losing so much that he was desperate to light a spark under them. "The Tiger manager meant to get mad, to explode, to scream and shout," Hawkins wrote in a column days after the incident. "He was determined to do it in front of the team to ensure maximum impact. He started plotting his plan of attack moments after he laid eyes on the infuriating article."[39]

If that was Houk's plan, it didn't work—at least at first. The Tigers lost the next five games in a row. But then something clicked. On July 1, five days following the incident, the Tigers finally won, stopping a five-game losing streak. From there, the team began doing something they had had trouble accomplishing for most of the season: winning.

Pitching had been the team's single biggest weakness all season, and starters Mickey Lolich, Vern Ruhle, and Joe Coleman now stepped up, pitching complete or near-complete games during that span. On the offensive side, no Tiger hitter was hotter than Ron LeFlore. Over the next three weeks, he hit .381 and collected twenty-four hits in sixty-three at bats, along with three home runs and six stolen bases. There was speculation that he might be chosen to be the Tigers' representative at the annual All-Star Game in Milwaukee, but he was passed over for veteran catcher Bill Freehan.

Still, Ron demonstrated how his bat and speed had the capability to push the Tigers into the win column. It was his two-run home run that broke the team's five-game losing streak on July 1. A week later, against the Kansas City Royals, it was Ron who was responsible for the deciding run in a tightly fought contest. To start the fifth inning, Ron hit a single and then stole second base. Now in scoring position, he advanced to third on a groundout by Gary Sutherland. (Royals second baseman Cookie Rojas, who fielded the ball, didn't even try to throw Ron out; he went after the slower Sutherland.) When the next batter, outfielder Leon Roberts, slapped a grounder to Royals shortstop Frank White, the fielder underestimated Ron's quickness and threw the ball to home plate. It was too late. Ron's run led the Tigers to a 3–2 win.

Beloved Tiger Willie Horton contributed as well, revitalizing a career that many believed was on the decline. Beginning July 3, the Tigers won nine games in a row. As far down as fourteen games out of first place prior to the turnaround, the team clawed their way to within 9.5 games. One could argue that Houk's outburst, staged or not, may have played a role in the Tigers' reversal of fortune.

The team was also coming into their own. They were more relaxed, both on the field and in the clubhouse, where they could be found playing cards, joking with reporters (not in Houk's case), and smoking cigarettes, including Ron, who smoked Kool, the preferred choice among Black players. The older players—Freehan, Lolich, and Gates Brown—mingled with the younger guys (Ron among them), a significant departure from past behavior.

When a young white reporter from an alternative weekly newspaper in Ann Arbor, Michigan, requested an interview with Ron, the two men rapped about his troubled childhood; life behind bars; and his wide-ranging musical tastes, from American jazz saxophonist Grover Washington Jr. to British rockers Elton John and David Bowie. With a reporter from *Sports Illustrated*, Ron discussed how he still lived with his parents at the house he had helped buy for them in East Detroit while expressing his annoyance with non-Tiger television broadcasters, who tried to be witty at his expense. He used the example of how one broadcaster had wisecracked that Ron had gone from "stealing cars to stealing bases."[40] But Ron had never stolen a car. He had stolen other things, but never cars.

When Houk found out that Phil Hersh of the *Baltimore Evening Sun* had dropped the charges against him, he was in a better mood, smiling in the dugout with tobacco hanging from his lip as his dark sunglasses hung over his nose.[§] The team had gone 15–4 during that winning period. The Tigers had defied everyone's expectations, including their own.

And then it all fell apart.

It started when Ron injured his knee while making a play in the outfield. He was out for nine games, six of which the Tigers would lose. When Ron returned, the team went on to lose their next nineteen games in a row. It got so bad that team owner John Fetzer—who never spent time with his players—made a rare appearance in the clubhouse, hoping to spark some life. When the team finally won a game on August 16, they had avoided tying the longest consecutive losing streak in American League history by one game. The team was so bad that fans would taunt the teenage batboy, "Hey bat boy! You need to get these guys new bats. They couldn't hit a beach ball!" Or, they would mock him, saying, "Why don't you bat for so-and-so? I'm sure you couldn't do much worse!"[41]

In the end, that spark in July did little to alleviate the team's woes. The 1975 Tigers finished in last place with one of its worst records in franchise history: 57–102, more than thirty-five games behind the first-place Red Sox.

Ron never fully recovered from his knee injury, perhaps returning too soon. In his final 200 at bats of the season, he managed to collect only forty-one hits (a .200 batting average) and steal a measly three bases, which reflected

---

[§] According to an email exchange with the author on April 16, 2024, Hersh said he "dropped the charges because I had fulfilled the reason for filing them: to let people like Houk see that laying hands on a journalist would not be tolerated and hidden."

how his nagging injury prevented him from terrorizing other teams on the basepaths. Even more troubling was the number of times he struck out. In his first full season in the majors, there was only one other player—Texas Rangers outfielder Jeff Burroughs—who struck out more than Ron. In those final 200 at bats of the season, Ron averaged one strikeout for every three at bats, an unheard-of figure for any MLB hitter, especially at leadoff.

During this period, Willie Horton, who was one of the few bright spots for the Tigers that season by winning the American League's Designated Hitter of the Year award, reached out to Ron in the locker room, hoping to impart the same type of positive advice that Kaline had done the previous season. But this time, Ron wasn't as receptive. After a few unsuccessful attempts, a frustrated Horton said to himself, "You know what, you're on your own. You're gonna do what you're gonna do."

During the second half of the season, teams had scouted Ron and identified his weaknesses. They knew he was susceptible to swinging at bad pitches—particularly the breaking ball, a pitch that looks like it will be a strike until it's unhittable and goes into the dirt. Houk had also counseled Ron to stop trying to hit home runs; it was only increasing his strikeout total.

Coaches and team personnel had noticed that Ron became more hardheaded as the season progressed. "He didn't want to be bothered," former batboy Dennis Clotworthy recalled. "He didn't want to be told about meetings with coaches when they told him you gotta do this or you gotta try that, like open up your batting stance or close it a bit."[42]

Despite Ron's and the team's woes, Houk still believed his young players had the tools to make the Tigers a winner. "People don't realize how hard these kids are trying," Houk let it be known to reporters. "[T]hey just don't realize how important the little things are until they have to do them under Major League circumstances. I've been at both ends of this game and, believe me, things can turn around so fast. You've just got to be patient."[43]

In Ron's case, Houk knew he possessed that rare capability to turn a game around. Once on base, Ron created a slew of problems for the opposition. This was why Houk was so patient with Ron. He could take a single—or even a walk—and turn it into a windfall of runs for his team. And it was why Jim Campbell took measures to ensure Ron avoided negative elements, even though he was no longer on probation.

Over the past year, two of Ron's friends had been killed. One had been shot twenty-one times when stepping out of his car, and another had been killed at a pool hall. If Ron was cruising through his old neighborhood, former acquaintances would tell him to leave. There was nothing there for him. For the most part, Ron listened and moved on. One fellow he did not disassociate himself from was former Jackson inmate and baseball manager, Jimmy Karalla, who had been released earlier that year.

Instead of turning his life around, Karalla went right back to organized crime. He reconnected with the Giacalone brothers, Anthony and Vito, who were now at the apex of their power in Detroit. One of the Giacalones' protégés was thirty-year-old Frank Lee Usher, a native of Detroit's East Side. Usher's initial contact with the Italian Mafia family began when he was fifteen, serving as an errand boy before moving up to "junior member."[44] As his responsibilities increased, so did the severity of his crimes. Known as Frank Nitti (the name of Al Capone's right-hand man), in 1974, Usher started his own "crime family" called Murder Row. It was financed by the Giacalones and specialized in the drug trade and murder-for-hire. Based on investigations by the US Department of Justice, Usher's heroin-dealing in the mid-1970s led him to be known as the "black godfather of Detroit."[45]

Around this time, Ron met Usher for the first time through Karalla. The two East Side natives took a liking to each other. Over the next couple of years, according to organized crime historian Scott Burnstein, "[they] were observed by federal agents hobnobbing with each other and additional nefarious characters emanating from the local gangland scene at various high-end restaurants and nightclubs."[46]

Ron was about to learn the price to be paid for keeping such company.

10

A Star Emerges

Despite the passage of time, Ron had not forgotten about Jackson Prison. And Jackson Prison hadn't forgotten about Ron.

"Ron used to return to prison on a regular basis to see his old buddies," recalled inmate Napolun Birdsong, who had announced the baseball games at Jackson when Ron had been competing there. "I['ve] never seen the prison [officials] allow a former inmate to come back as often as they did Ron. It seemed like he came back as often as he wanted to. And they would let him have access to his little crowd, his old buddies, and he'd be holding court."[1]

The prison administrators had their own reasons for rolling out the red carpet for Ron, whose legendary feats on the diamond were still the talk of the yard. Ron's redemptive story gave inmates hope for a new life, which to the staff meant they would be more inclined to exhibit positive behavior. Sports, especially baseball, became more popular now that Ron was playing for the Tigers.

"[LeFlore] was the instrumental force in revamping the [prison baseball] team," noted a reporter for *The Spectator*, the prison's newspaper.[2] Not only did Jackson field a highly competitive team, attracting the institution's best athletes but it also generated so many requests from visiting teams to play them that some had to be turned away. A few of the players hoped that they, too, would become the next Ron LeFlore, and there was reason to believe it.

The Pittsburgh Pirates, for example, sent "two scouts to four Illinois prisons . . . in search of baseball talent. 'We're looking for ball players,' said a team scout. 'Maybe some of them are behind the walls.'"[3]

During the 1975–6 offseason, when Ron wasn't making public appearances, he was active with the Detroit chapter of the Big Brothers of America and received the Big Brother of the Year Award. His personal life, however, was not as meritorious. He had been in an intermittent relationship with his fiancée, Deborah Lewis, until she had broken it off. Not long after, she had gotten married, but tragically her husband died (causes unknown). Deborah and Ron reconnected, though their relationship was destined to be short-lived once she announced that she was pregnant with his child. Ron wasn't willing to commit to a long-term relationship, not to mention helping care for a child.

Ron's focus was on himself and what suited him in the moment, and that was to hone his skills as a ballplayer. In late 1975, Ron got on an airplane and headed south to Puerto Rico. Similar to the MLB's Instructional League in Dunedin, Florida, Puerto Rico had since the 1950s served as a launching pad for rookies as well as veterans who were seeking further development, many of whom would become future stars.

When Hank Aaron came to Puerto Rico in 1953, for instance, he was a relatively unknown nineteen-year-old infielder. One of his coaches adjusted his swing, and Aaron eventually became the greatest home run hitter in major league history. When Maury Wills arrived in Puerto Rico in 1957, he had been stuck in the Los Angeles Dodgers' farm system for the past five years, and within a year, he secured the starting position as shortstop for the Dodgers, a position he held until 1972. Following the 1970 season, Reggie Jackson was sent to the island by the Oakland A's organization. His winter league team coach noticed he had trouble seeing the ball clearly and suggested he be fitted for glasses. When Jackson returned to the A's, he emerged as a dominating hitter of his era.

Like other teams, the Tigers had sent several players to Puerto Rico, including Willie Horton, Jim Northup, and pitcher Denny McLain. All three blossomed into their positions when they returned to the States. Detroit's front office was hoping Ron would experience similar success.

Once Ron arrived in Puerto Rico, he (not surprisingly) experienced a jolt of culture shock. But it was short-lived. Though hardly a world traveler, Ron had played ball in various parts of the United States and learned to adapt to new cities and regions. Besides, there were many English-speaking residents to help him navigate the island, including umpire Joe West, whom he would befriend and go to the bars with at night and sip Puerto Rican rum.

Ron took advantage of the year-round warm weather—in stark contrast to frosty Detroit at that time of year—staying in hotels by the beach, visiting the nearby island of Saint Thomas, and frequently patronizing various drinking establishments.

On the field, Ron was mentored by Harvey Kuenn, the manager of the Mayagüez Indians, a team in the Puerto Rican Winter League. Kuenn, a former Tiger and the 1959 American League batting champion, immediately identified Ron's weaknesses. When batting, Ron needed to plant his feet instead of lunge at the ball. Kuenn also advised Ron to avoid the temptation of wanting to hit every pitch out of the park—and, most importantly, to lose "some of his cockiness."[4]

Apparently, Kuenn's observations paid off. Ron hit over .300 that winter, earning a spot on the winter league's All-Star team.

When Ron returned to Detroit, the 1976 spring training season would soon begin. Like any new season, there were plenty of team personnel changes, none more significant than the trade of pitcher Mickey Lolich. The veteran pitcher—who had spent his entire career with the Tigers, including a vital role on the 1968 championship team, where he pitched three complete games in the World Series and was selected as the series' MVP—had been traded for the power-hitting Montreal Expos first baseman Rusty Staub. Near the end of his playing days, Lolich was deeply disappointed that he was leaving the team. No longer the ace among the starters, he was bluntly told by Jim Campbell, "We don't need you. You're not winning anymore."[5]

With Rusty Staub, Willie Horton (who was coming off his best season in years), and outfielder Ben Oglivie the Tigers had an abundance of riches at the plate. Understandably, Ron was concerned about whether he still had a role within the organization. It seemed that Detroit was no longer pinning its future on him.

While the Tigers' organization, like all teams in the offseason, was deciding which players to keep and who to let go, professional baseball itself was in the midst of significant change. Following the 1975 legal decision to abolish the reserve clause (which prevented players from changing teams unless management had given them an unconditional release), now they had greater freedom of choice, which would be known as "free agency." But there was a sticking point: When would a player become a free agent? The owners wanted it to take effect in the player's ninth season. Those on the field favored a sooner timeline. Unable to resolve the issue before spring training, the owners refused to open the spring training ballparks, locking out the athletes. While older players understood what was at stake and stood their ground, younger players, like Ron, were less committed to the cause.

"I wasn't aware of none of that stuff," he recalled. "I went to spring training to get in shape."[6]

Since he couldn't practice at TigerTown, Ron and a few other players went to Florida Southern College's Henley Field, where the team used to hold spring training. They stretched, hit grounders to one another, and worked on their hitting. They even created makeshift teams—Mickey Stanley's Scavengers versus Danny Meyer's Derelicts—and competed in seven-inning games. It wasn't all fun. Without a steady paycheck, Ron and some of his teammates feared that if the lockout went on much longer, they would have to find part-time jobs.

Fortunately for them, on March 9, a court of appeals ruled in favor of the players, allowing them to decide on free agency after six years of major league service. A week or so later, the spring training camps were opened. The ruling, however, had long-term implications for the game. Salaries skyrocketed, and sports agents became ubiquitous. It also diminished a player's loyalty to his team, causing some baseball fans to seek their sports entertainment elsewhere, namely the NFL and the NBA.

That same day, Ron, who thought his worries were behind him, was confronted with a new problem.

Detroit Free Press reporter Ron Ishoy—who normally covered local news, from IBM company picnics to small plane crashes—somehow stumbled upon Ron LeFlore's birth certificate. It indicated that his birth year was 1948, yet the Tigers listed it as 1952. It was a significant enough discrepancy that Ishoy contacted the *Press*'s Tigers beat reporter Jim Hawkins, who was in Lakeland, Florida, covering the team's spring training.

Ron "is not the 23-year-old flash he'd like everyone to believe he is," Ishoy and Hawkins wrote on March 9 in the lead article of that day's sports section.

According to their evidence, which included prison records and Ron's driver's license, the *Free Press* reporters claimed that Ron and the Tigers' organization had lied to the public about when he was born. When general manager Jim Campbell was asked for comment, he placed the onus on Ron. "In the [parole] documents," Campbell claimed, "there was a one-year discrepancy on his age. I asked Ron which age was the correct one, and we used the age he identified."[7]

Ron offered his own convoluted explanation:

The only record I've ever seen with my date of birth on it was the report from the parole board when I was released from prison. That said I was born in 1950. And that was the date I always went by before I went to prison. When I came up with the Tigers, they had a copy of the report and a sheet that said I was born in 1952. They asked me which one I preferred and I naturally took the lesser age. At that point I was just happy to have a chance to play pro ball. I think anybody with my background, who suddenly had the chance to improve himself into a respectable citizen, would have done the same thing. I didn't think I was doing anything wrong.[8]

In later years, Ron blamed fellow inmate and prison baseball coach Jimmy Karalla for the discrepancy. Karalla had advised him to "knock a couple of years off" his real age, which, he felt, would be to Ron's advantage.[9]

"When I asked the Tigers for a tryout, I lied about my age," Ron said in a 1979 interview. "I thought [based on Jimmy Karalla's advice] they would look more favorably on a 21-year-old rather than a 23-year-old which I was."[10] Thirty years later, Ron changed his tune and asserted that the Tigers told him "to lie and say I was 21 years old."[11]

Neither Campbell nor Ralph Houk were upset about it, at least publicly. "I could care less," Campbell explained, "the only concern I have is that he can play ball."[12]

Houk concurred. "One or two years—who the hell cares?" he felt. "I don't give a damn if he's 58 as long as he can run and hit and throw."

The GM's and the skipper's public statements did not put the controversy to rest. Attempting to do so, Campbell took the high ground. "[Ron has] paid his penalty," he pointed out. "He's trying to get a fresh start in life. He has conducted himself properly since he has been with us, and he's done everything we've asked."[13]

What neither Campbell nor Ron ever addressed was that the age discrepancy was not a matter of one or two years, but actually four. That had long-range consequences for the team and player: Ron's trade value to the Tigers dropped, and his negotiating power diminished accordingly. But for the moment, all eyes were focused on the upcoming season.

The goal of the 1976 Tiger club was simple: avoid ending up last for a third consecutive season. At the very least, finish with a better record than 1975, which one critic deemed was the "the most miserable year in Tiger history."[14] It wouldn't be easy. The American League East Division was stronger than its counterpart in the west.

Unlike the start of the previous season, those in the front office and on the field were less confident about Ron's potential. He would not be the franchise savior that they had hoped for. They knew he still needed to work on his fielding and inconsistent hitting. Whether he realized it or not, this was a make-or-break year for Ron LeFlore.

On opening day in Cleveland, Ohio, Houk did not include Ron in the lineup. Instead, he started Ben Oglivie in center field and replaced him later in the game with veteran Mickey Stanley, who was still on the roster and could literally play any position save pitcher. Ron rode the bench as he watched the Tigers win their first game of the season on the road. They then headed home to face the Brewers. Once again, Ron didn't see any action. Back on the road, the Tigers headed west to face the California Angels.

In this third game of the young season, Houk continued to start Oglivie, despite his measly .091 batting average. At the top of the eighth, the Tigers were down 4–2. Second baseman Gary Sutherland started the inning with a single. The tying run was at the plate. Houk replaced Sutherland with Ron as a pinch runner. This was Ron's debut of the 1976 season, a humiliating experience from being a starter to a pinch runner. Yet he maximized his opportunity, stealing second base. Willie Horton then belted a double and Ron scored, igniting a rally that led to the Tigers taking the lead, 5–4.

Later, the Angels tied and the game went into extra innings. The Angels won, but Ron showed Houk he was indispensable on the bases.

In the fourth game of the season, Ron finally had his first at bat and roped a double. But Houk continued to tinker with the lineup, using Mickey Stanley in one game and Oglivie in another. On April 20, six games into the season, with the Tigers' record at 3–3, Houk put Ron back in the starting lineup against the Oakland A's. Ron knocked in another double.

Just as he was on the cusp of earning back his starting role, Ron's life took a sudden and tragic turn.

While Ron had turned himself around in ways no one who knew him could have ever imagined, his younger brother Gerald struggled. He had so much promise. The family thought he would become a doctor. He was a gifted student and had an aptitude for science. He even attended college for a brief time, but the streets of Detroit's East Side took hold of him just as they had with Ron.

For Gerald, his difficulties began when he was a teenager, after Ron had been sent to the juvenile lockup facility in Ionia. The youngest and the last of the four LeFlore sons to live at home, Gerald went through an endless cycle of addiction, getting clean and then relapsing. During this period, he had a son, Gerald Jr., and would have two more children, all the while heavily involved in the drug trade. At one point, he couldn't pay his dealer and allegedly had been kidnapped and held for ransom—a ransom to be paid by his famous older brother. Somehow, Gerald was let go without harm, and no money was exchanged.

Around 2:00 a.m. on Friday, April 23, 1976, 26-year-old Gerald LeFlore was at home with his girlfriend in northeast Detroit. There were six other men present. About thirty minutes into the gathering, Gerald noticed his satchel was missing. Immediately, he became enraged, likely because he had a stash of drugs in the bag. Gerald yelled at the men, pointing a rifle at them. Three of the men grabbed Gerald, and a scuffle ensued. During the fight, the safety latch on the rifle was deactivated. Someone pulled the trigger, and a bullet went into Gerald's chest. He was taken to Detroit General Hospital, where he was pronounced dead.*

---

*There have been other versions of how Gerald died. The one told in this narrative is the police version. In another tale, Gerald's girlfriend was with him at the top of the stairs when the six men "busted in and shot Gerald." Then there's the story that Gerald tried to rob the six men, and they killed him in self-defense.

While the police were in the process of identifying the next of kin—which would have been Gerald's parents, since he wasn't married and his children were too young—Ron and his teammates were back home, following their road trip in California. The Tigers were about to begin a four-game series against the Texas Rangers. Game time was set at 2:15 p.m.

Before Ron headed to the ballpark, he stopped at his parents' home, totally unaware of what had happened to his brother. When he got out of his car, he saw his mom, Georgia, in front of the house in a daze. It was unlike her. When he spoke with his parents, it was clear that something was amiss. But Ron had a game to get to and left for Tiger Stadium.

While taking batting practice, a clubhouse attendant interrupted Ron and told him Deborah left him a message to give her a call. It was important. Ron probably thought she was in labor, since she was only a few weeks away from having their child. Instead, Ron returned the call and received the news. He immediately called his mother.

"He is gone," Georgia told him.

"You want me to come?" Ron asked her.

"No," she said. "You can't do anything for him now. He's gone. Go and play the ball game."[15]

Ron later found out that when he had seen his mother earlier, she had just returned from the city's morgue to identify Gerald's body.

Word spread throughout the clubhouse. When Ralph Houk got wind of what had happened, he assumed Ron was not going to play that afternoon.

"I made a new lineup with [Mickey] Stanley in center [field]," Houk informed Ron, who told the manager that he was *not* sitting out the game.[16] His mother's advice made sense. There was nothing he could do for his late brother but "play the ball game."[17]

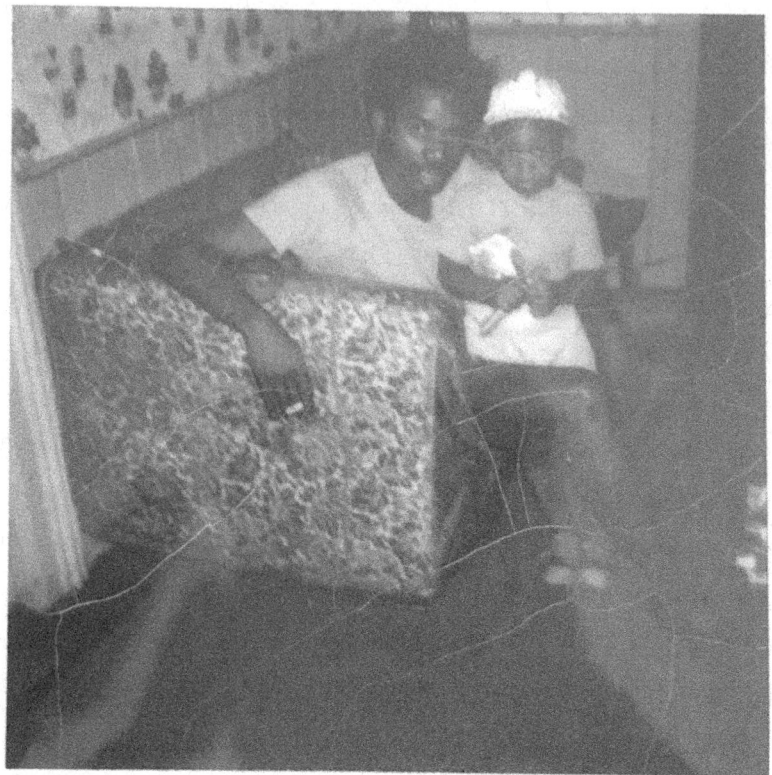

Ron's younger brother Gerald with his son, Gerald Jr. This photograph was probably taken not long before Gerald's untimely death on April 23, 1976. (Ron LeFlore's personal collection)

Those in the stands were unaware of Ron's tragedy and treated the game as any other by maliciously taunting Ron. "Go back to prison where you belong," a fan yelled at him that afternoon.[18]

Ron had become a master of compartmentalizing such insults, and now, he utilized that skill regarding Gerald's death so that he could focus on the task at hand. In his first at bat, he hit a single into the outfield. In the bottom of the second, with the Tigers down 1–0, the bases were loaded and Ron hit another single to tie the game. In the fourth inning, Ron collected his third single of the day. He also stole second. The Tigers won a nail-biter, 7–6. It was Ron's best performance of the young season.

After the game, word had spread that Ron's brother had been killed the day before. When he was asked by reporters why he played, he said, "I did it for my parents.... They tried to keep it [the news] from me as long as they could for my own good."[19]

Later, Ron went to his parents' house. They learned that the police, who had released the six men involved in the shooting, had ruled Gerald's death "accidental," which only angered Ron, who felt it was no accident. His brother had been murdered.[20]

The following day, Ron drove around his old neighborhood when he spotted the man he thought was responsible for killing Gerald. Without hesitation, Ron reverted to his old mindset. He began scheming how he could kill the man without being seen. But then he caught himself. What about his career? His teammates? His parents? His soon-to-be child? What about the inmates at Jackson who looked to him for inspiration? But what gave him pause more than anything was the thought of going back to prison. Ron drove off.

Gerald's funeral was held on Tuesday, April 27, at Mount Zion Baptist Church, in the neighborhood where he had been raised. Ron wasn't even thirty years old, and he had already buried two brothers. It was a lot to take in, but he didn't have time to sulk.

A week after Gerald died, Ron's daughter, LaRonda, was born. Ron's relationship with his child and her mother started out well, but his attention waned. He was neither ready nor willing to assume the responsibilities of fatherhood and a domestic partnership. His focus was on himself and baseball.

The first time that the *Detroit Free Press* mentioned the word "hitting streak" and Ron LeFlore in the same sentence was on May 8.[21] *Free Press* reporter Jim Hawkins was writing about how Ron, a week earlier, had stolen a career-high four bases against the Chicago White Sox, then casually noted that the center fielder currently had a ten-game hitting streak. At some point in a hitter's career, a player will likely develop a hitting streak that typically extends to thirteen, fourteen, or sixteen games. But Ron's streak didn't stop there.

"Look Out DiMag . . . Here Comes LeFlore" was the headline of Hawkins's piece when Ron's streak had extended to eighteen consecutive games, the longest by a Tiger since Al Kaline's twenty-two-game hitting streak in 1961.[22] Normally, a story like this would have been on the front page of the sports section, but it was buried on page four. Someone else had grabbed the spotlight.

Mark Steven Fidrych was born on August 14, 1954, in Worcester, Massachusetts. Like a lot of boys coming of age in the late 1960s and early 1970s, Fidrych played baseball, basketball, and football at his public high school. He was "not a highly touted prospect," though he did show glimpses of potential when he shut down Harvard University's freshman baseball team while in high school.[23] Still, the six-foot, three-inch, lanky right-handed pitcher hadn't been offered an athletic scholarship, nor was he heavily scouted. Only two teams were interested: the Boston Red Sox and Detroit.

During the summer of 1974, following high school graduation, Fidrych was earning three dollars an hour working at an industrial site that produced equipment for gas stations when he received a phone call. He was told he was being drafted. At first, he thought it was into the army (to fight in Vietnam). But the caller explained that the Detroit Tigers had drafted him in the tenth round. With nothing to lose, the eighteen-year-old Fidrych quit his job and packed his bags for Bristol, Virginia, where the Tigers' rookie ball club was located. Within a year, he was sent to the Tigers' Triple-A club in Evansville, Indiana. Fidrych's performance at Evansville was so impressive that he was invited to participate in the Tigers' 1976 spring training.

Sporting curly blond locks, Fidrych came to camp wearing shredded tennis shoes, a raggedy T-shirt, and cut-off shorts. His appearance might not have been in line with the conservatively managed Tigers front office, but all was forgotten once he was on the mound.

"When we saw him pitch, we realized how good this guy was," second baseman Gary Sutherland recalled.[24] Tiger fans would eventually agree.

Six weeks into the season, the Tigers faced the Cleveland Indians on May 15. The buzz surrounding the Tigers was focused on Ron, who was hitting .388 and among the American League leaders in batting average, runs scored, and stolen bases. Plus, the team was in second place in their division. Fans were holding their breath. The Tigers had been in a similar situation last year: hot early on and then they cooled off.

When Fidrych took the mound, his first as a starter, fans looked on with curiosity. Who was this tall, gangly, smiling, curly-haired pitcher? Any reservations they had were quickly erased as Fidrych allowed only two hits, pitching a complete game in a 2–1 victory against the Indians. But what made the rookie pitcher unforgettable to his admirers was his behavior: talking to the baseball while preparing for his next pitch, tidying up the mound by getting down on his knees, and swaggering around the diamond after getting a batter out while pumping his fists with gusto. In this era, pitchers never acted like he did, which was why kids gravitated to him, parents adored him, and girls swooned over him.

Fidrych and his antics became a sensation. He even earned a nickname: the Bird, given to him by a Tiger coach because he resembled the *Sesame Street* character Big Bird—tall, awkward, and gentle.

While fans waited for Fidrych's next start, Ron continued his incredible hitting streak.

So much of the allure of baseball is its historic recordkeeping. Among the most revered records at this time were the career home run category (set by the Atlanta Braves' Hank Aaron with 755) and home runs hit in a single season (held by the New York Yankees' Roger Maris with sixty-one). Then there were the records for consecutive games played (Lou Gehrig, with 2,130), and baseball's longest consecutive hitting streak (fifty-six, set in 1941 by the

Yankees' Joe DiMaggio). Of all these records, DiMaggio's would be the only one that would continue to stand the test of time.

While Tiger fans were giddy about Fidrych, the month of May 1976 belonged to Ron LeFlore. The first significant milestone he surpassed was Al Kaline's twenty-two-game hitting streak set in 1961. It would be eclipsed on May 21. At that point, it was no longer a Detroit story.

As Ron continued to hit in every game and inched closer to DiMaggio's seemingly unassailable record, the national media joined the parade in tracking the streak, to the chagrin of at least one of his teammates. Inside the team's less-than-impressive locker room, outfielder Alex Johnson, whose locker was next to Ron's, found non-Detroit writers sitting on his stool after each passing game, not realizing it wasn't for them.

Among Tiger fans, whenever Ron came up to bat, fans made sure to be in their seats. He was one of the only exciting hitters on the club to watch during this time. But during the streak, it was taken to a whole new level.

"In the Tiger dugout, in the press box, in the bullpen, in the grandstand, and in the centerfield bleachers, all eyes are on the hot hitting Tiger star every time he steps up to the plate," Jim Hawkins wrote.[25] Luckily for Ron, about half of the time during his streak, he would get a hit in his first at bat, suspending any anticipation. But when he didn't, that was when the nail-biting in the stands ensued. Once he got a hit, the fans sighed with relief. When the inning was over, Ron jogged to center field to a standing ovation from those in the bleachers, who were chanting, "LeFlore! LeFlore! LeFlore!"[26]

When the Bird was back for his second start on May 25, Ron was approaching the next milestone: twenty-seven games, the longest hitting streak in the American League since 1951, set by Boston Red Sox's Dom DiMaggio (Joe's younger brother). When Ron collected hit number twenty-eight, the focus turned to twenty-nine, which would tie the longest streak by a Detroit Tiger since Pete Fox in 1935.

Deemed by the *New York Times* as the "league's top hitter" two months into the 1976 season, Ron was hitting an American League-leading .392 batting average and was second in the league in hits and doubles, tied for third in triples, and eighth in stolen bases.[27] He was considered a lock for the 1976 All-Star Game in Philadelphia.

When Ron reached thirty consecutive hits on May 27 against the Orioles on the game's first pitch (he hit a stand-up triple), the talk of the streak became even more serious. Could he get to forty? Fifty? Fifty-six? Whether on radio or television, in the sports section or any bar, the "whole town" of Motor City was talking about it.[28] When Ralph Houk was asked how Ron measured up against past players he had managed such as Mickey Mantle and Yogi Berra, he said, "[I]t's too early to start comparing Ron LeFlore to baseball's all-time greats."[29] True, but it was pointed out that so few players had ever accomplished such a feat (Mantle and Berra not among them). Babe Ruth had never had a thirty-game hitting streak. Neither had Lou Gehrig, Ted Williams, or even Ron's former teammate, Al Kaline. Since 1900, only twelve players have had longer consecutive hitting streaks.

While it would be virtually impossible for anyone to compartmentalize that level of attention, Ron acquired an effective coping mechanism: transcendental meditation. "I meditate twice a day . . . usually about 15 or 20 minutes when I get up," Ron disclosed, "and then about 15 or 20 minutes a couple of hours before I come to the ballpark." He added, "It gives you a lot of relaxation."[30]

The regimen was inspired by John Fetzer, the 74-year-old owner of the Detroit Tigers. A spiritual man, Fetzer, who had an estimated net worth of $100 million, making him the wealthiest resident of the state of Michigan, was on the front lines of the new age movement.

Meditation played a role in helping Ron to attain one of the longest hitting streaks in MLB history. What also contributed was the time he had spent in Puerto Rico. There, he had learned to become a patient hitter, no longer lunging at pitches. It was telling that his first home run in 1976 did not occur until his thirtieth game of the season—and what a blast it was. During the second game of a doubleheader against Baltimore at Tiger Stadium, in the midst of the streak, Ron hit a "booming drive into the upper deck in right centerfield."[31]

On May 28, the Tigers were at home, taking on the league-leading New York Yankees, now led by former Tiger manager Billy Martin. With rain expected, the stadium was less than half-filled that evening. Nonetheless, the intensity between these two rivals that dated back seventy-five years was bitterly apparent. Before the game had even started, Yankee catcher Thurman Munson made it clear that the Yankees intended to stop Ron's thirty-game hitting streak.

"He ain't gonna get no hit tonight, so you guys can stop writing about it," Munson blurted to reporters ahead of the first pitch.[32]

In his first at bat, when Ron had gotten a hit nearly half the time during his streak, he tapped a fly ball in shallow right field for an out. In his second plate appearance, the Tigers were up 1–0, and teammate Jerry Manuel was on second base. The team was hoping to add a run, which they would need against the mighty Yankees. With a full count against him, Ron slashed the ball along the third baseline. It should have easily been a hit for Ron, but Yankee third baseman Graig Nettles happened to be covering the bag. Nettles normally played further away from the base to cover more ground—except that he saw Manuel stealing, and that forced him to move over to the third baseline.

"If I hadn't gone over to cover the bag, I probably wouldn't have fielded the ball quickly enough to throw LeFlore out," Nettles later said.

Now zero for two, Ron's third at bat, which came during the sixth inning, involved Manuel again. He hit a "slow chopper" to the shortstop. If no one had been on base, Ron would have likely beat the throw to first. However, since Manuel was on first base and heading to second, the Yankee's shortstop flipped the ball to the second baseman, forcing Manuel out. Ron was safe, but his at bat was ruled a ground out, not a hit.

With the Tigers down 9–5 in the bottom of the eighth, not only was the game slipping away from them but Ron's thirty-game hitting streak was also in danger of ending.

Yankee reliever Tippy Martinez was on the mound. Ron led off the inning. He swung at the first pitch. Strike one. Ron sensed he was reverting to his old habits: chasing the ball, not exercising patience. Before he took his next pitch, he noticed Yankee first baseman Chris Chambliss was playing deep, so he tried something different: a bunt.

Martinez delivered the pitch. Ron went into a bunting position. He made contact, but it went foul. Strike two.

Munson called time and went to talk it over with his pitcher. "Throw him a good fastball, but keep it inside," he told Martinez.[33]

Ron went back into the batter's box. The pitch came across the plate—right down the middle, like Munson wanted it. It was Ron's favorite pitch, but he didn't swing at it. Home plate umpire Jerry Neudecker raised his fist. Strike three.

Ron walked slowly back to the dugout. He knew. His teammates knew. The fans knew. The streak had ended.

When the eighth inning ended (all three batters went down one, two, three), Ron jogged out to center field. The fans in the bleachers gave him a standing ovation, and it quickly spread to the rest of the stadium. Twenty thousand fans were on their feet. They weren't stopping until Ron acknowledged it by pulling on his baseball cap. Once the crowd settled down, the game went on, and the Tigers lost.

Ron's thirty-game hitting streak—which really was thirty-one games, if you factor in the last game he played from the previous season—was the longest in the American League since Dom DiMaggio in 1949 and the longest by a Detroit Tiger since 1930. Ron, who was awarded the American League's Player of the Month for May, had solidified his credentials and accomplished something that only a handful of players had ever done.[†]

[†]Two years later, Pete Rose would eclipse Ron's streak and break the National League's record of thirty-seven. At forty-four games, Rose came the closest to DiMaggio's record thus far.

When players were later asked about the excitement surrounding Ron's historic hitting streak, pitcher John Hiller's response reflected the team's overall sentiment: "I just wish we were winning more because then it would be even more fun."[34] It wasn't even June yet, and the Detroit Tigers were in last place in the AL East standings. They had lost eleven of their previous thirteen games. At one point during Ron's streak, the team was flirting with a record of its own: consecutive scoreless innings. The record was forty-eight. The team went without scoring a run for thirty-one straight innings. Part of the problem was that Ron and newly acquired right fielder Rusty Staub accounted for the bulk of the offense. One out of every three Tiger hits was from Ron's or Staub's bat. Yet Ron might have had "as much to do with the Tigers' last-place standing . . . as anybody," explained a *Sports Illustrated* reporter in a profile piece.

In a previous game against the Yankees, for example, Ron dropped a fly ball in the outfield that led to three unearned runs. Then, three innings later, he did the same thing, and it led to three more unearned runs. On the offensive side, Ron led his team in strikeouts even though he was hitting .392. Even on the basepaths, which was considered his biggest asset, Ron demonstrated he still needed to learn when to go and when not to. In a game against the Orioles, the score was tied in the top of the ninth inning when there were two outs. Ron was on second base and Willie Horton, who could hit the long ball, was at bat. Most players would have known not to steal in this situation. But Ron didn't adhere to baseball wisdom and attempted to steal third base. He was tagged out, ending the inning prematurely. The Orioles loaded the bases in the bottom of the ninth and beat the Tigers 8–4.

As impressive as his streak was, it was widely acknowledged, as Rusty Staub noted, that Ron still needed to "discipline his thinking and be more attentive to the little things."[35]

"He just hasn't played baseball that long," Houk said when asked about Ron's mistakes on the field. "When he does things it's often on instinct. So sometimes he does things a more experienced player wouldn't do. But he's learning."[36]

Hitting wasn't the Tigers' biggest concern. Their pitching was even more anemic. By early June, it seemed the team was heading toward posting a worse win–loss record than the abysmal 1975 season. Fortunately for them, the Bird was on their roster.

Three days after Ron's hitting streak came to an end, the spotlight shifted to the Bird. After losing his second start, Fidrych pitched a complete game that went eleven innings, allowing eleven hits and four runs in a 5–4 win against the Brewers. Five days later, he was back on the mound and went the distance again, but this time he only allowed seven hits and two runs. During the month of June, Fidrych didn't lose a single game, going 6–0, and by the end of the month, he had the third-lowest ERA (Earned Run Average) in the American League.

Despite the Bird's remarkable statistics, it was his personality that caught the attention of the nation. On June 28, in the ABC-televised *Monday Night Baseball* game of the week, followers of the national pastime across the country would learn what all the fuss was about in Detroit. Nearly 50,000 fans were on hand at Tiger Stadium, watching the Bird take on the first-place Yanks. That day, he pitched a complete game, allowing only one run against the Pinstripes.

From that moment on, and throughout the remainder of the 1976 season, the Bird became an American phenomenon. Wherever and whenever he was pitching, baseball stadiums filled up.

Ralph Houk, who had played with and managed the best players in modern history, was surprised. "Mickey Mantle used to draw crowds," Houk commented, "but I've never seen a rookie do anything like this."[37]

For the second month in a row, the American League selected a Tiger (Mark Fidrych) as its Player of the Month. Although Ron's hitting streak didn't lead to more team wins, the Bird's domination did. In May, during Ron's streak, the Tigers went 10–17. In June, with Fidrych leading the way, the team went 17–12 and were no longer at the bottom of the American League East standings. They had moved up from sixth place to third.

Although Ron's hitting dropped slightly in June, he was still one of the American League's top performers at the plate, batting .351 and leading the league in hits. He was even showing improvement on defense. In the twenty-seven games he played in May, Ron committed four errors. In the twenty-nine games during June, he made only one. In addition to Ron and the Bird, other Tigers stepped up. Outfielder Rusty Staub proved his worth to fans, hitting .316. Willie Horton and catcher Bill Freehan produced impressive numbers, and rookie first baseman Jason Thompson was contributing, leading the team in home runs. Across the country, baseball aficionados had taken notice of what was happening in Motor City.

Three Tigers—Bird, Ron, and Staub— were voted by fans to be starters in the annual All-Star Game on July 13 in Philadelphia at Veterans Stadium. For Ron, in particular, it was an important milestone. He was no longer just an ex-con who had made it to the majors. As he saw it, being an All-Star "means that I'm part of society now. I'm part of something I've never been a part of before."[38]

Among the 64,000 attendees at the game was President Gerald R. Ford. For the former college athlete and avid sports fan who began his daily reading every morning with the sports section, there was no way Ford would pass up an opportunity (especially during this election year) to throw out the first pitch and have a front-row seat at the forty-seventh MLB All-Star Game that would be viewed on television by some seventy-five million Americans.

The Tigers also took pride in their loyal fan base. Hundreds of Detroiters made the nine-hour drive to Philadelphia's recently built Veterans Stadium to watch their Tigers heros. Among those who made the trip were Ron's parents, John and Georgia, and two of Ron's childhood friends, Kenny and Casey.

As Ford's motorcade came roaring through the streets of Philadelphia, Ron's buddies waited outside the stadium with thousands of other fans, hoping to get a glimpse of the thirty-eighth president. Out of nowhere, a Secret Service agent pulled Casey aside. Initially, Kenny couldn't figure out why his friend was singled out, but then he noticed that Casey was wearing a long, leather trench coat on a warm, summer day. Casey was patted down and cleared.

Ford's entourage finally arrived, and the president headed to the players' locker room. Standing in single file, the American Leaguers, in uniform, waited patiently to shake hands with the most powerful man in the world.

When Ford approached Ron, the president joked, "We Michiganders have got to stick together."[39]

Standing next to Ron was Mark Fidrych. "The Bird, how are you?" Ford said to the 21-year-old phenomenon, who would be the second-youngest pitcher ever to start an All-Star Game.[40]

Fidrych was unimpressed. "Fuck the president. I got a game to pitch," he whispered to Ron.[41]

The Tiger pitcher should have savored the moment. Little did he know that it would be the highlight of his day; he gave up four hits and two runs and was the losing pitcher as the National League pounced on the American League 7–1.

Regardless of Fidrych's performance, the estimated 200 reporters on hand were there for one reason only: the Bird. His youth, charming features, odd antics on the mound, and early pitching success had mesmerized the media— to the neglect of Ron, whose rise to baseball fame, one could argue, deserved equal attention. After all, only five years earlier, Ron had been watching the All-Star Game in a prison mess hall and was now a participant. Aside from the *Free*

Press's Joe Falls, who, the day after the game, penned a column, "LeFlore Knows Just Where He's Going," no one else bothered to cover the Tiger center fielder.

The 1976 season ended prematurely for Ron when he ruptured his knee on September 12 at Yankee Stadium. He had surgery on it the next day and missed the final three weeks of the season. Even though it ended on a down note, 1976 was his best season to date in the majors. In addition to his thirty-game hitting streak, he finished the year with a .316 batting average, which was a team high and nearly sixty points higher than his average the previous season. He also led the Tigers in triples and runs scored (and ranked tenth in the American League for the latter) and was second in hits (four hits behind Staub) and tops in stolen bases (second in the AL). His fifty-eight swipes were the most in a single season by a Tiger since Ty Cobb had stolen sixty-one in 1912. To Ron's credit, he had also decreased his number of strikeouts from the previous season by more than 20 percent.

But the 1976 season belonged to the Bird, who was the dominant player on the club. Mark Fidrych's superb performance on the mound led him to earn the American League Rookie of the Year Award, be named runner-up to the Cy Young Award, and be voted by Detroit writers as "Tiger of the Year."

After coming off their worst season in nearly a quarter of a century, the 1976 Detroit Tigers had improved despite the bumps along the way. This squad had won seventeen more games than they had the year before, increased their attendance by nearly a third (much of it thanks to the Bird), and established a new generation of Tiger superstars: the Ace (Mark Fidrych), the Slugger (rookie Jason Thompson, who smacked seventeen home runs), and the Speedster (Ron LeFlore).‡ Team manager Ralph Houk was compensated with a three-year contract worth $255,000 (equivalent to $1.35 million today). Houk wasn't the only Tiger rewarded for his efforts, though.

---

‡Ironically, the future of each of those three players with the club was short-lived. Not one of them was part of the team's later successes.

A STAR EMERGES

During the 1976 All-Star Game in Philadelphia, Ron was among the players in the locker room who shook hands with US president Gerald R. Ford. When Ron's teammate and fellow All-Star Mark "The Bird" Fidrych met President Ford at the All-Star Game, he was not as impressed. After Fidrych shook hands, he whispered to Ron, "Fuck the president. I got a game to pitch." ("Trip to Pennsylvania," Frames 19A and 21A, White House Photographic Collection, Gerald R. Ford Presidential Library)

In the winter of 1966, there had been only two people in the office during Tiger pitcher Earl Wilson's contract negotiation: Wilson and general manager Jim Campbell. Like every athlete during the era before free agency, Wilson was not allowed to have someone physically present to represent him during his player contract meeting. Prior to 1975, managers, coaches, and players had been at the mercy of the team's general manager. Teams wanted it this way, knowing the vast majority of players were ill-equipped to effectively negotiate for themselves. Campbell, however, was unaware that Wilson, during their meeting, had someone helping him; he just wasn't in the room with him.

Robert "Bob" Woolf was a 38-year-old, Boston-based criminal defense attorney when he negotiated his first contract on behalf of a professional athlete, and that was Earl Wilson. During the meeting with Campbell, Wilson would excuse himself from the GM's office, find a telephone, and call his apartment, where Woolf was waiting. After a brief telephone conversation, Wilson would return and resume the negotiation. Woolf was on the front lines of an industry that was to become quite lucrative when free agency was officially allowed in Major League Baseball less than a decade later. By then, Woolf had developed an impressive clientele that included Ron LeFlore. The era of player representatives absent from the bargaining table was over. So were the minuscule salary increases.

Ron went from making $23,500 a year in 1976 to signing a three-year deal worth $270,000 (equivalent to $1.5 million today). Ron actually could have signed a contract with another team that was worth more money, but as he put it, he was a Detroit native and loyal to the team who had given him an opportunity when no one else would. He was especially devoted to his manager, Ralph Houk, who continued to play him early in his career even though fans were riding him for it.

"Get that convict out of there," fans would yell at Ron from the stands.[42] Houk ignored the taunts, and Ron never forgot that.

Detroit Tiger General Manager Jim Campbell was at the helm of the organization when Ron joined the club. Although Campbell tried to steer Ron away from negative distractions off the field, he ultimately was unable to keep his star player out of trouble. (Society for American Baseball Research)

Afterward, Ron treated himself to a shiny blue Mercedes as well as a home in a middle-class (predominately white) neighborhood. Although his newfound wealth was clearly a blessing, it also had the potential to be a curse. Jimmy Butsicaris, co-owner of the Lindell AC, tried to shield Ron "from the bad influences" that suddenly swarmed around him more so than ever.

Given Ron's limited formal education and strong ties to his buddies still living in the East Side, Butsicaris made a strenuous effort to provide a haven for Ron. "That's why so many athletes hung out at the Lindell," Mel Butsicaris

(Jimmy's nephew) explained in later years. "My dad and uncle would protect them from people who would try to take advantage of them." On more than one occasion, Ron would mention a possible business deal, but Jimmy would tell him, "That sounds a little shady. Don't get involved with that."[43]

A deal that wasn't fraudulent was the one his agent was working on with a Hollywood producer about Ron's life journey. "What a story that kid is," Woolf said of his client.[44]

What a story, indeed.

11

One in a Million

"All I [ever] wanted to be was a sportswriter," Jim Hawkins once said. When the native from Superior, Wisconsin, graduated from the state's flagship college, the University of Wisconsin–Madison, in 1966, the next logical step for him was to find a newspaper to hire him. He settled for an internship with the *Milwaukee Journal* before landing his first full-time job writing sports for *The News Journal* in Wilmington, Delaware, which was followed by a brief stint at *The Baltimore Evening Sun*. He was at the bottom of the pecking order, covering local sports or whatever else was thrown at him. When the *Detroit Free Press* hired him in 1970 to cover the Tigers, he became the "youngest regular baseball writer in the country."[1]

Known for his "clever leads" and unconcerned about the reaction from the Tigers' front office, Hawk (the nickname Hawkins went by) was fiercely competitive, always the first writer to arrive at the ballpark.[2] If it was an 8:00 p.m. start, he'd be there at 3:00 p.m. He'd talk to the players, the coaches, anyone who could provide him with a scoop on a potential story. Ralph Houk in particular was always a source of information. Since Hawkins was with the team nearly every day throughout the season, the two men got to know each other well. Houk would "talk about players, possible moves, and tell him things off the record."[3] Because there were rival newspaper writers covering the Tigers, Hawkins made sure to get the goods first. Once he got his story (this was in addition to covering the game itself), he'd head up to the open-air press box, take a whiff of the freshly cut grass, and type away on his typewriter.

Hawk did have his critics. Bill Brown, a former Tigers assistant public relations director, thought the *Free Press* reporter could be "a little loose with the facts."[4] Willie Horton once went after Hawkins with a bat in the clubhouse over an article that didn't reflect well on him. He screamed, "I'm gonna kill you, motherfucker. I'm gonna kill you."

Hawkins came of age during what is arguably the last decade when writers had unlimited access to players. He traveled everywhere with the team, either by plane or bus. He stayed in the same hotels, drank at the same bars, and even carpooled with one of them—pitcher Mickey Lolich—to Tiger Stadium.

When Ron LeFlore joined the club, Hawkins was elated. Since Billy Martin had departed in 1973, Hawk needed a new subject to keep his stories engaging. The current crop of Tigers, whom he covered every day for eight months out of the year, was not giving him enough ideas for a story. Ron made Hawkins's job far more exciting, as did the Bird.

Following Fidrych's extraordinary rookie season, Hawkins teamed up with the Bird (as well as another author) and published *Go Bird Go!* with Dell Publishing Company, a major publishing house in New York. The book was light on depth and went straight to paperback, the type of sports biography that proliferated in the 1970s. Since Fidrych had pitched only one season, for Hawkins it was a "quickie, overnight book." Still, Fidrych's story was in high demand; and *Go Bird Go!* reportedly sold 75,000 copies in the first month alone, an extraordinary figure in the publishing world. With that success, Hawkins was hoping to replicate that success by telling another Tiger's story, which was even more astonishing and potentially more profitable. But there was one problem: Joe Falls.

By the 1970s, *Free Press* columnist Joe Falls was an "institution" in Motor City, the dean of Detroit's sports writers, having covered the city's sports teams since the 1950s. He was nationally recognized and could easily land a major publishing deal with favorable terms. He also saw the potential in Ron's story. When Hawkins found out that he might be competing against his senior colleague for the ghostwriting gig, he assumed Ron would go with Falls. But Ron was unaware that Joe Falls was interested. The columnist wasn't a mainstay in the Tigers' locker room like Hawkins was and that gave Hawk an advantage. Ron had gotten to know Hawkins well and trusted him to tell his story.

Since Ron was recovering from knee surgery during the 1977 offseason, it was an ideal time for writer and subject to collaborate. Using a tape recorder, Hawkins conducted his interviews at Ron's house. The reporter delved into Ron's childhood, his parents, his brothers, the crimes he had committed as a youth, life in prison, and when he had received the call from the Tigers. These information-gathering sessions were interspersed with research trips. They drove by Dee's (the bar where the robbery took place), schools Ron attended, parks he played at, and his parents' home. As a white man, Jim was unaware of what life was like in a Black, impoverished neighborhood. He was about to get an education.

When Ron and Hawk arrived at the LeFlores' house in the East Side, Hawk naturally pulled up to the curb and parked the car.

"You can't park out front," Ron said.

"Why?" Jim asked. "There's all kinds of spots on the street."

"Go around here, and go down the alley," Ron told him.

When they approached the alley, Ron got out and opened a metal gate. Jim pulled forward and parked his car in the LeFlores' backyard. Ron then locked the gate.

"What's this all about?" Hawk asked. He still didn't understand why he couldn't park in front of the house.

To Ron, it seemed so obvious: "If you park your car out front, when you come out, you won't have any tires."

Before going inside, Hawkins observed that the exterior of the house—a simple, two-story, post–Second World War structure—was shabby at best, with an overgrown lawn and in desperate need of a paint job. To his surprise, however, the interior was spotless and well-maintained. After they left, Hawk wanted to know why his parents didn't take care of the outside of their home the same way they had done so inside.

"If they did that," Ron explained, "people would think they have money, and they would break in."

Ron's explanation surprised Hawkins—a reaction that obviously revealed the reporter's insularity. He was living primarily in a white man's world, with hardly any exposure to economically stressed, crime-ridden Black neighborhoods. The only people of color he associated with were at the ballpark: the players, the ground crew, and the handful of Black fans who were brave enough to endure sitting through a game where others around them made subtle and not-so-subtle racist remarks.

The entire Detroit Tiger ecosystem was white-centric. There were no people of color in the front office, nor among the media. Among the forty-six writers and television broadcasters who covered the Detroit Tigers that season, only one was Black: Frank Saunders, who worked for the *Michigan Chronicle*, a weekly Black newspaper. This wasn't just a Detroit problem; it was common throughout Major League Baseball. Since Jackie Robinson's debut in 1947, the press corps remained white and male—and hostile to anyone who wasn't. Astonishingly, even as recent as 1971, *Sports Illustrated*, the gold standard for sports writers, had published a 6,000-word article by its editor, Martin Kane, inquiring why Black athletes had attained so much success in such a short amount of time in professional sports. It must have been, he theorized, because Black players were built differently—a view, whether Kane realized it or not, was racist and not physiological. This was the world Jim Hawkins operated in.

"Pull in," Ron told Hawk as they went on another field trip to do more research, this time at Jackson Prison. In the parking lot of a McDonald's restaurant, Hawk went inside with Ron, who ordered a cheeseburger. He paid for it with a fifty-dollar bill. That caught the writer's attention. Hawk pulled out his wallet and offered to pay for the forty-cent burger so that Ron wouldn't have to break a fifty.

"No, no, I got it," Ron insisted.

They continued on their way when Ron asked Hawk to pull over again. This time, it was at a convenience store. They went in, and Ron picked up a six-pack of beer. Again, he paid using a fifty-dollar bill. This time, Hawk didn't offer to pay for it, but he was still puzzled by Ron's transaction with the cashier.

When they arrived at Jackson, before checking in, they sat in the parking lot as Ron gulped down the beer. The strangeness of the situation did not escape Hawkins. Here, they were sitting in the "parking lot of the largest walled prison in the world, home of the most notorious prisoners, including a mass murderer," and Ron—a wealthy, professional baseball player—was sitting beside him, wearing an expensive leather jacket and a matching hat, drinking a six-pack of beer.

Once they went through security (Hawk couldn't bring in his tape recorder), it felt more like a class reunion than a visit to a penitentiary. All his old buddies were "coming up to him," while Ron was handing out cash.

"I don't want to have to be giving them twenties and fifties," he told Hawkins. "I want to have a pocket full of fives and tens," which clarified why he had used fifty-dollar bills for minor purchases.

Even the guards were smitten with Ron. Everyone wanted his autograph and to take a photograph with him. It was obvious why Ron enjoyed returning: he was treated like a king, walking around without any escort. No guard, no warden. Just Hawkins, Ron, and 5,000 inmates.

When they entered the gymnasium, they saw a young man sweeping the floor.

"This is John Norman Collins," Ron informed Hawkins, who recognized the name right away. They started up a conversation and then, without warning,

Hawkins realized that Ron had disappeared. There was no one else in the gym except him and a "guy who probably killed twenty people."

Hawkins's mind was running wild. "Should I turn and run?" he thought to himself. "I didn't want to talk to him anymore."

Hawk eventually excused himself and went outside into the yard to look for Ron, whom he caught sight of.

"You were scared. Weren't you?" Ron teased him.

"Goddamn right, I was scared!"

After they met more inmates, one of them began shouting at Hawk as he and Ron were leaving: "Hey, Jim! Write a book about me. . . . Hey, Jim!"

As they were about to exit the prison, Hawk asked Ron if he was uneasy about returning to a place where he had been incarcerated for three and a half years. "Not a bit," was Ron's quick reply. At first, Hawkins was baffled by his answer, wondering whether the ex-convict was truthful. When they discussed the issue further, Ron pointed out that the "worst part in being in prison [is that] you can't leave." As long as he could turn around and walk out the door, in his view, Jackson was simply a place to visit. Not so for Hawkins, who, for weeks following his trip to the prison, experienced nightmares.

Hawkins spent the remainder of the offseason and spring training typing up the manuscript. When it was time for Ron to review his autobiography, according to Hawkins, he read a couple of chapters while sipping on a beer in his apartment in Lakeland, Florida.

"Okay, I've had enough," Ron said, handing back the copy to his ghostwriter. "Where do I sign? This is all fine. Let's go to the bar."[5]

It was no secret that Ron was writing a book. Ever since Yankee pitcher Jim Bouton had published *Ball Four* in 1970—the first bona fide, tell-all book about what happened inside a major league locker room that became a bestseller—a new genre had been born. Following Bouton's success, scores of books had been published that focused similarly on the inner workings of professional sports and what occurred behind the scenes. Ron's book would add to the growing glut. But what made Ron's situation unique was that his agent had a movie deal tied to it, which guaranteed that the book would become a top seller. It seemed everything was falling into place except for one thing: Ron's playing.

Like in 1976, Ron got off to a slow start in 1977. So did the Tigers. With veterans Bill Freehan retired and Wille Horton traded, the team had all but shredded its 1968 World Series championship squad (outfielder Mickey Stanley and pitcher John Hiller were the last men standing). Once again, the Tiger faithful were being asked to learn new names donning the Old English D uniforms, such as shortstop Alan Trammell, second baseman Lou Whitaker, catcher Lance Parrish, and pitcher Jack Morris. Despite the personnel changes, fans still had a few players they could cheer for, notably Mark Fidrych, who the *New York Times* hailed as the "biggest box office draw in baseball in years."[6]

And then, just like that, the Bird's season came to a premature end. During spring training, the All-Star pitcher found himself at Henry Ford Hospital in Detroit, being operated on for a torn cartilage in his left knee. He was expected to be out until June. If the Tigers were hoping to be saved in the standings as well as at the box office, Ron would have to come to the rescue.

Following his own surgery, Ron spent months at the University of Detroit's sports facilities, working with a private trainer to rehabilitate his knee. "I went through hell, getting ready for spring training," he said afterward.[7]

Lakeland was his first opportunity to get back in baseball shape, and he took full advantage of it, arriving at 7:00 a.m. every morning and staying until the dinner hour. Eventually, he was just as fast and strong as he had been prior to the injury, but the team could not coalesce. April and May were dismal for the Tigers. Ron was of no help, making errors, getting picked off, and hitting a paltry .230 through May 30. By then, Houk had had it and benched him for two games.

"He's all screwed up at the plate," the frustrated manager told reporters. "This game isn't that tough. I don't know what else I can do. He's been pressing [putting unnecessary pressure on himself] at the plate and pressing on the bases too. The way he's been playing, I had to do something."[8]

When Ron returned, he and the Tigers were facing the Oakland A's and Vida Blue, a Cy Young Award-winning pitcher. Blue held the Tigers to one run and four hits, but two of those hits came from Ron's bat. Four days later, Ron hit two home runs in a single game. He was back.

While the 1977 Tigers finished a disappointing fourth place in their division and twenty-six games out of first place, Ron had an even better season than he'd had in 1976, when he had been a starter in the All-Star Game. He had career-highs—a .325 batting average and sixteen home runs—in a single season. He was also the first Tiger to reach the 200-hit mark in a single season since Al Kaline in 1955; the first Tiger to score 100 runs in a season since 1961; the first Tiger in nearly twenty years to maintain a .300 batting average for two consecutive seasons;* and the first Tiger since Ty Cobb to have stolen twenty or more bases in four straight seasons. And he was among the top ten American League hitters in several offensive categories: batting average (fifth), hits (second), runs scored (ninth), at bats (second), triples (eighth), and stolen bases (fifth).

Despite the team's unimpressive record, there were glimmers of hope for the struggling Tigers. Second-year first baseman Jason Thompson hit a staggering thirty-one home runs and had over 100 RBIs. Veteran Rusty Staub smacked twenty home runs and also knocked in 100 runs. Still, the 1977 season belonged to Ron.

"No Tiger in history—not even the immortal Ty Cobb—ever did as many things in a single season as LeFlore did this year," Jim Hawkins pointed out in his column.[9] Ron was selected as "Tiger of the Year" by the Detroit chapter

---

*Harvey Kuenn, who was Ron's manager in Puerto Rico, did it in 1958 and 1959.

of the Baseball Writers Association of America (BBWAA), the only award he received that year. Because of his poor performance at the beginning of the season, he wasn't selected for the All-Star team. He also wasn't considered a serious contender for the American League MVP Award. Rod Carew of the Minnesota Twins was the obvious choice, hitting an incredible .388 and leading the American League in multiple other categories. Yet there were eighteen other players who were ranked higher in the balloting than Ron, even though his stats were superior (i.e., higher batting average, more hits and runs scored) to the majority of them. In fact, when it came to strikeouts, which was something Ron continued to struggle with, there were two other MVP candidates—California Angel Bobby Bonds and Yankee Reggie Jackson—who had more.

Perhaps it had to do with Ron not playing for a contender, nor was Detroit a team most writers followed as closely as the Yankees or the Red Sox. Whatever the reason for Ron's lack of recognition, his situation was about to take a dramatic reversal.

Ron LeFlore and Jim Hawkins's book, *Breakout: From Prison to the Big Leagues*, had all the trappings of a bestseller. One author was the starting center fielder for the Detroit Tigers, while the other wrote for one of America's largest circulated daily newspapers. Upon its launch during the 1978 spring training season, *Sports Illustrated* ran a ten-page excerpt in its weekly magazine. The *Detroit Free Press* used the book as a means to advertise its own newspaper. Harper & Row, the book's publisher, sent Ron on a five-city book tour, where he made appearances in Philadelphia, Boston, Minneapolis, Chicago, and New York. While in the Big Apple, he was interviewed on the popular television show *Good Morning America*. Newspapers throughout the country ran book reviews and mentions in their sports sections.

With an initial printing of 25,000 copies, the book sold out quickly, leaving publishing insiders scratching their heads, wondering why Harper & Row had not been better prepared for the expected windfall of sales. A second printing was underway within a month of the first edition's release. The hiccup didn't slow Ron down. Everywhere he went, fans shoved the book into his hands, asking for an autograph, which he was more than happy to oblige. At the downtown Detroit department store Hudson's, Ron's book signing looked like an Elvis sighting, as lines for the Tiger outfielder's signature snaked around shopping aisles.

Not that it affected or even slowed sales, but the reviews of *Breakout* were mixed. Naturally, sports writers praised the book. Jim Selman from *The Tampa Tribune* called it "a heck of a story, worth your reading."[10] Jim Hawkins's colleague, Joe Falls, noted that it was "not your usual sports book." Describing several scenes in the book as "shocking," Falls confessed his cluelessness about life in the inner city.

"Unless you've lived it, how can you possibly understand it. I know I can't," he wrote in a column. "The Ron LeFlore I know is a quiet, smiling, friendly guy who sits in the front row of lockers on the left as you enter the Tigers dressing room in Detroit."[11]

On the other hand, there were those who saw nothing unique about Ron's biography. "For the first 21 years of his life, Ron LeFlore's story was as predictable as a computer program," said a reviewer from the *New York Times*.[12] *Library Journal*, the trade publication for librarians, curiously maintained that the book provided "little explanation as to why his early years were so crime-ridden" and should only be "recommended for very comprehensive sports collections."[13]

In essence, *Breakout* was a chronological tale of Ron's life, focusing primarily on his childhood and incarceration. The book concluded with his sensational 1976 All-Star season. Ron's account of his drug use, crime sprees, and troubled family upbringing was reviewed by the baseball commissioner's office prior to publication, and according to one newspaper, the book would have been even more graphic without "some editing" from the league's top official.[14] Even Jim

Campbell played a role in the editorial process, requesting that Hawkins not publish "the more 'racier episodes.'"[15]

For fans expecting a trajectory from obscurity to fame similar to Mark "The Bird" Fidrych's memoir that was published a year earlier, or a behind-the-scenes, tell-all diary like *Ball Four*, *Breakout* stood out from the pack. The vast majority of sports books that came out prior were mostly written by white players (or, rather, their white ghostwriters) about their experiences in the white community. Bouts with racism or living in America's inner city were not as well-documented among baseball players, which was why the book was jarring to its readers and demand was high.

Ron went into vivid details about the first time he took heroin, his father's alcoholism, his exposure to street prostitutes, and, of course, the armed hold-up responsible for his imprisonment. It was written in a similar style and shared common themes with another best-selling coming-of-age memoir. Published in 1965, *The Autobiography of Malcolm X* was about a troubled Black young man from Michigan who was sent to prison and found redemption. Unlike that autobiography, Ron didn't have Alex Haley as his ghostwriter, nor was he as engaged as Malcolm X was in the project. He also didn't view his world through a racial lens. For example, *Breakout* did not explain why Ron's parents fled the Jim Crow South, nor why they were forced to live only in Detroit's predominantly Black neighborhoods. In fact, there was hardly any mention of racism until he entered the penal system and the minor leagues—and only in those instances, it was lightly discussed.

Ron also intentionally withheld stories that he was uncomfortable sharing, such as his mother sleeping with her landlord to cover the month's rent. Georgia didn't read her son's memoir, disclosing in an interview with *People* magazine that "there were too many painful things in it."[16] There were other stories and statements that were omitted or incorrect as well. Ron barely mentioned his older siblings Harry and Marvin; he still clung to an incorrect birthdate (1950 instead of 1948); the number of people involved in the robbery was four, not three; and he failed to mention that he had been a looter in the 1967 Detroit riots.

Regardless, Hawk and Ron enjoyed the spotlight and the money they were raking in. They playfully started calling each other Ticket, signifying they were each other's "meal ticket." When they were at a book signing together, sitting side by side, Hawk would holler over, "Ticket!"[17] Ron would respond accordingly. It became a running joke between the two, confusing those who were present.

Ron especially was taken in by the glamour. When he wasn't on the field, he could be found wearing fashionable clothes, sporting aviator sunglasses, and cruising in his Mercedes along the streets of Detroit. Emboldened by his good fortune, he was more inclined to take risks. When a local sportscaster caught a ride with him leaving the players' parking lot at Tiger Stadium, Ron took out a marijuana joint and lit it.

"Ronnie," radio broadcaster Eli Zaret said, "the fans are right there. Can you wait a hundred feet before you light it?"

"This is my town," Ron answered. "I do whatever I want."[18]

In 1978, Detroit was Ron's town. He was recognized wherever he went. Women were throwing themselves at him, and he happily obliged their requests. Children were in awe of his presence and begged him for an autograph. He had more money than he could have imagined, and even more was coming his way.

The book had been out for only two months when it was announced that Ron's agent, Bob Woolf, finalized a deal with CBS to acquire the rights of *Breakout* to become a made-for-television movie. The actor playing Ron would be 21-year-old LeVar Burton, who had starred one year earlier as Kunta Kinte in the most-watched television program of all time, the miniseries *Roots*.

During the 1970s, movies that were made exclusively for television had become a new trend among the three major networks, which were ABC,

CBS, and NBC. Made-for-television movies like *Brian's Song* (ABC, 1971), *Duel* (ABC, 1971), *The Autobiography of Miss Jane Pittman* (CBS, 1974), and *Roots* (ABC, 1977) had proven to network executives that these modest-budget projects that bypassed the theaters could be lucrative. Early on, these movies were mostly fiction. But by 1978, as the *New York Times* reported, the networks expanded into stories that were based on show business personalities such as Judy Garland, Florenz Ziegfeld Jr., and Scott Joplin. When Ron's book was released, it was ideally positioned to be picked up by one of the three networks.

The filming of *One in a Million*—the screen title of the adaptation of *Breakout*—began in late spring and would air at the end of September, right before the 1978 World Series. When the Tigers were on a road trip in California that May, Ron met the young man who would be playing him.

"We really hit it off," actor LeVar Burton recalled of their first encounter.[19] He had tried to maximize his time with Ron, "absorb[ing] as much as I could" of his subject's physical mannerisms.

"That's part of my job as an actor," Burton later commented. "That was why they hired me to play the role."[20]

Burton was an actor, not an athlete. Since he had never attended a professional outdoor sports venue prior to filming *One in a Million*, the role of playing a baseball player was new territory for the Emmy Award winner. What wasn't foreign to him was playing a prisoner. Having depicted an African slave who was brutally beaten from the moment he was taken from his family in *Roots*, Burton understood what it was like to be shackled, beaten, and exposed to excessive violence.

At one point in the film, while Burton is depicting Ron at Jackson Prison (which was filmed in a real prison in Joliet, Illinois), there is a scene when Ron is taken against his will to solitary confinement. When the white guard walked a handcuffed Burton through a dark hallway, an eerie feeling came over him.

"So many of the body positions and postures were the same as I had as a slave in *Roots*," Burton remembered. "Then the guard threw me into the cell and it was just like the same thing 200 years later."[21]

Other scenes that were included were Ron's stint in the minors and his homelife, the latter partly filmed in Ron's East Side neighborhood. But it is the baseball episodes at Tiger Stadium that the movie is best remembered for.

On May 20, the day of filming at the ballpark, the Tigers were scheduled to play their division rival, the Boston Red Sox, that Saturday afternoon. The crew was on a tight schedule. Although they needed to finish fifteen minutes before the game started at 2:15 p.m., the movie director had to time it just right so that they could maximize the fans who were already in the stands. By attending the game that day, they had agreed to serve as movie extras.

The production company, EMI, worked with the Tigers' organization to recruit retired Tigers Al Kaline, Norm Cash, Jim Northrup, and Bill Freehan to play themselves in the movie. The rest of the actors playing Ron's teammates were local college athletes from nearby Wayne State University and Oakland University. Filming began early that morning. The plan was to shoot the scenes of Ron's tryout at Tiger Stadium—when fans were not present—and then, as game time approached, capture the scenes when he was playing in front of a crowd. Everything went smoothly until Burton stepped up to the plate.

Whiffed.

Whiffed again.

Burton kept missing the pitches that one reporter described as "patty-cake deliveries." It took him "a dozen swings before he was able to hit the ball into fair territory."[22] When he finally made contact, he hit what was described as "a blooper" over shortstop.[23]

Then it was time to show off Ron's speed, which was what had really dazzled the Tigers when they had first seen Ron on the diamond. The plan was for Burton to run to first base.

Ready. Set. Action.

Burton took off—sort of.

One observer jokingly said, "LeFlore moves that slowly only when he's sleeping." Nonetheless, the crew got what it needed. Now it was time for Hollywood to take over. From a different angle, they had one of the college players who looked similar to Ron do the same thing. Al Kaline, playing himself, uttered his line, "He's faster than anyone on our club. He sure can move."[24]

After the tryout scene was declared a wrap, Burton was prepped to play in the outfield, replicating an actual game. With some 30,000 fans in the stands, Ron, who was serving as a technical adviser for the film, and Billy Martin, who was portraying himself, advised Burton how to play center field. Apparently, it paid off; the actor "caught on real well."[25]

For those in the stands, it was a treat. The making of a movie was not an everyday occurrence in Detroit. Nor was seeing Kaline, Cash, Northrup, and Freehan back together for the first time since 1974. For fans, it was a "Mount Rushmore of real-life Tiger greats" in the flesh, though a bit grayer.[26]

Ralph Houk, who was not in the film and not "particularly pleased with the proceedings," was reminding everyone that there still was a game to play. With rain in the forecast, the Tigers' manager feared that if they didn't start on time, there would be a delay. The film crew was supposed to be off the field at 2:00 p.m., but they weren't—and sure enough, the game started eleven minutes behind schedule, and the rain came later that day. Houk fumed.

"I didn't even watch [the filming] I was so mad. They said they'd be completely off the field by 2 p.m. Here's a big ball game and we're fooling around."[27]

Movie extra Mark Orr on the film set of "One in a Million." (Mark Orr's personal collection)

That day, Detroit wound up losing to the Red Sox by one run.

The loss didn't dim the mood. After the game, the partying got underway. Booze and drugs, including cocaine, were flowing among the TV crew, actors, and players, even though they were filming again the next day. Sure enough, the following morning, a crew member knocked on Burton's hotel room door to let him know it was time to be on set. Nobody responded. The crew member kept knocking and knocking. No one answered. Concerned, a hotel clerk was summoned to unlock the door. Fortunately, the actor was present, but it was obvious "he had a long night."[28]

Apart from Houk, no one in Tiger management expressed concerns about Hollywood's invasion of Detroit. Perhaps the distractive potential it might pose was overlooked by the fact that the team was playing extraordinarily well.

At this point in the new season, the Tigers were 22–11 and tied for first place in the American League East Division. Rusty Staub, Steve Kemp, and

Jason Thompson, along with rookies Lou Whitaker and Alan Trammell, were providing the offensive firepower. The pitching, which had always been suspect, was making headway, especially with the Bird back in action, albeit temporarily. Ron, who always got off to a slow start, was banging out home runs and hitting successfully in the clutch. The fans obviously took notice; attendance was up 30 percent from this point last year.

But once Tinseltown arrived, everything went downhill.

By the end of June, the Tigers plunged to fifth place (out of six teams) in their division. The team was dropping balls, not getting on base, and blowing leads. Ron's performance took a nosedive as well. During this period, he went from a respectable .286 batting average with forty-two hits and sixteen stolen bases, to dropping his average twenty points and stealing half the number of bases. Even Jim Hawkins, who was still covering Ron despite the obvious conflict of interest, took his coauthor to task with a large dose of sarcasm:

> Maybe Ron LeFlore was right. Maybe Hollywood should've let the Tiger center fielder play himself, as LeFlore suggested, in the TV movie currently being made about his remarkable life, instead of hiring actor LeVar Burton. Certainly, in the past three weeks, LeFlore has done a much better job of imitating Burton than Burton has done portraying LeFlore.[29]

Ralph Houk could not have agreed more. "I don't know if it's all the hullabaloo over the movie or what," the manager told Hawkins, "but [Ron's] mind has not been on baseball, I'll tell you that."[30]

There were rumors that Ron might be traded. And then, similar to previous seasons, following a dip in his performance, he rose to the occasion.

That moment came at the end of June. Ron stopped swinging for the fences and began getting on base more frequently, which, as the leadoff hitter, was his main objective. On June 27 against the Cleveland Indians, Ron led off the game with a single (followed by a stolen base) that ignited

In May 1978, former Tiger manager Billy Martin, Ron, and actor LeVar Burton on the set of the made-for-television movie, "One in a Million." Burton portrayed Ron in the movie that aired in September 1978 on CBS. (Everett Collection, Inc.)

a six-run rally, and the Tigers never looked back on that game. Although the team itself was unable to replicate its performance earlier in the season (a revisit of its anemic pitching, exacerbated by the Bird's departure due to another injury), Ron showed no signs of slowing down. He maintained a .328 batting average following his midyear drought and finished the 1978 season at or near the top of every hitting category in the American League. He led the league in runs scored and stolen bases. He was among the top ten in batting average, hits, at bats, and total bases. And he managed to put together another impressive hitting streak (twenty-seven games) at the end of the season.

For the second year in a row, Ron was voted by the Detroit chapter of the BBWAA as "Tiger of the Year." He and Ty Cobb became the only Tigers with multiple hitting streaks of twenty-five games or more. He also finished sixteenth in the MVP voting, four spots higher than he had the previous season.

Off the field, Ron remained actively involved with Detroit's March of Dimes chapter. He served as the chairperson of the annual Bike-a-Thon fundraiser held at Belle Isle Park and was often seen with the afflicted children at Tiger Stadium, welcoming them on the field before games. As selfish as he could be at times, Ron could also be counted on to support organizations that focused their mission on serving Detroit's youth, especially those growing up in similar conditions that he had once endured.

His volunteer work went beyond the March of Dimes. In early June 1978, with the Tigers on the road, Ron received the following note from a hotel clerk: "Message from the White House, from the staff of Jimmy Carter."

"This is bullshit," he initially thought—and justifiably so. Ballplayers—with Ron being no exception—were known for pranking one another. Still, it piqued his interest. He called the phone number.

"I'll be dammed," he said afterward. "It was the president's office."[31]

At the peak of his fame, Ron shaking hands with a security guard, most likely at Tiger Stadium. (Ron LeFlore's personal collection)

Ron was selected by President Jimmy Carter to serve on the National Advisory Committee on Juvenile Justice and Delinquency Prevention, a twenty-one-member panel composed of academics, judges, lawyers, social workers, prison officials, and those who had direct contact with the justice system. Its task was to provide recommendations on federal policies, legislation, and programs regarding youth and their exposure to the justice system. To balance the varying views of its members, the committee was required to have a third of them under the age of twenty-six, of whom at least three should have had direct exposure to the juvenile justice system. Ron, who was actually thirty years old when the announcement was made public on June 28, was still officially using 1952 as his birthdate, allowing him to fulfill the age requirement.[†]

[†] If someone from President Carter's administration had closely read *Breakout*, they would have immediately realized that Ron was not twenty-six years old, since he cited his birthdate as June 16, 1950, which would have made him twenty-eight years old. Of course, that was inaccurate, too.

The committee was scheduled to meet four times a year, with half of the meetings held in Washington, DC. Of course, that posed a problem for Ron, who was on the road for half the year; the president's staff told him not to worry, as long as he made an appearance or two each year.

When Ron attended his first meeting of the National Advisory Committee, he caused quite a commotion.

"Everyone wanted to meet him; everyone wanted to talk to him," recalled Kenneth McClintock-Hernández, a committee member who was then a twenty-year-old, second-year law student at Tulane University. Like Ron, McClintock-Hernández stood out from the majority of those who served on the committee, who were older, mostly white, and well-established in their careers. Unlike Ron, however, McClintock-Hernández had experience in the policy matters under discussion, having served on Puerto Rico's juvenile justice advisory committee.

In truth, Ron lacked the formal education to contribute anything of substance to the discussion of policy and legislative items and was there more as "a symbol, as a token of a former juvenile justice client who did well in life."[32] Symbol or not, it was notable that the kid who had grown up in the East Side of Detroit was a member of that distinguished committee.

On September 26, *One in a Million* aired across the nation on CBS. The streets of Detroit were quiet that Tuesday evening as residents and fans saw Tiger Stadium, former Tiger players portray themselves, and their neighborhoods depicted in a two-hour television movie. The *Detroit Free Press* celebrated the occasion by providing readers with a special pullout section featuring the script, photographs from the movie set, and news articles to promote the film (and one of its reporters). Local resident Tom Sherry, who lived in the same neighborhood as Ron and his girlfriend Deborah, recalled how the "neighborhood was charged up.... Everyone is watching the same thing, at the same time, about the same guy who is our neighbor."[33] The Lindell AC, which

John LeFlore Jr. admiring his son's celebrity status as he signs autographs for fans. (Ron LeFlore's personal collection)

was featured as well as its owner, Jimmy Butsicaris, who played himself, saw an immediate spike in patrons.

Although locals thought *One in a Million* was a "grand slam," the movie's ratings were not as impressive.[34] It wasn't even the top-rated program that evening, which was ABC's television show, *Three's Company*, followed by two other popular ABC programs, *Taxi* and *Starsky & Hutch*.[35]

Still, the film had an enormous impact on Ron's author royalties. The book rights were purchased by Warner Books, the movie studio's publishing division, which printed another edition in mass paperback and retitled it after the film. And since the movie was part of CBS's programming, it would be

Ron's mother, Georgia LeFlore, posing with her grandson, Gerald Jr., whose father was killed two years prior. (Ron LeFlore's personal collection)

shown in syndication for years to come, which was essentially free promotion for the book.

Wherever Ron went, so did the cameras, the glitz, the women, and the drugs. In New York City, when the Tigers were in town, Ron was a frequent guest at Studio 54, *the* place to be seen during this disco music era. He'd be joined by Yankee right fielder Reggie Jackson, who would pick him up at the airport in his Rolls-Royce whenever the Tigers were in town.

Ron enjoyed the unrestrained life of a celebrity. At concerts, he would go backstage and hang out with singers such as Rod Stewart and Bob Marley. He was given mink coats and men's suits to advertise. Back in Detroit, Ron enjoyed attending boxing matches at Olympia Stadium and was seated in the front row before being mobbed by admirers and autograph hounds.

With such fame, Ron was inevitably a target of those who sought to exploit him. "I knew I had to put my guard up," he said, but it was harder than he realized.

"You grow up in a neighborhood, and something good happens to you. Everyone comes knocking at your door, thinking you're going to give them a handout.... I gave a few guys some money because I know they didn't have anything."[36]

Unfortunately for Deborah, who was living in Ron's house and raising their daughter, he was not present. Nor did he seem to appreciate that Deborah also took care of his late brother Gerald's three children. It was only a matter of time before their fragile relationship dissolved entirely, resulting in legal troubles that would follow Ron for decades. But for the moment, that was the least of his concerns.

12

Le Expos

When Ralph Houk retired at the end of the 1978 season, the Tigers hired the manager of the Triple-A Evansville Triplets, Les Moss. Known as an "organization man," Moss spent thirteen seasons as a backup catcher, then went on to become a batting coach, a scout, and manager of various teams in the minors for ten seasons.[1] On paper, he was an ideal pick, someone who had paid his dues and come up through the ranks. But his boss, Jim Campbell, soon had regrets about the mild-mannered Moss and began looking for a replacement.

For the first time in decades, Sparky Anderson, the former Cincinnati Reds skipper who had led the team to four World Series appearances and two championships, was not in uniform. He had been let go the previous season by the Reds for not making it to the playoffs two years in a row. Anderson was planning to take a year off while contemplating his next move. It was well-known within the league, however, that Anderson wouldn't be away for long.

Campbell began pursuing Anderson that spring. Once they reached an agreement, in an unusual move on June 11, fifty-three games into the 1979 season, Campbell fired Les Moss and replaced him with Sparky Anderson.

"He was exactly what we needed," according to third-year Tiger shortstop (and future Hall of Famer) Alan Trammell. "We needed to be corralled. We needed direction."[2]

Campbell was of like mind—and even more optimistic: "Sparky was the man who could take it to the top. He was the final piece of the puzzle."[3]

In his first meeting with the team, Anderson made it clear there was a new sheriff in town. He was not soft-spoken like Moss. Nor was he patient like Ralph Houk. The 45-year-old, white-haired Tiger manager had a larger-than-life personality and a ferocious "winaholic" attitude, similar to Billy Martin.[4] Yet, unlike Martin, he was disciplined and didn't exhibit unpredictable behavior. Nor would he ever be insubordinate, which made him a perfect fit in Campbell's world.

Anderson was taking over a team loaded with "good young prospects," including the highly touted rookie outfielder Kirk Gibson.[5] This emboldened the new manager to remind veteran players, who were used to a more relaxed, freewheeling atmosphere, that they were expendable. If he had to "trade every player in this room" to win, he'd do it.[6]

Additionally, Anderson insisted that players and coaches not only perform on the field but also look like sports professionals off it. He expected all personnel to wear a sports coat and tie when on the road. Hair past the ears was unacceptable and so were mustaches—which pertained to Ron, Aurelio Rodríguez, Rusty Staub, and Jason Thompson, all of whom were starters.

Despite all the bravado and recent policy changes, the Tigers were actually losing more games under their new manager than with the previous one. By the end of Anderson's first month on the job, the Tigers went from eight to fifteen games out of first place in their division.

Ron, who was hitting well above .300 and stealing as many bases as he could to compensate for the team's fifth-place standing, was offended by Sparky's "lack of respect toward the players."[7] Regarding himself as a superstar, there was no way he was going to adhere to Anderson's rules.

The inevitable clash of personalities was first ignited by Ron's refusal to take batting practice before the game. Ron argued that he didn't need it; Sparky disagreed. Each time Ron showed up after hitting drills took place, he was fined fifty dollars. It became so frequent that Ron would simply walk into his manager's office, take out a 100-dollar bill, slap it on his desk, and leave. Fifty dollars for today, the other fifty for tomorrow.

"Ron got away with a lot of stuff that other people wouldn't," recalled Irwin Cohen, baseball freelance writer and later a team official.[8]

When the Tigers were on the road, for example, they would take a bus from the hotel to the ballpark. The team was on a schedule, but that was of little concern to Ron, recalled the team's traveling secretary Bill Brown. Right after the bus departed the hotel, "Ron would come out of the hotel lobby and try to make it stop for him and him alone," Brown remembered.[9] The bus pulled over and picked him up the first time. The second time it happened, and anytime afterward, it would not.

Then there was the July 24 incident. In a home game against the Milwaukee Brewers, Ron didn't show up at the clubhouse. He had missed the previous day's game because of the flu, but team officials assumed he was feeling better, since they hadn't heard otherwise. When Ron didn't show up at gametime, his name was scratched from the lineup, which caught the beat reporters' attention. When they inquired, the team was unable to provide an explanation. According to Ron, he was still under the weather; nonetheless, he had failed to contact the front office. It was an embarrassing moment for the team, as evidenced the next day in a *Detroit Free Press* headline: "Where's LeFlore? The Plot Thickens."[10]

"As in all sports," Brown maintained, "if you had a good year, you got privileges that others didn't get. The stars were treated differently. Ron thought he was a star ... [and] assumed he was better than he was and should have had more privileges because of it."[11]

That did not sit well with Anderson. "[We] do things my way or hit the highway," he was known for saying during his first season with the Tigers.[12] No player on his team was "untouchable."[13]

"It was evident he [Ron] wouldn't last long under the Anderson regime," observed Ernie Harwell, the team's radio announcer.[14]

Ron didn't make it easy for the club to want to retain his services. With his contract expiring at the end of the season, the star center fielder did not hide the fact that he was seeking a "mountain of money."[15] To Jim Campbell, the thought of paying Ron LeFlore several millions of dollars—twice as much as he was making—was never going to happen.

In the first place, Ron was thirty-two, which in baseball was already considered past one's prime, especially when your most important physical attribute was speed. Then there was Ron's public image. According to *Jet* magazine, Ron was "slapped with a lawsuit because he allegedly stopped making support payments [to former fiancé Deborah Lewis] for the care of their 2-year-old daughter," LaRonda.[16] When asked for comments, Ron did not provide any while in the Bahamas with his new girlfriend. There was also the growing speculation about his increasing drug use.

In the 1970s, recreational drug use was on the rise among Americans, impacting all sectors of society, including professional sports. Baseball players took drugs for a variety of reasons. Younger athletes would do it to fit in with their new teammates or alleviate the stress of trying to make the team. Others took part to cure the "loneliness [and] boredom" on the road.[17] It was a problem for every club. The Tigers were no exception, though its management was under the misimpression that Ron was the "only Tiger regular to have ongoing drug problems."[18]

Once Ron had been released from prison, it wasn't long before he had started smoking marijuana again. Toward the end of the decade, when he became famous and had money, Ron started using cocaine. It was believed, by the end of the 1970s, that nearly half of all ballplayers had or were using the substance. In Ron's case, drug use was likely the contributing factor to his unexpected absences and frequent tardiness to the ballpark. But that wasn't even the worst of his off-field troubles.

Sometime in July 1979, Ron was at the ballpark when Jim Campbell summoned him to his office. When he arrived, an FBI agent was waiting to speak with him.

Campbell greeted Ron with a photograph of a murder victim. "Do you know about this guy being dead?" he asked.

"Why are you asking me?" Ron responded defensively. "I don't know why this guy is dead. I didn't know that guy. I dropped him off at the house of Frank Nitti [an alias used by Frank Lee Usher, a notorious mobster]. They were doing a golf tournament."[19]

For months, the FBI had been "following" Ron because they thought he was "linked" to the most gruesome Detroit killing in recent memory.[20] In July 1979, two men and a woman, all of whom were involved in the illegal drug trade, had been "shot in the head and decapitated."

"The men's hands had been chopped off, and one of the woman's hands had been cut off. . . . The heads of the victims were put into brown plastic garbage bags and placed next to the bodies."[21] Ron had picked up one of the two men earlier that day from the airport.

Prior to this incident, Campbell had had his own suspicions about his star player, which was why he had hired a private investigator "to tail" him. The investigator "encountered LeFlore meeting and dining with Usher on a semi-regular basis."[22] In the end, law enforcement officials were not dependent on Ron to bring a case forward against Usher. A random tip from a neighbor provided "the first break" in the case.[23] It took government officials three months to gather a sufficient amount of evidence before an arrest warrant was issued for Usher and four of his associates.

On December 7, 1979, Ron was at home, shaving in the shower, when the phone rang. His girlfriend, Sara Garrabrout, picked it up. It was Bill Lajoie, who had met Ron five years earlier, when he had driven him to Decatur,

Illinois, to play for the Clinton Pilots. Lajoie had since been promoted from head of scouting to assistant general manager.

"Hi, is Ron there?"

"Honey, it's for you," Sara informed Ron, who was in another room.

"Who is it?" Ron asked.

"Bill Lajoie," she said.

"Tell him I'll call him back."

"Can he call you back?" Sara asked Lajoie.

There was a pause before Sara told Ron, "He says it's important. He says to tell you you've been traded."

"Gimme that phone," Ron said, grabbing the receiver. "Where? Who for?" he asked Lajoie.

"I've traded you to Montreal," Lajoie replied.

"Who for?"

"Dave . . . uh, what's his name?" Lajoie had trouble remembering it. "Dave? Dan? Dan Schatzeder [pitcher]."

"Who else?"

"Nobody."

There was silence.

"I had never even heard of Schatzeder," Ron thought to himself when he got off the phone.[24] His whole life has been upended by a single phone call from the man, who, as a scout, considered Ron to be one of his greatest success stories.

It should not have come as a surprise to Ron. First, his other mustached teammates, Rusty Staub and Aurelio Rodríguez, had also been let go by the Tigers. Second, Ron and his new agent, Ken Fishkin, who used to work for Robert Woolf, had been negotiating with Campbell and Lajoie during the offseason and were at an impasse. Campbell offered Ron $3 million for six years; Ron wanted $4 million for five years. "I didn't think we were that far apart, really," Ron confided to Hawkins hours after the trade was announced.[25]

Detroit Tiger manager Sparky Anderson and Director of Player Development Bill Lajoie, both of whom had an impact on Ron LeFlore's career. (Anupam Sinha's personal collection)

His agent concurred. "I didn't think we were asking too much," Fishkin said. "Now, he'll [Ron] have to learn to speak French."[26]

"We tried desperately to sign him," Campbell went on record, perhaps to appease fans more than Ron.[27*] The Tigers' GM knew that there was going to be fallout; he just didn't realize the extent.

Before there were online chat groups and Facebook comments, fans voiced their frustration in their local newspaper.

---

*On November 29, 1979, less than ten days before Ron's trade to the Expos, Baseball Commissioner Bowie Kuhn wrote a list of topics under the header "Security Review." One of the topics was Ron LeFlore, which made mention of "his file" and that "Sandy [Hadden, Kuhn's chief deputy] will talk to Jim Campbell." At this point, Campbell had most likely already made up his mind that he no longer wanted Ron on the Tigers. Perhaps Sandy Hadden conveyed there was additional information held in this file that may have given Campbell more confidence in his decision to trade his star center fielder.

"I'm just stunned. How can you put that into words? That's an obscene trade."

"I'm sick about it. You don't give away a guy who steals 80 bases and get a guy with a 10 and 5 record."

"Is Jim Campbell on drugs?"

"Let's face it, they traded away the most exciting player on the bases for somebody we never heard of."

"You mean they traded one for one? Are you positive? You're not pulling my leg, are you?"

"I think it's ludicrous."[28]

Not surprisingly, sports writers joined the fans' chorus of outrage. *Detroit Free Press* columnist George Puscas ripped the team's management: "The Tigers are an organization that refuses to compete." Why would Jim Campbell trade "one of the few sparks on his dismal fifth place club?"[29]

Former Detroiter Donald Kaul, who was now working for the *Des Moines Tribune*, went further, proposing (tongue-in-cheek) that it was a citywide conspiracy, given the lackluster records of the three other professional sports teams in Motor City: the Lions (football), the Pistons (basketball), and the Red Wings (ice hockey). "It's a plot," he sarcastically wrote. "The owners of Detroit athletic teams don't wanna win and will go to any lengths to avoid it."[30]

The anger at the Tigers' organization did not cease. On Monday, December 10, three days after the trade was announced, three Ron LeFlore fans dumped a two-foot-high pile of horse manure on the steps of the Tigers' offices on Trumbull Avenue. When it was reported by the *Free Press*, the caption said it was "some fan's way of letting Campbell know what they think of the LeFlore trade."[31]

The following day, Ron LeFlore was in Montreal. Dressed in a suit and wearing an Expos baseball cap, he smiled for the cameras as he was introduced to the Canadian media. He was joined at a team press conference by two other newly named yet lesser-known Expos, pitcher Fred Norman and backup outfielder Rowland Office. To anyone who attended the session, it was obvious who the audience had come to see.

Ron did his best to accommodate the media, but it had been a rough week for the ex-Tiger. He was shipped off to Montreal, a town known more for hockey than baseball. Everything about Montreal was different: language, food, music, and especially the sports. Ron went from playing for a storied franchise that had recently celebrated its seventy-fifth anniversary, to one that was marking its twelfth season of existence and had never had a winning record until the previous year. Then he was informed by Expos manager Dick Williams that he was *not* going to displace the team's current center fielder, Andre Dawson. Instead, Ron would be in left field, a position he had rarely played.

Furthermore, Montreal's Olympic Stadium had synthetic turf, which in the previous decade had become popular among team owners for its low maintenance costs. Shaky on defense to begin with, Ron would be playing in a different position on terrain he was unfamiliar with. But the Expos didn't bring Ron in for his glove.

"We've never had speed like that at the top of our order," Expos general manager John McHale boasted to reporters. With the addition of Ron, the Expos would arguably have the most explosive lineup in Major League Baseball. They had three base stealers (Ron, Dawson, and second baseman Rodney Scott) and four hitters who could hit the long ball (Dawson, right fielder Ellis Valentine, first baseman Warren Cromartie, and catcher Gary Carter). With Ron at the plate and on the bases, Montreal's management hoped that he would be the catalyst for the team, improving everyone's performance.

The Expos offered something that Ron hadn't experienced before: winning. Unlike the Tigers, who had never been in serious contention for a pennant while Ron had played for them, the Expos had narrowly missed the playoffs at the tail end of the 1979 season.

RON LeFLORE

After six seasons with the Detroit Tigers, Ron was traded to the Montreal Expos on December 7, 1979. (Rucker Archive, Society for American Baseball Research)

For his one year of service, Ron was paid $500,000 (equivalent to $2 million today), which at the time made him one of the highest-paid players in the game. "We're gambling that this fellow can make us a champion right now," said McHale.[32]

The Montreal Expos, who were favored to win its division, got off to a dismal start, going 6–10 and finding itself in fifth place in the National League East Division. Ron struggled, too, committing four errors in the first eleven games of the season, causing Dick Williams to substitute him for a stronger fielder late in games when the score was close. But starting in May, the Expos settled in and started winning more games than they lost, battling back from the bottom of the division to second place. By early June, they were at the top of the standings.

Still adjusting to the new league, Ron hadn't been consistent at the plate despite the team's success. He started June with an embarrassing .227 batting average, yet he still managed to lead the league in stolen bases. On June 6, Ron broke the spell. At home against the St. Louis Cardinals, Ron singled in the first inning and then stole second base. The pitcher, who was rattled, went on to walk Andre Dawson. Both players scored off Gary Carter's two-run double.

Later, in the sixth inning, Ron doubled, stole third, and scored his second run of the day. And in the eighth inning, with the Expos up 4–2, Ron showed why the team had taken a chance on him. With one out, Ron singled and then stole second base. Unnerved, the pitcher walked second baseman Rodney Scott. Now, with two men on who were both capable of stealing, the pitcher tried to pick off Scott, but he threw the ball out of reach to his infielder. Scott advanced to third, and Ron scored his third run of the game. In the end, the Expos beat the Cardinals 7–2.

The next day's headlines in the Canadian newspapers summed it up: "LeFlore Runs Wild Against Cards" and "LeFlore 'Steals' the Show."[33] Ron went on a hitting tear for the next three weeks, helping to solidify the Expos' top position in their division. He continued to lead the National League in stolen bases (and was among the leaders in runs scored), doing exactly what the Expos had hired him to do: firing up the team, not to mention distracting virtually every opposing pitcher in the league.

As a team, the Expos were living up to the preseason hype. *The Sporting News* had them on its cover, and *Sports Illustrated* ran a feature about their speedsters (Ron, Scott, and Dawson), tagging them "The Burglars" for their mass thievery. Stealing bases impacts the game, sometimes in ways fans don't always appreciate. It increases the likelihood of an error, can lead to more walks, decreases the number of double plays, and helps the batter at the plate, since the pitcher is less focused and more likely to make a throwing mistake. It also affects a pitcher's psyche, as Expos pitcher Steve Rogers explained to *Sports Illustrated*: "When one of these guys comes to bat, the pitcher thinks, 'Don't walk him, because if he gets on first, it's like walking a double.'"

Canadians were warming up to the Black Detroiter with a French-sounding surname. Just like in Detroit, fans at Olympic Stadium chanted, "Go, go!" anytime Ron got on base, knowing he was, at any moment, going to take off.[34] By the season's midpoint, Ron had surpassed the Expos' single-season stolen base record of fifty. In fact, he was on track to break the all-time MLB single-season record of 118 set by St. Louis Cardinal Lou Brock, who had retired the previous year.

As the season progressed, Ron found his groove. By August, he was unstoppable on the basepaths, as he demonstrated in a doubleheader against the New York Mets at home. The largest crowd of the season was on hand at Olympic Stadium, among them Prime Minister Pierre Elliott Trudeau and his three sons, including eight-year-old (future prime minister) Justin.

Ron made an immediate impact in Montreal, but he wore out his welcome by the end of the season, and the team released him. (Rucker Archive, Society for American Baseball Research)

In the first of two games, the Mets were up 3–0 in the bottom of the eighth. The Expos were six outs away from ending their six-game winning streak. The Mets' Pat Zachry, who was July's National League Pitcher of the Month, faced the bottom of the order. Shortstop Chris Speier led off with a single. Jerry White pinched-hit for pitcher Steve Rogers and was walked. At the top of the order, Ron was at the plate and slashed a grounder that got past Mets third baseman Elliott Maddox and scored Speier and White. The score was now 3–2.

Afterward, Rodney Scott bunted, which advanced Ron to third. With Dawson—their best hitter—up, the Expos could take the lead for the first time in the game . . . except he popped up to third. One out.

Then Ellis Valentine, another hot hitter, struck out. Two away.

At that point, first baseman Warren Cromartie stepped to the plate. Even though Cromartie was a .300 hitter, Ron was getting nervous. He wanted to tie this game—now.

Attempts to steal home were rare in 1980, partly because pitchers no longer wound up their body like they used to, allowing the runner an extra second or two to steal. For the first time in his career, back in June, Ron had done the impossible: stealing home successfully. Ready to try it again while Cromartie was at bat, Ron tempted the Mets pitcher, moving as far as the halfway point on the baseline before the pitch was thrown.

At that very moment, he decided that he "had better than an even chance to steal."[35]

Pat Zachry didn't think Ron would run. But when he saw Ron galloping down the basepath, he had to adjust his throw while in a pitching motion. Meanwhile, Cromartie was at the plate and focused on the pitcher, not Ron.

"Cro!" someone yelled from the Expos' dugout. "Don't swing!"[36]

Cromartie turned slightly, saw Ron, and fell to the ground to avoid colliding with his teammate. The ball sailed past the catcher. Cromartie, who was underneath the catcher and still holding his bat, watched Ron cross the plate.†

---

†Since Ron's steal of home was later ruled a balk, he didn't get credit for stealing home.

The game was now tied 3–3, and it would go into extra innings. In the bottom of the tenth, Ron walked, stole second, and scored the winning run off Dawson's single. The Expos' fans were ebullient. The team had never been this exciting to watch before.

In the locker room in between games, Ron was congratulated by everyone, including Prime Minister Trudeau, who made his way to Ron's locker to shake his hand and introduce his sons.

"He's a fast runner—eh, guys?" remarked Trudeau.[37]

A couple of days later, a profile in the *New York Times* compared Ron to Jackie Robinson, who was also known for stealing home when it counted. One of Robinson's Brooklyn Dodger teammates, the great Duke Snider, who was now a broadcaster for the Expos, said that Ron reminded him of Jackie when he was on the basepaths.

Shaking hands with the Canadian prime minister; appearing in the most prestigious and widely read newspaper in the country; being compared to the legendary Jackie Robinson; playing for a serious contender; and possibly breaking the all-time, single-season stolen base record—Ron LeFlore had become the toast of Montreal. It sure looked like the Tigers had gotten the short end of the deal.

Unfortunately, Ron had a way of sabotaging his own success.

The short-lived monthly magazine *Inside Sports* rode the wave of the era's sports magazine boom. Established in 1979, *Inside Sports* was billed as the "*Esquire* of sports magazines" and was promoted to readers as a "more literate" publication than the industry leader, *Sports Illustrated*.[38] If there were any doubts about *Inside Sports*'s assertion, one only had to read its articles by acclaimed writers such as David Halberstam and Studs Terkel.

When Ron LeFlore met New York-based freelance writer Mark Ribowsky at Olympic Stadium during the All-Star break in July, neither knew this unassuming interview for *Inside Sports* would land on the gossip pages of sports sections throughout North America. The interview lasted five hours, which took place in Ron's car as well as over food and drinks at a downtown restaurant called the Rib Tickler. When they parted ways, Ron went about his normal routine and did not think anything of the interview, probably because he was distracted by Montreal's nightlife.

Expos pitcher Bill Lee and other players always looked forward to the end of each home game because that was "when the town opened up. Everybody was out at discos and partying."

"The reason we were so good," Lee joked, was that visiting teams "partied harder than us," thereby weakening themselves.[39] Bars were plentiful in downtown and the Old Montreal neighborhood. A typical night out for Expo players started at a pub, then they'd head to a disco, stay until three or four o'clock in the morning, get a cheeseburger, go back to their apartment, sleep until 10:00 a.m., have breakfast, take a nap, and then go to the ballpark.

Ron especially had a reputation for being "one of the first players out of the clubhouse" so he could get a jumpstart on the nightclubs.[40] Montreal was not only known for its bars but also for "being a hot spot for drug and cocaine use in baseball circles."[41] During this era, cocaine was ubiquitous in clubhouses across the league. Ever since he had arrived in Montreal, Ron's use of cocaine had dangerously escalated, occasionally spanning multiple days. "I'd stay up all night long," he said. "I remember one time I was up for five or six days straight."[42] It reached a point, following a night of partying, that he needed cocaine to wake himself up before a game.

Like most users, Ron thought he had it under control. He wasn't fooling anyone.

When Ron's friend Kenny Brown visited Montreal that season, he overheard a teammate tell Ron, "You got to slow this down. This ain't going to work."[43]

Although Ron was performing at a high level on the field, there were signs that his cocaine use was taking its toll. During the season, manager Dick Williams wondered why Ron typically played better at night than during the day, likely a result of his excessive nighttime partying, leaving little rest for day games. He would often show up late at the clubhouse. Once, when there was a doubleheader, Ron arrived minutes before the first pitch, claiming that he thought the game began at 1:00 p.m. (instead of noon).

Williams also was concerned about Ron's errors on the field. When Ron misplayed a flyball, his excuse was that he "lost it in the lights." Williams didn't believe him. After the game, Williams went to left field to see if that was the truth.

"Son of a bitch," he muttered after looking up at the stadium's ceiling. He moved five feet and looked up again. "Goddamn it."[44]

The lighting did not pose a problem. Williams knew Ron was lying.

Ron had yet another explanation for his erratic behavior on and off the field: "personal problems."[45] His girlfriend, Sara, was in the final days of what turned out to be a complicated pregnancy, their first together. There were several false delivery starts, which Ron claimed contributed to his tardiness. On August 14, 1980, Sara gave birth to a healthy eight-pound, one-ounce baby boy, Ronald Alexander LeFlore Jr.

When the September edition of *Inside Sports* was published at the end of August, Ron's interview wasn't the lead article, but it certainly was the one that grabbed all the attention. Issues were "disappearing rapidly" from newsstands.[46]

Why the unprecedented interest? In the interview with Ribowsky, Ron had vented about his former team, calling Sparky Anderson a "dictator" and saying that Tiger general manager Jim Campbell had treated him as "a dumb black boy." He also went after his ghostwriter and biggest cheerleader, *Detroit Free Press* columnist Jim Hawkins: "He was nothing then and he's been nothing since. Yeah, he stabbed me in the back too." Ron then went on record facetiously saying that MLB Commissioner Bowie Kuhn should take a hit of marijuana because so many of his players were engaged in rampant drug use.

If Ron's comments about Detroit's management and Commissioner Kuhn did not create enough of a stir, the remarks he made about his current situation were even more inflammatory. After stating that the French-Canadian press knew "nothing about baseball," he accused his teammates and the city of Montreal of racism.

"This town is 80, 90 percent white. And regardless of how many [B]lacks are on the team, you still feel like you're a nigger here," Ron told Ribowsky.[47] Never mind that Jackie Robinson, when playing for the Brooklyn Dodgers' farm team in Montreal thirty-five years earlier, had noted in his memoir that Montrealers "were warm and wonderful to us [him and his wife, Rachel]."[48]

To support his accusation, Ron cited an example of how a Black Expo had a racially charged run-in with law enforcement. He even went after some of his white teammates, calling them "rednecks." When Ribowsky pressed him to identify who they were, Ron responded, "Go down the roster. Take your pick. Some of these guys are from the South and all Southerners are rednecks. They've been brought up to hate niggers."[49]

Ron's Black teammates disagreed. Center fielder Andre Dawson said, "This is my fourth year here and his first. I can't recall a single incident of a black player being put down. Montreal fans accept [B]lacks as well as any other city in the National League. . . . They haven't shown any prejudice."[50] And first baseman Warren Cromartie? "[N]ever had any issues" when it came to racism in Montreal, and he had actually found it to be a "safe haven for Blacks."[51]

When asked about the backlash generated by his interview, Ron disingenuously expressed disbelief over the commotion. "After all the nice things I've said about Montreal, I hope people don't get the wrong impression about me," he told Michael Farber, a *Montreal Gazette* reporter. His feigned naivety was one thing, but given how "incensed" his teammates were, he had to seriously address the damage he had done within the clubhouse. Hoping "to clear the air," he announced that he planned to call a team meeting.[52]

Later, Ron decided to shift gears, denying that he had made some of those contentious comments to Ribowsky. "Well, there are a few words in there I didn't say," he declared lamely, "and a lot of things I said were left out, but I guess I'll just have to live with it."

Now it was Ribowsky who was fuming at Ron.

"LeFlore made the charges," Ribowsky said, defending the accuracy of his interview. "It didn't matter how hard I tried to steer the conversation back to base-stealing. . . . And LeFlore talked. Drinks? Oh definitely, we were having a few drinks, but it was a sober interview. There's not a slurred word in six hours of tape."

The Canadian media, once in awe of Ron's playing capabilities, now jumped all over him. "LeFlore Can't Duck Attack on Expos" was the headline in *Montreal Gazette's* column written by Ted Blackman.[53] In the *Ottawa Citizen*, the lead article in the sports section was "'Nigger' LeFlore Blasts Expos," while out west, the headline in the *Vancouver Sun* read, "'Racist': LeFlore Attacks Montreal."[54]

Most of those in the Expos' front office sought to put the controversy behind them. General manager John McHale told reporters, "All I'm interested in is seeing him [Ron] help us win the championship." Team owner Charles Bronfman was not as diplomatic: "I find LeFlore's statements so ridiculous they make me laugh."[55]

By and large, Montrealers followed McHale's lead, seeking victory rather than vengeance. On September 9, in their first game back in Montreal since the interview had been published, the Expos took on the New York Mets. In his first at bat, Ron received a "scattering of boos," but virtually no one in the stands wanted him traded or benched. Expos fans wanted their team to go to the playoffs, and they knew Ron was integral to their success, as he demonstrated in a 3–0 win over the Mets that day. He had two hits, including a triple and a stolen base.

Despite the off-field distractions, it did not impact his play. Ron continued to rank among the National League's leaders in stolen bases, triples, and runs scored.

Still, he needed to bring his self-created controversy to a close. On the advice of his agent, he issued a prepared statement to the press, apologizing to fans and the team. "I love Montreal," he went on. "I have been made to feel welcome and at home here in ways that I never dreamed possible."[56]

MLB Commissioner Bowie Kuhn also demanded that Ron provide a formal expression of regret. Presented with a pre-typed apology letter from the commissioner's office, Ron signed it without protest.

Years later, as he looked back on the interview, Ron admitted, "I was so stupid."[57]

That summer of 1980 posed other challenges for Ron.

On September 11, against the Chicago Cubs, Ron was tracking down a Dave Kingman fly ball into foul territory. Following its trajectory, Ron approached the outfield wall and was about to collide with it when he instinctively put his hands out to prevent the collision. Although he stopped what could have been a very serious injury, he nearly fractured his left thumb and sprained his wrist in the process.

With only three weeks left in the season, how could Ron play in the outfield? How could he swing a bat? But there was one way he could help his team: run the bases.

At the time of his injury, Ron was the league leader in stolen bases, with ninety-two. Pittsburgh Pirates center fielder Omar Moreno was the next closest, with eight-six. There was a good chance that Moreno would pass him, which was all the more reason for Ron to serve as a pinch runner.

The Expos powered their way through September, tied for first place with Pittsburgh and the Philadelphia Phillies for the National League East title. The Pirates would eventually fall back, and it would end with a showdown in the second to last game of the season between the Expos and the Phillies, led by superstar third baseman Mike Schmidt. Ron had already pinched-run in four games and was available if the Expos needed him.

The game remained close throughout; and in the seventh inning, the Expos were down 3–2 when Ron came in to pinch-run for third baseman Chris Speier, who was on first base.

"Ron LeFlore is coming out, and you know what that means," the broadcaster said as Ron stretched his legs while the hometown crowd began cheering, anticipating that he would ignite a late-inning rally.[58]

Ron wasted no time and took off for second. He landed safely, but the infielder misplayed the catcher's throw and the ball rolled into center field. Ron got up and went to third. He eventually scored a run on a sacrifice fly to tie the game. The game went into extra innings, but the Phillies prevailed, winning 6–4 thanks to Schmidt's game-winning home run in the eleventh inning. It was the second year in a row that the Expos narrowly missed the playoffs.

With one game to go—a meaningless one, since the Phillies had captured the NL East's playoff spot—Ron was prepared to sit it out, along with the other starters. Except Ron did so in the visitors' locker room, sipping sparkling wine with the Phillies' Pete Rose and Mike Schmidt. In the middle of the game, Rose mentioned to Ron that Moreno hadn't stolen a base in the Pirates' finale. He ended the season with ninety-six stolen bases, while Ron was at ninety-five.

"Hey," Rose told him, "you only need two more stolen bases to win the [NL] title."[59]

Expos manager Dick Williams was well aware that the stolen base title was up for grabs. Besides, he wanted a victory in this final game of the season: "It doesn't mean much, but we wanted to win this for the fans. They've been terrific all year."[60]

With the Expos down 5–4 in the eighth inning, Williams seized the opportunity to replace backup catcher Bobby Ramos on first with Ron. When Williams signaled for Ron, no one knew where he was. The Expos skipper had forewarned Ron that he would use him if the game was close. Now that it was, he was nowhere to be found. A noticeable delay ensued.

Then, all of a sudden, Ron appeared with a cast on his left arm, coming out of the opposing team's dugout, running across the backstop and into the Expos dugout.

"What the hell was he doing over there?" wondered Williams. "A little ninth inning socializing?"[61]

"I've never seen a guy come out of the other team's tunnel to pinch-run," recalled *Montreal Gazette's* Michal Farber, who was covering the Expos that season.[62]

"It was kinda weird . . . [but] that was Ron," Cromartie remembered.[63]

With the crowd on its feet, all eyes were on Ron LeFlore, possibly for the final time in Olympic Stadium, given the speculation about whether he would return the following season.

On the first pitch, Ron took off. Phillies catcher Ozzie Virgil Jr.—who, like any NL catcher, was ready for Ron to steal—threw the ball to second base, except the ball landed in the outfield. Ron slid and began dusting himself off. He pretended not to have seen what happened. If he continued to third base, he would only be credited with one stolen base, tying Moreno. But he would have no possibility of surpassing it, since there was no way he could steal home plate with a cast on his hand.

As play resumed, Ron took his lead off second. The crowd was on its feet. Once the pitcher released the ball, he raced to third. Safe!

Ron LeFlore won the National League title for most stolen bases in the 1980 season. He also became the first player in MLB history to win the stolen base title in both the American and National Leagues.

Ron eventually scored and tied the game, sending it into extra innings. The Expos won it in the tenth.

"That was the greatest year of my career," Ron said years later. "Not stats-wise, but fun-wise."[64]

Ron wanted to remain in Montreal, but he was oblivious about how much resentment he had caused with the Expos.

Shortly after the end of the 1980 season, in an interview conducted by a journalist from *Toronto Globe and Mail*, Ron expressed the "hope that the article [in *Inside Sports*] can be overlooked."[65] Ignoring Ron's comment, the reporter was far more interested in discussing the future of the Expos, having fallen short of making the playoffs for the second year in a row. Ron was supposed to be the decisive difference; he hadn't been.

The interview raised more questions about Ron's future, instead of solidifying his position with the Expos. And as for his disastrous comments in *Inside Sports*, it served only to confirm the negative views held by those in the front office.

"You wouldn't believe all the problems we had," said team General Manager John McHale. "He was a talent, but he brought with him baggage that was not good."[66]

According to team manager Dick Williams, Ron was "constant[ly] bitching about the food or the laundry or the managing, even though I played him in every game." His reputation for "late-night forays into strange parts of town," in Williams's opinion, had affected Ron's performance on the field. What made it worse was that he brought along "the team's younger players with him."[67]

Similar to Detroit, Expos management blamed Ron for being a bad influence on the team's up-and-coming Black stars.

In fact, General Manager McHale thought that Ron "was eventually the guy who led Tim Raines into it [cocaine]."[68] Raines, who would go on to have a spectacular career and be voted into the Hall of Fame, had developed a serious addition to cocaine while playing for the Expos, entering rehab in 1982. Did Ron draw Raines into drugs? Raines did not place the blame on Ron, whose interactions with the nineteen-year-old were minimal, which was likely true given that Raines had only played in fifteen games with the Expos that season and spent most of it in the minors.

Despite his drug problem, Raines had enormous potential. As the front office saw it, he could perform as well as Ron—and without the attitude. Raines could play outfield, hit leadoff, and steal bases, all of which convinced the Expos that they no longer needed Ron's services.

Undaunted, Ron and his agent, Ken Fishkin, were under the impression that he was a hot commodity in the off-season market. To their chagrin, only one club expressed interest—the Chicago White Sox.

Perhaps, it wasn't surprising that the Sox signed him. Their owner, Bill Veeck, was regarded as a rebel rouser and an anomaly among his cohorts. Referred to by another team owner as a "god-damn-socialist," the 67-year-old was an early advocate of integration.[69] As owner of the Cleveland Indians in the 1940s, his club became the first in the American League to have an African American on its roster, Larry Doby and, shortly thereafter, pitcher Satchel Paige. A proponent of racial justice, Veeck was also an unapologetic showman, reminiscent of P.T. Barnum, known more for his gimmicks over the years than for being a strategist. On one occasion, he hired a little person to pinch hit. He also allowed his son to organize the legendary Disco Demolition game, where a Chicago DJ burned disco music records at the ballpark; it tuned into a riot and the game was suspended. Was Ron just another one of Veeck's stunts, a means to fill more seats at Comisky Park?

"He'll put the go-go back into the White Sox," Veeck said upon signing the former Expo to a three-year, $2.4 million contract, making him one of the highest-paid players in the league.[70] Two months later, Veeck sold the team.

With Veeck gone, Ron found a new advocate—the Sox's 36-year-old manager, Tony La Russa. The Tampa, Florida, native played professional baseball, but his future was in management. After working as a minor league team manager (while attending law school), the White Sox hired him midway through the 1979 season. Less flamboyant than Veeck, the serious-minded and unflappable La Russa was convinced that Ron could provide the Sox with the necessary spark to improve the team's previous season's fifth place finish in the AL West.

"He's going to generate a lot of excitement, a lot of runs," La Russa said before spring training. "When Ron gets on, he disrupts everyone—the defense, the pitcher, the catcher, the manager. Everyone but me."[71]

Before the 1981 season started, however, La Russa's confidence in Ron was shaken. His star player showed up at spring training in Sarasota, Florida, overweight, "the heaviest of his career."[72] He missed practices. When he did appear, he was late. He arrived an hour and fifteen minutes late for a game in Lakeland against his former team, the Tigers. La Russa had a lengthy discussion with Ron, hoping the situation would turn itself around. But the young manager was unaware of problems beyond his control.

Ron was deeply involved in drugs. Frequently out all night, partying, he continued to miss practices, missed team flights, and showed up late to games. He was suspended and issued fines, but none of them had the desired effect. Ron finished the 1981 season with a career low .246 batting average. He was no longer hitting leadoff; he wasn't even a full-time starter. He had become a pinch hitter, sharing outfield duties with a lesser-known (and less expensive) player.

The following season was just as dismal and actually got worse. As the 1982 season was drawing to an end, Ron was arrested at his Chicago residence for unlawful possession of amphetamines and two unregistered pistols. The team suspended Ron, this time for the final three games of the season (not that it mattered much; he only played in one game in all of September). LaRussa and the White Sox wanted nothing more to do with Ron LeFlore.

At the peak of Ron's earning power, he was making $735,000 in a single season (equivalent to $2.5 million today). By 1983, after two disappointing seasons with the White Sox, Ron failed to make the forty-man roster and was cut on the last day of spring training, even though he still had a year's salary left on his contract. He fought it and won compensation, but that would be his last victory in baseball.

EPILOGUE

On any given day in 1987, at five in the morning, a dozen or so skycaps (the modern-day train porter) would stand on the curb of the sidewalk under the Eastern Airlines banner at the Sarasota-Bradenton International Airport in Sarasota, Florida, and wait for the next car to pull up. Dressed in a white dress shirt, gray slacks, and a captain's hat, he (they were nearly all men) would assist customers with tagging their luggage, checking it in, and answering any number of questions about their flight: Is it on time? Am I going to make my connection? What gate am I going to? Can you help me with my luggage? All the while, the skycap would be methodically calculating what type of tip he was going to receive. On a slow day, he would assist a couple of hundred passengers. But during the holiday season, it could spike to 500.

Among those assisting the travelers was 39-year-old Ron LeFlore, the once-magnificent base-stealing champion, former All-Star, and best-selling author.

"It was good money," Ron recalled.[1] Good money, but it was challenging work, both mentally and physically. You had no choice but to take insults and slights and endure covert racism (most of the skycaps were people of color), all the while lifting heavy luggage and inhaling toxic fumes from idle vehicles.

Ron was likely making minimum wage, which was $3.35 an hour (or close to it), so tips were what kept a skycap motivated to assist customers. On average, one could expect to receive about a dollar per bag, but customers were not obligated to tip and as many as half chose not to. Those who did might have given as little as a quarter per bag. On a rare occasion, Ron would have a customer—often traveling from or heading to New York—slip him a hundred-dollar bill for three or four bags. Sometimes, he would encounter someone he knew from his past, such as college basketball broadcaster Dick Vitale, whom

Ron had met during the 1976 offseason when he was undergoing physical therapy for his injured knee. At the time, Vitale was the basketball coach at the University of Detroit, where Ron had worked out with the players during their practices.

"Ronnie was always good to me when I was in Detroit," Vitale recalled. "Any time I'd go to the ballpark at Tiger Stadium, Ronnie would send over to me a nylon sock with baseballs and autographs."

"I feel bad about his career," Vitale went on to say. "I know, he has no one to blame but himself, but at least he is trying to make a living."[2]

The once-darling of Detroit and toast of Montreal was no longer part of Major League Baseball. He went from signing autographs, riding in limousines, and meeting heads of state, to waking up at four in the morning, hustling for a dollar here, a dollar there, and asking men and women, "Can I help you?"

Ron LeFlore had experienced three dark periods in his life. The first was the loss of his brother, Harry. The second was his years of incarceration. And the third was the period following the end of his playing career. After a stint in Puerto Rico during the winter of 1983, at which time he failed to resuscitate his career, he went home to his residence in Sarasota, Florida, where he lapsed into a downward spiral: "I started using drugs real hard."[3]

Day after day, high on cocaine and isolated in his Sarasota mansion, which he had purchased upon signing with the White Sox, Ron spent his time sitting in front of the television with now two children in tow, Ronald Jr. and Georgia. His relationship with their mother, Sara, who was also using drugs, had ended; they were now separated.

Ron's rampant drug use undoubtedly contributed to his financial woes. With his judgment impaired by substance abuse, "people were taking advantage of him," according to Johnny Butsicaris's son, Mel.[4] Like most drug addicts, Ron failed to hold himself responsible for his money troubles; instead, he lashed out at his agent, Ken Fishkin, whom he claimed was withholding his financial statements, which Fishkin denied.

Aside from relationship and money problems, Ron also had to wrestle with personal tragedies. His father, John LeFlore, died in September 1981. Less than a year later, in May 1982, Ron's one-year-old son, Ronald Jr., almost died from a near drowning in the family pool.

Five months later, Ron was arrested in Chicago for possession of a controlled substance and an unregistered firearm. It led to a suspension from the White Sox (the charges were later dropped). In December 1982, Sara and Ron had another baby, John, named after his late father. Only six weeks old, John died from sudden infant death syndrome (SIDS). The pool incident, Ron's arrest, and the SIDS episode triggered an investigation by the Sarasota County Sheriff's Office and the Florida Department of Health and Rehabilitative Services, who considered (but never filed) charges against Ron and Sara for child neglect and endangerment.

On top of all of this, Jimmy Karalla, the former inmate who had arranged for Ron's tryout with the Tigers, filed a lawsuit against him, claiming they had made a verbal agreement in prison that he would receive 20 percent of Ron's earnings. According to Karalla, Ron told him, "When I sign my next big contract, I will give you a percentage of it. Without you, I'd be dead or in jail. I owe you."[5]

Ron denied making the statement. The suit was eventually dismissed.

Somehow, there was a silver lining during this tumultuous period in Ron's life. In his final year with the Chicago White Sox, Ron had met Emily Zafer, a twenty-year-old college student who was studying interior design. They were polar opposites. She was white and came from a stable family. She was fourteen years his junior. Despite their differences, however, the relationship got serious. Emily had tried to convince Ron to seek help for his addiction, but to no avail. When she moved with him to Sarasota, she hadn't realized how bad it was.

"[He] wasn't the same person [as] when I met him," she later said. In Chicago, she was at home and could retreat to friends and family. But in Sarasota, it was just her, Ron, and his "cling-ons" and "moochers."[6] Ron had violated the one rule that Al Kaline, Jim Campbell, Gates Brown, and Jimmy Butsicaris had all warned him about: keep the hangers-on away.

It had been more than fifteen years since the Detroit Tigers had made an appearance in the World Series. But when they did in October 1984, it was without "Go, Go!" Ron LeFlore. Watching his former team play in the championship series on television, Ron sank into a deeper depression—one that he thought he might not ever recover from. Here, he was, out of shape, overweight, and lying on his couch, with nowhere to go and lines of coke at an arm's length, watching his former team win a World Series.

Emily, who was working at a fine furniture store in Sarasota at the time, sensed she made a mistake by moving to the Sunshine State to be with Ron. She gave him an ultimatum: "It's either me or the drugs."[7]

Ron seriously considered ending it all. Whether it was jumping from Tampa's Sunshine Skyway Bridge or shooting himself in the head, he considered all his options.

In July 1986, at approximately one o'clock in the morning, Ron was behind the wheel on his way home with two friends. Traveling at 110 miles per hour, he passed out and smashed his car against a road barrier, where it flew into a plowed field and rolled over several times. All three passengers were thrown from the vehicle and taken away in an ambulance. Ron suffered a concussion and was hospitalized for four days with three broken ribs. The other two passengers had significantly more serious injuries and spent months in recovery.

"I took that as an omen," he said. "It was time to straighten out my act."[8] And he did, to some extent.

Like most professional athletes who didn't end their career in the Hall of Fame or with endorsement deals lined up, it was hard for Ron to transition from sports star to blue-collar worker. By the end of the 1980s, he was no longer living in a mansion. He was in drug counseling, and he had to find a job to support Emily (whom he married) and his two children, who were living with Sara. He was also legally obligated to provide child support to his ex-girlfriend, Deborah Lewis, for their daughter, LaRonda. So Ron worked as a skycap, a security guard, and a municipal recreation league official. He even tried his hand at becoming a professional umpire.

Although Major League Baseball wanted nothing to do with Ron LeFlore, there were still opportunities for him to capitalize on his past glory. In 1989, Ron and a few hundred other retired ballplayers were hired to play in the first (and only) Senior Professional Baseball Association. Players such as Rollie Fingers and Vida Blue, as well as Ron's former teammates Steve Kemp and Bill Lee, participated in the league. It was an ideal situation for Ron. Since games were held in towns throughout Florida, he wouldn't need to relocate. He would also be well-compensated financially. Best of all, he would be back in the game.

Yet Ron was unable to seize the occasion. When he arrived at training camp, the guy who said he would do anything to play again, even if it was for one dollar, showed up twenty pounds overweight and obviously out of shape. The lightning-quick Ron LeFlore was no more; he was older and slower. He was unable to chase down fly balls like he used to, and it took too much time for him to get on base. His manager "ordered him on a weight-loss regimen," but he didn't lose the amount needed to improve his performance. And even in this less-than-competitive league, Ron had difficulty getting along with the higher-ups and was viewed by the team's front office as a "pain in the ass."[9]

Whether Ron would have survived longer than a year turned out to be a moot question. After one and a half seasons, the league folded.

Ron continued to look for opportunities to get back into baseball, no matter how small they might be. He became an instructor at former Red Sox star Jim Rice's and former White Sox Chet Lemon's baseball schools, gave inspirational speeches, umpired high school and college games in Florida, traveled throughout the South to give baseball lessons to aspiring high school athletes, and even ran a Ron LeFlore Baseball Camp for youth in St. Petersburg. But Ron's most consistent stream of revenue, like most former players of his era, was signing his autograph at baseball card and memorabilia shows. For hundreds—and in some cases, thousands—of dollars per appearance, Ron would go to a mall, a hotel, or a community center, and sit in a folding chair at a six-foot-long table for two hours, writing his name on photographs, baseball cards, bats, gloves, hats, or jerseys. Anything that could be written upon. It was easy, but not satisfying. Ron wanted to get back to *real* baseball.

Ron's first opportunity came in 1995 when he was hired to manage the Newburgh Night Hawks, who were part of the new Class-A-level Northeast League. Unaffiliated with a specific Major League Baseball club, the goal was for the league to produce players who would eventually be picked up by MLB teams. A first-time manager, Ron coached a team that played in a stadium that had no locker rooms, no permanent restrooms, and only about 500–600 fans in the stands on any given evening. Like his players, Ron saw this assignment as a stepping stone. Most of the players were former college athletes who didn't get drafted but still held onto that dream of playing in the majors.

Among them was Jim DeRosa, who, at first, was thrilled to learn that the great Ron LeFlore was his manager. "He knew a lot about baseball. That was the best part about it," DeRosa recalled.

True, Ron knew the game well. But he wasn't cut out to manage others. During a losing streak, for example, he told members of his team to get drunk together, hoping it would loosen them up and improve their performance on the field. Nor did Ron demonstrate a willingness to get to know the players. DeRosa was convinced that Ron never learned the names of any of the players, including his. Instead, he would call everyone "motherfucker."

"Why didn't you get to that ball, motherfucker?" Ron was known for shouting at his players during practice.[10] He was let go after one season.

Over the next eight years, Ron coached two other minor league teams, neither of which were affiliated with a MLB club. He knew his players "didn't have the talent" to make it to the big leagues, and these managerial assignments weren't going to take him there.[11] Even with Jim Campbell retired, the Tigers were uninterested in bringing Ron back as a coach or in the front office, as they had with Willie Horton, Gates Brown, Bill Freehan, and Al Kaline. When Ron was invited back to Tiger Stadium, it was merely for ceremonial purposes—and even that did not end well.

After eighty-seven years, Tiger Stadium was scheduled to close its doors following the final game of the 1999 season. The historic venue on the corner of Michigan and Trumbull Avenues was moving to the city's downtown district. To celebrate the stadium's farewell, dozens of former Tigers were invited to attend the finale and be honored after the game, with their name announced by the voice of the Tigers, Ernie Harwell. Ron was among them.

After the game, Ron—accompanied by his wife, Emily, and his 79-year-old mother, Georgia, now in a wheelchair—headed back to their car. In the parking lot, police officers placed Ron under arrest for failure to pay child support for LaRonda, who was now twenty-three years old. Her mother, Deborah Lewis, had been battling with Ron ever since LaRonda's childhood because of his refusal to maintain payments of $250 a month. Nearly a decade earlier, Ron had been arrested for failure to follow the court's order. To avoid jail time, he had agreed to pay $5,000 in outstanding child support and continue the monthly payments. But after a brief period, he stopped making them. At the time Ron was arrested outside Tiger Stadium, he owed approximately $56,000 (equivalent to $115,000 today) in back payments to his daughter.

"I don't have anything except my pension," 51-year-old Ron told the judge.[12] He claimed his only source of income was his $20,000-per-year MLB pension, which he used to support his wife, two other children, and medical bills.

"It's some crock again," Deborah Lewis argued. "This man makes money signing autographs. He'll pay the money, and he'll be gone again."[13]

In order to avoid spending forty-five days in jail, Ron agreed to make the payments.

The episode was not only a public embarrassment for Ron, who was roasted in the US and Canadian press ("Leflore Arrested For Being Deadbeat Dad" was one of many similar headlines).[14] It also permanently sealed his fate with the Tigers' organization.

"You don't become a coach unless you're a solid citizen," according to Bill Brown, the team's traveling secretary during the 1970s and 1980s. "I don't know if anyone could depend on him [LeFlore]."[15]

Part of the reason for that is Ron couldn't trust anyone. He believed everyone was out for themselves, which helps to explain his self-destructive behavior. Growing up in his environment, you had to act tough, always be on guard, and protect yourself above anyone else, whether it be at school, on the street, or incarcerated. It was a matter of survival. When you have that mindset, it inevitably creates blind spots.

For example, Ron felt no one ever assisted him in baseball; he did it all by himself. "Whatever they said about helping my progress was a lie. No one helped me," he insisted over and over in interviews I conducted with him.[16] He failed to see that, throughout his playing career, there were more than a handful of individuals who put their faith in him: Jimmy Karalla, Bill Lajoie, Jim Leyland, Hoot Evers, Stubby Overmire, and especially Ralph Houk, who arguably played the most important role in Ron's development as a player. In addition, there were plenty of players like Al Kaline, Mickey Stanley, and Willie Horton who offered their expertise. But Ron, plagued by trust issues, never fully embraced it, foregoing a set of worthy advisers who could have steered him to a Hall of Fame playing career. And there's no doubt Ron had the mechanics and the talent to be one of baseball's best.

Between 1976 and 1980, Ron LeFlore terrorized every pitcher he faced in the major leagues. When he hit safely in thirty consecutive games, he was one of only thirteen other players in the history of the game to have ever accomplished it. He followed it up with a twenty-seven-game hitting streak two seasons later. He batted over .300 in 1976, 1977, and 1979, scored 100 runs in three consecutive seasons; ranks fourth in total stolen bases in Tiger franchise history, and was the first (and now one of two) players in MLB history to lead both leagues in stolen bases.[17] He is often ranked as one of the fifty best Tiger players in the team's 125-year history.

When Hall of Fame infielder Rod Carew was asked who was the fastest player he ever went up against was, his response was Ron LeFlore: "He hit a one hop line to the SS [shortstop] and beat it out. I couldn't believe my eyes."[18] Award-winning *Detroit News* sportswriter Tom Gage also ranks Ron as one of the "most iconic Tigers."[19]

"Whenever that guy came to the plate," longtime Detroit-based broadcaster Bob Page recalled, "you were not going out to get a hot dog or go to the restroom. He was electrifying."[20]

And when Paul Giamatti, the two-time Oscar-nominated actor and son of the late MLB commissioner A. Bartlett Giamatti, was asked during a 2016 interview with the *New York Times* if he was a Red Sox fan, since he had grown up in New Haven, Connecticut, he answered:

> I had to, but I was also a Tigers fan. They had a player named Ron LeFlore, who was my hero. I was obsessed with that guy. He had been in prison. I remember I got his autograph when my father took my brother and me to spring training. He was a good player, but part of the appeal was that I thought his story was so cool.[21]

Raised by his Southern parents in a Detroit ghetto, serving a three-and-a-half-year sentence in a maximum security prison, getting a tryout with the Tigers, and then, not only getting signed but also becoming an All-Star and one of the game's top players—Ron's story is best described by the title of his TV biopic, *One in a Million*. Baseball author and co-founder of *Spitball* magazine, Mike Shannon, took it a step further, calling Ron's journey, "not a million-to-one

In 2010, 62-year-old Ron LeFlore watches the action in the MLB Alumni Legends Game at Bright House Stadium in Clearwater, Florida. (Photograph taken by Joseph Garnett Jr., ZUMA Press Inc / Alamy Stock)

but a billion-to-one shot."[22] What is agreed upon is that Ron LeFlore overcame insurmountable odds. He is a survivor. No one with his background should have reached the heights he did, let alone survive past the age of twenty-five. (The tragic fate of many his childhood friends is a testament to that.) He might not have achieved everything he wanted, but what he did accomplish is nothing short of a miracle.

"I made a mark in baseball," Ron told his old friend and ghostwriter, Jim Hawkins, in 2013. "Nobody can take that away from me. But I could have made a much bigger mark in baseball than I did. I could have done so much more."[23]

Ron might not have made it to the Hall of Fame or received a Ron LeFlore Appreciation Day at Comerica Park, where the Tigers now play. However, he finally got his dues after all these years, though it was not how he envisioned it.

On Saturday, August 17, 2019, Ron was sitting alone at a fold-up table in the social hall of the Balkan American Community Center in the Detroit suburb of Troy. On the opposite side of the table was a line of a dozen or so middle-aged white men, each of whom had paid ten or fifteen dollars to meet Ron. They were clutching baseballs, wooden bats, and eight-by-ten-inch photographs, all of which would soon be inscribed by the ex-major leaguer. Ron knew the routine. Each fan would step up to the table, wait for his acknowledgment, then proceed to tell the former All-Star how wonderful a player he was and what he had meant to him when he was a youngster. Ron would smile, sign his name, shake hands, and pose for a photograph. Then, on to the next guy. The 71-year-old was on autopilot until an unannounced visit from former teammate Willie Horton broke the momentum. Past tensions had dissipated as the two joked with one another like a couple of old friends.

Since Ron's highly publicized arrest in 1999 for failure to pay child support (and another arrest in 2007 for the same offense), the once-fleet footer now had grayed hair and walked with a limp and a cane. Suffering from arterial vascular disease, which was caused by a lifetime of smoking, Ron had to have his right leg amputated below the knee in 2011. The stolen base king now had to worry about his balance constantly and paid extra careful attention when he walked across a room. And on a day like the one in Troy, during long periods of sitting, Ron would take off the prosthetic for his right leg because it was uncomfortable.

"See the Movie, Meet the Legend" was the tagline for the other event Ron would be appearing at that weekend in Detroit.[24] The plan was that he would attend the card show on day one, and the next day he would be the guest of honor at a fortieth anniversary screening of *One in a Million* at the Detroit Historical Museum.

There was some discussion about also inviting actor LeVar Burton, who had portrayed Ron in *One in a Million*, to the screening. Burton was actually scheduled to be in Detroit two weeks before Ron; however, other previous engagements kept him from making an appearance that Sunday. "Give Ronnie a hug for me," Burton told a go-between.[25]

When the card show concluded, Ron—once again accompanied by Emily, his wife of thirty-plus years—turned his attention to Dave Mesrey, an associate editor of *Detroit Metro Times*, who was the promoter of the screening and the LeFlores' tour guide for the next twenty-four hours.

Mesrey encountered his first dilemma: transportation. He didn't want to drive the couple around town in his rusty, old van, which looked like it had been used in a 1980s teen horror movie.

"I needed someone who had a nice set of wheels," he explained.

Enter Tom Derry, a close friend of Mesrey's who had also grown up idolizing Ron and was happy to chauffeur the LeFlores to their downtown Detroit hotel, about a twenty-minute drive from Troy. Museum staff had booked Ron and Emily at a historic boutique hotel along the Detroit River (which runs through the border between the United States and Canada) that was a ten-minute drive from the museum. Ron may have been persona non grata in Major League Baseball, but he still was a professional athlete and was used to being catered to.

"Hey, where are all the white people at?" Ron asked tongue-in-cheek as they pulled up to the hotel entrance, where the majority of people outside were predominately African Americans.[26]

EPILOGUE

In August 2019, former teammate Wille Horton (left) surprises Ron, who is in Troy, Michigan, signing autographs at a sports memorabilia show. (Dave Mesrey's personal collection)

The LeFlores sat in the hotel lobby while Mesrey attempted to check them in. Between the early morning flight and the on-the-go itinerary, it had been a long day for the couple. They were ready to unwind in their room. But the hotel reservation had never gone through, and there were no extra rooms available. Meanwhile, Derry had left, saying that he had plans with his wife.

Mesrey walked over to Ron and Emily, pretending everything was fine. Then he excused himself to call his museum contact, Tracy Irwin. Normally even-tempered, Mesrey had no time for niceties: "Where else can we get a hotel for Ron and Emily on such short notice?"

While Ron and Emily waited, Mesrey noticed the current issue of the *Detroit Metro Times*. On the cover was a photo of twenty-five-year-old Ron LeFlore as a lead-in to Jimmy Doom's article that promoted the big event. Ron indicated to the person sitting across from him that it was a photo of himself. As Emily knew all too well, a retired professional athlete loved nothing more than adoration.

Meanwhile, Irwin managed to secure another hotel—which was located in Troy, of all places. Mesrey reached out to his friend, Mark Orr, to see if he could give the LeFlores a ride to the new hotel. Orr was a real estate agent based in Grosse Pointe, another Detroit suburb. He was also a former collegiate baseball player who had been an extra in *One in a Million* and was a serious Tigers fan.

"One minute, Mark is sitting at home, watching *SportsCenter*. Next thing you know, he's driving Ron LeFlore to his new hotel," Mesrey said, recalling the unanticipated turn of events.[27]

Orr couldn't have been more excited. Nostalgia took hold of him. While driving to Troy, Orr told Ron about his experience on the movie set and how he had hit a home run during batting practice. When they arrived at the hotel, a large crowd was roaming the streets.

"Ron, this is all for you," Orr said in jest.

Everyone laughed. In reality, the streets were blocked off for a car show.

After Ron and Emily were given a key to their room, Mesrey and Orr drove back to Detroit. On their way home, the two talked, mostly about Ron. Like other fans of his generation, Orr remembered Ron as muscular, powerful, and fast. "He partied a lot, and it shows," Orr said to Mesrey.[28]

Ding. Mesrey had a text message. It was Ron's agent, Mark Dehem.

"What happened?" Dehem asked. "Ron hasn't had a proper dinner yet. They don't have a car. Hotel doesn't have a restaurant."[29]

Mesrey was back in crisis control. He was ready to head back to Troy, this time in his van. But fortunately, Dehem was able to take care of the LeFlores. Mesrey finally had a break, the first and only of the day.

To help promote the event, Mesrey had arranged for Ron to be interviewed by a couple of radio stations. When the producers called Ron's room to arrange for it, no one picked up. They called Mesrey, who called Ron. No answer.

This was not a good sign. Should Mesrey, who was already at the museum, head to the hotel? Had Ron skipped town?

EPILOGUE

Once Mesrey received confirmation that Ron and Emily were en route to the museum, he breathed a sigh of relief. But when the LeFlores arrived, he noticed that Ron was less than chipper.

Mesrey met the couple at the building's back entrance and walked them to a freight elevator, where they encountered Elana Rugh, the museum's new president and CEO, who greeted the LeFlores. Hoping to expand the museum's audience, she was excited about the afternoon event.

"How's it going, Ron? Are you enjoying your stay?" she asked as the elevator ascended, unaware of the events of the past twenty-four hours.

There was a long pause before Ron responded. "Not good, not good," he said. "The hotel sucked. I didn't get a proper dinner. But whatever. It's good to be back home."

Rugh looked at Mesrey, then handed Ron an envelope containing his appearance fee. Maybe she thought it would have made him feel better to receive it now, rather than afterward.

When they arrived at Rugh's office, Ron and Emily kept to themselves, munching on snacks and drinks. Mesrey remembered observing the discontented couple and thinking, "Months of organizing, cajoling, hustling, all down the drain."

A museum usher arrived and alerted the group that the auditorium was filling up. Most museum screenings on Sundays were fortunate to have a half-filled auditorium. This event would be full.

Mesrey had reserved seats in the front row for Ron and Emily, but he assured them that there was no need to sit through the whole movie. After all, Ron had probably seen the film more times than he could count.

"Nah, let's watch this thing. Let's go. Let's do this!" Ron said, to the great relief of his host.

Ron had "every right to be pissed off by the way things were going. [Yet] he took it all in stride," Mesrey remembered.[30]

In August 2019, the Detroit Historical Museum hosted a screening of the movie, "One in a Million." Ron, who was the guest of honor that afternoon, stands in front of his Detroit Tiger jersey on display. (Tom Sherry's personal collection)

While none of his immediate family members were alive to witness the celebration after the movie (his older brother, Marvin, and his mother, Georgia, had since passed away), about 140 people were in attendance for the screening. Among them, Ron's estranged daughter LaRonda Lewis; fellow inmate and political activist John Sinclair; former *Free Press* sports reporter Joe Lapointe; former Lindell AC waitress Roxanne Foster; ex-Tiger Ike Blessitt; and the children of Jimmy and Johnny Butsicaris (Mel Butsicaris and Liz Jackson) showed up to offer their congratulations.

No one wanted to leave, as the event turned into a mini-reunion for everyone who was present. Make no mistake: Ron was the guest of honor, and he enjoyed every moment of it. He smiled, laughed, posed for photographs, and sat for interviews. It may have taken forty years, but it was finally *his* day.

ACKNOWLEDGMENTS

The biography had its genesis in 1988. I was eight years old. My mother, an elementary school teacher, had always encouraged me to read, something I was reluctant to do on my own (not anymore!). Knowing I loved baseball, she used the subject matter to lure me to our local library. It worked. One day, my mom checked out a book, *From Prison to the Major Leagues*, which was a children's biography of Ron LeFlore. I was fascinated by his story because it was so different from any of the other players. It stuck with me ever since. Nearly forty years later, now grown with a family of my own, and seeking a new subject to write about, I was curious what happened to Ron LeFlore.

It started with a search on Google. And then an email to Bob Page, who had recently interviewed Ron for his show, "No Filter Sports Podcast." Page was kind enough to reach out to Ron on my behalf. Ron consented and I made the first of what would be dozens of phone calls to him over a four-and-a-half-year period.

As of this writing, Ron and I have never met in person. In fact, even in the age of Zoom, we have yet to meet virtually face-to-face. All of our conversations had been conducted by phone 3,000 miles away over a span of three time zones (fortunately for me, Ron was a night owl). I am grateful to Ron for the hours he spent answering my numerous personal and often uncomfortable questions, many of which took him back sixty, sometimes seventy years. I like to believe he benefited from our talks as much as I did.

Even though this book centered on Ron LeFlore, it was the people around him that help piece together this 76-year-old jigsaw puzzle. I would like to thank the following individuals—some of whom have passed since I have spoken with them—for taking time out of their busy lives to share their stories about Ron, the Tigers, the Expos, and the city of Detroit: Al Userau, Anup Sinha, Betty Bolden, Bill Brown, Bill Lee, Dennis Clotworthy, Dick Tracewski, Emily LeFlore, Frank Howard (thank you to Kyle Brostowitz of the Washington Nationals for connecting me), Frank Rashid, Gary Gillette, Irwin Cohen, James Derosa, Jerry Green, Jimmy Karalla Jr., Joe Lapointe, John Sinclair, Honorable Kenneth McClintock-Hernández, Kenny Brown, Larry Paladino, Linda Walter, Mark Orr, Matthew Franklin, Mel Butsicaris, Michael Farber, Pat Jano, Philip Hersh, Ray Herbert, Steve Kemp, Tom Sherry, Tom Tuley, Tracy Irwin, and Warren Cromartie.

In addition to the above, there were four individuals that deserve special mention.

When I spoke with Jim Hawkins, Ron's autobiographical ghost writer and Tiger beat reporter for the *Detroit Free Press*, his stories were fascinating and his ability to recall the most minute details from a half-century ago confirmed why he was one of the best in the business. I also want to acknowledge Adam Motin of Triumph Books for connecting me with the "Hawk."

Bill Dow, a freelancer with the *Detroit Free Press*, not only shared his extensive knowledge about the Tigers and his interactions with Ron (and Ron's mother, Georgia) but also delved into his own personal experiences of growing up in the Detroit area, which helped me gain a better understanding of the Motor City.

Napolun Birdsong was the hardest interviewee to reach and the most unlikely. Birdsong was a fellow inmate of Ron's at the State Prison of Southern Michigan in the 1970s. I was able to track him down by mail, and he was kind enough to respond my request. Birdsong was a lively storyteller, who vividly recalled Ron's days on the prison's baseball diamond. But what I found equally as helpful was his willingness to share what life was like behind bars. Sadly, he passed away in 2023, two years after I interviewed him.

As I have experienced with my previous books, every biographer needs a generous soul to guide them along their journey, introducing them to key contacts and providing geographical and historical context for their subject.

Dave Mesrey was that person. In addition, Dave unintentionally made it into the narrative. When he shared the wild tale that led up to Ron's appearance at the Detroit Historical Museum in August 2019, I knew at that moment it would somehow find a way into this book.

I would also like to acknowledge the following individuals for their assistance in my research: Carolyn Chun, Interlibrary Loan Coordinator at California State University, East Bay; Rachel Wells, Reference Librarian at the National Baseball Hall of Fame Museum in Cooperstown, New York; LuAnn Mims, Librarian Supervisor for the City of Lakeland History and Culture Center; baseball historian Jim Sargent; and Jacob Pomrenke of the Society for American Baseball Research. In addition, a thank you to fellow biographers for their support and encouragement: Jonathan Eig, Andrew Maraniss, and John W. Miller. In addition, I am appreciative of Georgia LeFlore, Ron's daughter, who graciously assisted her father in gathering his personal photographs for this book.

I am especially grateful to Sara Letourneau, a freelance editor, who did a superb job, sharpening my writing and correcting my mistakes that would be career-ending in this trade. And my thanks to Christen Karniski, acquisitions editor at Bloomsbury, who has been a pleasure to work with.

I am not the person I am without the love and support of my family: my sister, Jen Adams (and Russ, and their daughters, Lyla, Ashlyn, and Brooklyn), and my sister Becca Dietor (and Matt, and their daughter, Leah); my in-laws, Frank and Evelyn Muro, and all members of my extended family; and, of course, my smart, creative, and beautiful wife Jennifer, and our precious and inquisitive sons, Jacob and Alex. I am so lucky to have all of you in my life.

This book nor any other I have penned over the past decade would not have come to fruition without my dad and fellow author, Gerald Henig. He is my primary editor, my advisor, and my friend. No person has been a bigger cheerleader when it comes to my writing. The amount of time he has spent editing my work and listening to my progress is incalculable and for that I am both grateful and fortunate.

NOTES

Prologue

1 Milton Richman, "Ron LeFlore: 'Inside' Story," *The Evening Sentinel* (Carlisle, PA), March 17, 1978.

Chapter 1

1 See Arthur F. Raper, *The Tragedy of Lynching* (Chapel Hill, NC: University of North Carolina Press, 1933), 1; Isabel Wilkerson, *The Warmth of Other Suns: The Epic Story of America's Great Migration* (New York: Random House, 2010), 39.

2 Billy Staples and Rich Herschlag, *Before the Glory: 20 Baseball Heroes Talk About Growing Up and Turning Hard Times into Home Runs* (Deerfield, FL: Health Communications, 2007), 113.

3 Ron LeFlore, in an interview with the author, May 19, 2021.

4 Staples and Herschlag, *Before the Glory*, 113.

5 Staples and Herschlag, *Before the Glory*, 113.

6 Ira Berlin, *The Making of African America: The Four Great Migrations* (New York: Viking, 2010), 166–7. Information about Ron's parents, aunt, and uncle was provided by Ron LeFlore during interviews with the author on December 27, 2020, and May 15, 2021.

7 For information about how African Americans decided on where to go, see Wilkerson, *The Warmth of Other Suns*, 178.

8 Ron LeFlore, in an interview with the author, May 15, 2021.

9 Staples and Herschlag, *Before the Glory*, 114.

10 Richard Bak, *Turkey Stearnes and the Detroit Stars: The Negro Leagues in Detroit, 1919–1933* (Detroit: Wayne State University Press, 1994), 36.

11 Bak, *Turkey Stearnes and the Detroit Stars*, 38.

12 Ulysses W. Boykin, *A Hand Book of the Detroit Negro* (Detroit: Minority Student Associates, 1943), 53.

13 Gunnar Myrdal, *An American Dilemma: The Negro Problem and Modern Democracy* (New York: Harper and Brothers, 1944), 366.

14 Staples and Herschlag, *Before the Glory*, 114.

15 Staples and Herschlag, *Before the Glory*, 115.

16 Staples and Herschlag, *Before the Glory*, 117.

17 Ron LeFlore, in an interview with the author, March 13, 2022.

18 Staples and Herschlag, *Before the Glory*, 115.

19 Ron LeFlore, in an interview with the author, August 9, 2020.

20 Staples and Herschlag, *Before the Glory*, 118.

21 Staples and Herschlag, *Before the Glory*, 115–16.

22 Ron LeFlore, in an interview with the author, January 15, 2023.

23 Useni Eugene Perkins, *Home Is a Dirty Street: The Social Oppression of Black Children* (Chicago: Third World Press, 1991), vii.

24 Bill Dow, in an interview with the author, September 12, 2020.

Chapter 2

1 Ron LeFlore with Jim Hawkins, *One in a Million: The Ron LeFlore Story* (New York: Warner Books, 1978), 47.

2 LeFlore with Hawkins, *One in a Million*, 49.

3 LeFlore with Hawkins, *One in a Million*, 50.

4 LeFlore with Hawkins, *One in a Million*, 51.

5 Ron LeFlore, in an interview with the author, June 24, 2023.

6 Staples and Herschlag, *Before the Glory*, 119.

7 "Detroit Heavy Casts Eyes on Gloves Crown," *Detroit Free Press*, March 4, 1956.

8 Staples and Herschlag, *Before the Glory*, 119.

9 Linda Walter, in an interview with the author, November 20, 2020.

10 Ron LeFlore, in an interview with the author, October 23, 2020.

11 LeFlore with Hawkins, *One in a Million*, 51.

12 LeFlore with Hawkins, *One in a Million*, 48.

13 Thomas J. Sugrue, *The Origins of the Urban Crisis: Race and Inequality in Postwar Detroit* (Princeton, NJ: Princeton University Press, 2014), 149.

14 Joe T. Darden, Richard Child Hill, June Thomas, and Richard Thomas. *Detroit: Race and Uneven Development* (Philadelphia, PA: Temple University Press, 1987), 221.

15 Eddie Muller, "80 Olympic Stars Invade S.F.," *San Francisco Examiner*, May 17, 1960.

16 Curley Grieve, "Sports Parade," *San Francisco Examiner*, March 16, 1961.

17 Ron LeFlore, interview, March 13, 2022.

18 Ron LeFlore, in an interview with the author, August 16, 2020.

19 Eddie Muller, "Rodriguez Winner by Unanimous Decision," *San Francisco Examiner*, November 29, 1960.

20 Eddie Muller, "Shadow Boxing: Martin Seeks Recognition as State Champion Today," *San Francisco Examiner*, December 16, 1960.

21 Grieve, "Sports Parade."

22 Associated Press, "NY Asked to Outlaw Or Suspend Boxing," *San Francisco Examiner*, February 6, 1961.

23 Bentley Kassal, "Letter to the Editor," *New York Daily News*, December 24, 1960.

24 Associated Press, "NY Asked to Outlaw."

25 Mel Bowen, "Medrano Will Substitute for Campbell in SC Bout," *Santa Cruz Sentinel*, January 27, 1961.

26 Eddie Muller "A Good Year in Bay Rings," *San Francisco Examiner*, December 18, 1960.

27 Eddie Muller, "Shadow Boxing: Campbell's Future on Line in Rematch With Medrano," *San Francisco Examiner*, May 14, 1961.

28 "Campbell in Coma; Hope Growing Dim," *Spartan Daily* (San José State University), May 17, 1961.

29 Todd Phipers, "Harry Campbell Loses Fight For Life," *Spartan Daily* (San José State University), May 17, 1961.

30 "Indiscriminate," *Spartan Daily* (San José State University), May 18, 1961.

31 Eddie Muller, "Ring Injury Proves Fatal," *San Francisco Examiner*, May 17, 1961.

32 Associated Press, "Boxer's Death Probe Seeks Other Causes," *St. Petersburg Times*, May 18, 1961.

33 Phipers, "Harry Campbell Loses Fight."

34 "Ex-Olympic Boxer Dies of 'Massive Blood Clot,'" *Jet*, June 1, 1961.

35 Associated Press, "Boxer's Death Probe."

36 "Dead Fighter's Spartan Mates at Rite Tonight," *San Francisco Examiner*, May 19, 1961.

37 Staples and Herschlag, *Before the Glory*, 123.

38 The mention of Ron's recurring dreams about Harry derived from the author's interview with him on March 13, 2022.

Chapter 3

1 Ron LeFlore, interview, June 24, 2023.

2 Staples and Herschlag, *Before the Glory*, 123.

3 LeFlore with Hawkins, *One in a Million*, 33–4.

4 Ron LeFlore, interview, June 24, 2023.

5 Staples and Herschlag, *Before the Glory*, 125.

6 LeFlore with Hawkins, *One in a Million*, 45.

7 Edward Shanahan, "The Needle That Costs Detroit $40 million Yearly," *Detroit Free Press*, February 15, 1970.

8 Staples and Herschlag, *Before the Glory*, 122.

9 LeFlore with Hawkins, *One in a Million*, 64.

10 Staples and Herschlag, *Before the Glory*, 121.

11 Ron LeFlore, interview, August 16, 2020.

12 "Ex-Con Ron LeFlore Does His Time in Tiger Stadium Now," *People*, September 30, 1974.

13 Kay Masini, "The Question: Where Do We Go From Here?" *The News-Herald-Palladium* (Benton Harbor, MI), September 24, 1969.

14 Staples and Herschlag, *Before the Glory*, 128.

15 Kenny Brown, in an interview with the author, August 28, 2020.

16 Staples and Herschlag, *Before the Glory*, 128.

17 Ron LeFlore, interview, October 23, 2020.

18 Perkins, *Home Is a Dirty Street*, 130.

19 Staples and Herschlag, *Before the Glory*, 128.

20 LeFlore with Hawkins, *One in a Million*, 67.

21 Milton Richman, "LeFlore Knows Meaning of Freedom," *Beckley Post-Herald and Register* (Beckley, WV), April 20, 1975.

22 Ron LeFlore, interview, May 15, 2021.

23 LeFlore with Hawkins, *One in a Million*, 21.

24 LeFlore with Hawkins, *One in a Million*, 69.

Chapter 4

1 Adrienne Eaton et al., *A History of Jackson Prison: 1920–1975* (Ann Arbor: University of Michigan, 1979), 3.

2 Eaton et al., *A History of Jackson Prison*, 96.

3 Charles E. Silberman, *Criminal Violence, Criminal Justice* (New York: Random House, 1978), 414–15.

4 Eaton et al., *A History of Jackson Prison*, 97.

5 Eaton et al., *A History of Jackson Prison*, 96.

6 Eaton et al., *A History of Jackson Prison*, 98.

7 Tom Milsom, "Jackson Prison Outbreaks Unlikely," *Battle Creek Enquirer*, October 10, 1971.

8 Eaton et al., *A History of Jackson Prison*, 116.

9 Milsom, "Jackson Prison Outbreaks Unlikely."

10 LeFlore with Hawkins, *One in a Million*, 76.

11 Leanne Smith, "Peek Through Time: From Bountiful Gardens to 'Ponderosa,' Jackson Prison Farms Were Fruitful," *Michigan Live*, June 4, 2014, https://www.mlive.com/news/jackson/2014/06/peek_through_time_from_lush_ga.html.

12 LeFlore with Hawkins, *One in a Million*, 78.

13 LeFlore with Hawkins, *One in a Million*, 79.

14 LeFlore with Hawkins, *One in a Million*, 84.

15 Richman, "LeFlore Knows Meaning of Freedom."

16 LeFlore with Hawkins, *One in a Million*, 81.

17 Ron LeFlore, interview, June 24, 2023.

18 Milsom, "Jackson Prison."

19 LeFlore with Hawkins, *One in a Million*, 79.

20 LeFlore with Hawkins, *One in a Million*, 96.

21 Ron LeFlore, interview, May 15, 2021.

22 LeFlore with Hawkins, *One in a Million*, 96.

23 Napolun Birdsong, in an interview with the author, January 27, 2021.

24 Richard Herr, *Inside-Outside: To Be Continued* (Bloomington, IN: iUniverse, 2011), 71.

Chapter 5

1 James Karalla III, in an interview with the author, December 28, 2021.

2 Mel Butsicaris Jr., in an interview with the author, November 11, 2020.

3 Karalla III, interview.

4 United Press International, "Arrest Five Detroit Men on 'Juice' Racket Charge," *Petoskey News-Review* [Petosky, MI], May 14, 1968.

5 Tom Ricke, "Vito Giacalone Gets His First Jail Term," *Detroit Free Press*, December 6, 1968.

6 "Two Arraigned in Extortion Plot," *Detroit Free Press*, December 21, 1968.

7 Karalla III, interview.

8 Maury Allen, "From Prison Cage to Batting Cage," *Sports Today*, April 1975.

9 Eaton et al., *A History of Jackson Prison*, 6.

10 Ken Kelley, "From Jackson Prison to Center Field: Ron Comes Home," *Ann Arbor Sun* 3, no. 15, July 17-July 31, 1975.

11 LeFlore with Hawkins, *One in a Million*, 97.

12 Gerald Sternberg, "One in a Million: Kermit Smith and the Ron LeFlore Story," *Michigan State University Football Players Association News*, February 2, 2021, https://msufpa.com/one-in-a-million-kermit-smith-and-the-ron-leflore-story/.

13 Herr, *Inside-Outside*, 88.

14 "Letter from Inmate #128008," in "From the Big House to the Big Leagues," Joe Falls (author of article), *Popular Sports*, May 1975, 28.

15 Herr, *Inside-Outside*, 91.

16 LeFlore with Hawkins, *One in a Million*, 100.

17 Sternberg, "One in a Million: Kermit Smith and the Ron LeFlore Story."

18 LeFlore with Hawkins, *One in a Million*, 97.

19 LeFlore with Hawkins, *One in a Million*, 103.

20 Sternberg, "One in a Million: Kermit Smith and the Ron LeFlore Story."

21 Birdsong, interview.

22 Birdsong, interview.

23 Birdsong, interview.

24 Jeff Pearlman, "Nearly 45 years ago, Ron LeFlore Went from Prison to the Big Leagues," *The Athletic*, June 28, 2018, https://www.nytimes.com/athletic/411275/2018/06/28/nearly-45-years-ago-ron-leflore-went-from-prison-to-the-big-leagues/.

25 "Ron LeFlore?" Spartan Tailgate [forum], https://247sports.com/college/michigan-state/board/93/Contents/ron-leflore-136174337/?page=1, accessed on September 27, 2019.

26 LeFlore with Hawkins, *One in a Million*, 98.

27 LeFlore with Hawkins, *One in a Million*, 99.

28 LeFlore with Hawkins, *One in a Million*, 100.

29 Bob Mee, *Ali and Liston: The Boy Who Would Be King and the Ugly Bear* (New York: Skyhorse Publishing, 2010), 26.

30 David Remnick, *King of the World: Muhammad Ali and the Rise of an American Hero* (New York: Random House, 1998), 53.

31 Dave Gagnon, "Gates Brown," *Society for American Baseball Research*, https://sabr.org/bioproj/person/gates-brown/, accessed on September 29, 2024.

32 Jimmy Karalla to Jimmy Butsicaris, April 11, 1973, provided by Tom Sherry's personal collection.

33 "Field of Dreams," Kiners Korner / SportsTalkNY, April 1992, YouTube, https://www.youtube.com/watch?v=xDeQ8wJdZW0.

34 Matt Helms and Brian Murphy, "Big Hearted Bar Owner Served Sports Legends," *Detroit Free Press*, November 21, 1996.

35 Lou Prato, "Tales of Booze, Bets, and Brawls at America's No. 1 Bar For Superjocks," *Detroit Free Press*, September 21, 1975.

36 Butsicaris Jr., interview; and Prato, "Tales of Booze."

37 Prato, "Tales of Booze."

38 Kelley, "From Jackson Prison to Center Field."

39 Todd Masters, *The 1972 Detroit Tigers: Billy Martin and the Half-Game Champs* (Jefferson, NC: McFarland & Company, 2010), 235.

40 Bill Pennington, *Billy Martin: Baseball's Flawed Genius* (New York: Houghton Mifflin, 2015), 179.

41 Masters, *The 1972 Detroit Tigers*, 234.

42 Masters, *The 1972 Detroit Tigers*, 237.

Chapter 6

1 Ernie Harwell, *Tuned to Baseball* (South Bend, IN: Diamond Communications, Inc. 1985), 207.

2 Harwell, *Tuned to Baseball*, 208.

3 Harwell, *Tuned to Baseball*, 208.

4 Earl McRae, *The Victors and the Vanquished* (Toronto: Amberley House Limited, 1981), 179.

5 Allen, "From Prison Cage to Batting Cage."

6 Harwell, *Tuned to Baseball*, 208.

7 Billy Martin and Peter Golenbock, *Number 1* (New York: Dell, 1980), 288.

8 Harwell, *Tuned to Baseball*, 208.

9 Jim Hawkins, in an interview with the author, September 14, 2020.

10 Budd Wilkinson, "Billy Martin Has a Tough Role in Film about Baseball Player," *The Arizona Republic*, August 5, 1980.

11 LeFlore with Hawkins, *One in a Million*, 116.

12 Michael Betzold, John Davids, Bill Dow, John Pastier, and Frank Rashid, eds., *Tiger Stadium: Essays and Memories of Detroit's Historic Ballpark, 1912–2009* (Jefferson, NC: McFarland & Company, 2018), 225.

13 Jimmy Doom, "Ron LeFlore's Unlikely Journey from Prison to the Detroit Tigers Honored 45 Years after His Big-league Debut," *Detroit Metro Times*, August 14, 2019.

14 Frank Howard, in an interview with the author, December 22, 2020.

15 Anup Sinha and Bill Lajoie, *Character Is Not a Statistic: The Legacy and Wisdom of Baseball's Godfather Scout Bill Lajoie* (Xlibris Corporation, 2010), 52.

16 Howard, interview.

17 Betzold et al., *Tiger Stadium*, 225.

18 Sinha and Lajoie, *Character Is Not a Statistic*, 52.

19 Curt Sylvester, "Tigers Fulfill His 'Dream'—Sign ex-Jackson Prisoner," *Detroit Free Press*, July 3, 1973.

20 Dick Groch and Bill Lajoie, *Baseball: The Major League Way* (Dubuque, IA: Kendall Hunt Publishing Company, 1976), 24.

21 Wilkinson, "Billy Martin Has a Tough Role in Film about Baseball Player."

22 Dick Tracewski, in an interview with the author, July 9, 2021.

23 Jim Hawkins, "LeFlore Speeded Bat Pace by Waiting," *The Sporting News*, June 26, 1976.

24 Howard, interview.

25 LeFlore with Hawkins, *One in a Million*, 119.

26 Doom, "Ron LeFlore's Unlikely Journey."

27 Hawkins, interview.

28 Martin and Golenbock, *Number 1*, 289.

29 Allen, "From Prison Cage to Batting Cage."

30 Hawkins, interview.

31 LeFlore with Hawkins, *One in a Million*, 119.

32 Ron LeFlore, interview, May 15, 2021.

33 Sinha and Lajoie, *Character Is Not a Statistic*, 52.

34 Allen, "From Prison Cage to Batting Cage."

35 Joe Falls, "From the Big House to the Big Leagues," *Popular Sports*, May 1975, 28.

Chapter 7

1 Falls, "From the Big House to the Big Leagues."

2 Birdsong, interview.

3   Sinha and Lajoie, *Character Is Not a Statistic*, 52.

4   LeFlore with Hawkins, *One in a Million*, 128.

5   Sugrue, *The Origins of the Urban Crisis*, 147–8.

6   Sylvester, "Tigers Fulfill His 'Dream.'"

7   Groch and Lajoie, *Baseball: The Major League Way*, 25.

8   Sylvester, "Tigers Fulfill His 'Dream.'"

9   Allen, "From Prison Cage to Batting Cage."

10 Sinha and Lajoie, *Character Is Not a Statistic*, 27.

11 Sinha and Lajoie, *Character Is Not a Statistic*, 36.

12 Sinha and Lajoie, *Character Is Not a Statistic*, 269.

13 Ron LeFlore, in interviews with the author, May 15, 2021, and August 23, 2020.

14 Ron LeFlore, interview, May 15, 2021.

15 Bill Dow, "Jim Leyland On How to Speed Up the Game: Get in the Batter's Box!", *Detroit Free Press*, July 28, 2020.

16 Paul Hemphill, "Ron LeFlore, Flying Tiger," *Sport*, August 1975.

17 Associated Press, "Bill Lajoie Dies; He Really Knew Talent," *Public Opinion* (Chambersburg, PA), January 1, 2011.

18 Doug Wilson, *The Bird: The Life and Legacy of Mark Fidrych* (New York: Thomas Dunne Books, 2013), 193.

19 Joe Gergen, "They Sure Weren't Much as Players, but McIlvaine, Leyland are Now," *Newsday*, July 31, 1988.

20 LeFlore with Hawkins, *One in a Million*, 129–30.

21 "Clinton Pilots Plan Workout Thursday," *The Times-Democrat* (Davenport, IA), April 18, 1973.

22 LeFlore with Hawkins, *One in a Million*, 133.

23 LeFlore with Hawkins, *One in a Million*, 130.

24 Dow, "Jim Leyland On How to Speed up the Game."

25 "LeFlore Batting 1.000," *Detroit Free Press*, July 9, 1973.

26 "C.R. Astros Lose 10-2," *The Gazette* (Cedar Rapids, IA), July 8, 1973.

27 "LeFlore Batting 1.000."

28 Hemphill, "Ron LeFlore, Flying Tiger."

NOTES

29. Benjamin Hill, "Gimenez's Time in Clinton Goes beyond Ball," *MILB.com*, June 3, 2015, https://www.milb.com/news/gcs-128334908.
30. Jim Benagh, "The Slugger Who Came in from the Cold (of a Prison Cell)," *Popular Sports: Baseball*, May 1978.
31. Ron LeFlore, interview, May 15, 2021.
32. LeFlore with Hawkins, *One in a Million*, 133.
33. Staples and Herschlag, *Before the Glory*, 136.
34. Dave Johnson, "When Cell Door Opened, LeFlore Took Off, Never Looked Back," *Evansville Courier & Press*, June 20, 1999.
35. William Zinsser, *Spring Training* (Pittsburgh, PA: University of Pittsburgh Press, 2003), 175.
36. Groch and Lajoie, *Baseball: The Major League Way*, 130.
37. Staples and Herschlag, *Before the Glory*, 136.
38. Ron LeFlore, in an interview with the author, November 20, 2020.
39. McRae, *The Victors and the Vanquished*, 175.
40. Falls, "From the Big House to the Big Leagues."
41. Pennington, *Billy Martin*, 182.
42. Jimmy Keenan and Frank Russo, "Billy Martin," *Society for American Baseball Research*, https://sabr.org/bioproj/person/billy-martin/, accessed on October 10, 2024.
43. Arthur Daley, "The Dismissal of Billy Martin," *The New York Times*, September 4, 1973.
44. United Press International, "Tigers Dismiss Martin For 'Policy' Infractions," *The New York Times*, September 3, 1973.

Chapter 8

1. William Leggett, "Anyone Finding Fountain of Youth, Call Detroit," *Sports Illustrated*, November 26, 1973.
2. LeFlore with Hawkins, *One in a Million*, 128.
3. Terry Foster, *100 Things Tigers Fans Should Know & Do Before They Die* (Chicago: Triumph Books, 2013), 57.

4   Stephen V. Rice, "Ed Katalinas," *Society for American Baseball Research*, https://sabr.org/bioproj/person/ed-katalinas/, accessed on October 11, 2024.

5   Groch and Lajoie, *Baseball: The Major League Way*, 37.

6   Groch and Lajoie, *Baseball: The Major League Way*, 39.

7   Bill Dow, "Fernandez Paved Way as Tigers' First Latino Position Player," *Detroit Free Press*, August 1, 2015.

8   Tom Gage, "Tiger Trail Blazers Still Are Standing Tall Today," *Detroit News*, March 2, 2010.

9   Kimberly C. Moore, "Tigers' Willie Horton Recalls Segregated Lakeland, Gives Thanks for Progress," *Lakeland Now*, January 20, 2023, https://www.lkldnow.com/tigers-willie-horton-recalls-segregated-lakeland-gives-thanks-for-progress/.

10 "Letter from a Detroit Tigers representative (unnamed) to Frank Scott," August 19, 1961, Goldin Auctions, Lot #9, https://goldinauctions.com/Historically_Significant_Lot_of_Letters_to_General-lot5337.aspx [link no longer available], accessed on July 1, 2015.

11 Tracewski, interview.

12 "Tigers Host Bosox, 3,500 Expected," *The Tampa Tribune*, April 15, 1974.

13 "Tigers Pound Tarps," *The Tampa Times*, April 23, 1974.

14 Tom Duffy, "Lakeland Has Eyes on Division Title," *St. Petersburg Times*, April 26, 1974.

15 Rick Wolff, *What's a Nice Harvard Boy Like You Doing in the Bushes?* (Englewood Cliffs, NJ: Prentice Hall, Inc., 1975), 41–2.

16 Irwin Cohen, "Rapping with Ron LeFlore," *Baseball Bulletin* [monthly newspaper], May 1975.

17 Ron LeFlore, in an interview with the author, December 27, 2020.

18 Ron LeFlore, interview, May 15, 2021.

19 Larry Paladino, "Gates Could Pinch Hit As Preacher Man Too," *The Times Herald* (Port Huron, MI), July 6, 1974.

20 Jim Selman, "On Their Second Chance," *The Tampa Tribune*, June 18, 1974.

21 Patrick Zier, "LeFlore: No Run of the Mill Farmhand," *The Sporting News*, July 27, 1974.

22 "Tigers Entertain Cards," *The Tampa Tribune*, July 11, 1974.

23 Tom Tuley, in an interview with the author, July 24, 2022.

24 Tom Tuley, "Ex-Convict Flying Free with Triplets," *The Evansville Press*, July 23, 1974.

25 Tuley, interview.

26 Tuley, "Ex-Convict Flying Free with Triplets."

27 Tom Tuley, "Those Flying Feet," *The Evansville Press*, July 27, 1974.

28 Pete Swanson, "LeFlore like Bob Hayes," *The Evansville Press*, July 28, 1974.

29 Tuley, "Those Flying Feet."

30 Tom Tuley, "Detroit Eyes Watch Trips End Home Stand," *The Evansville Press*, July 31, 1974.

31 Joe Falls, "Tigers Get the Razz from the Laughing Fans," *Detroit Free Press*, July 27, 1974.

32 Pete Swanson, "Hernandez and Hill Spark A.A. Talent Gush to Majors," *The Sporting News*, October 5, 1974.

33 Tom Tuley, "Triplets Rest," *The Evansville Press*, August 1, 1974.

34 Swanson, "Hernandez and Hill."

35 Tuley, interview.

36 Ron LeFlore, in an interview with the author, July 24, 2022; and Kelley, "From Jackson Prison to Center Field."

37 Hawkins, interview.

38 Tuley, "Triplets Rest."

39 Johnson, "When Cell Door Opened."

40 Larry Paladino, in an interview with the author, February 19, 2021.

41 Attendance information for 1974 provided by Baseballreference.com and Jim Hawkins, "Bleak Message to Tiger Fans: 'Bite the Bullet,'" *The Sporting News*, January 18, 1975.

42 Tuley, interview.

43 Jim Hawkins, "Tigers Call Up Whiz Kid LeFlore," *Detroit Free Press*, August 1, 1974.

44 LeFlore with Hawkins, *One in a Million*, 146.

45 Hawkins, "Tigers Call Up Whiz Kid LeFlore."

46 Watson Spoelstra, "Tigers Are Red-Faced on Dead-End Street," *The Sporting News*, March 6, 1971.

47 Tuley, "Triplets Rest."

48 Hawkins, "Tigers Call Up Whiz Kid LeFlore."

49 LeFlore with Hawkins, *One in a Million*, 146.

Chapter 9

1. LeFlore with Hawkins, *One in a Million*, 144.
2. Johnson, "When Cell Door Opened."
3. LeFlore with Hawkins, *One in a Million*, 144.
4. Jim Hawkins, "How Baseball Saved Ron LeFlore," *Detroit Free Press*, August 2, 1974.
5. Dennis Clotworthy, in an interview with the author, October 29, 2020.
6. Jerry Green, in an interview with the author, February 14, 2021.
7. Dennis Clotworthy, *Al Kaline's Last Bat Boy* (Pickney, MI: Wynwidyn Press, 2014), 160.
8. LeFlore with Hawkins, *One in a Million*, 144.
9. Benagh, "The Slugger Who Came in from the Cold."
10. Tom Hawley, "Fryman Stifles Brewers, 2–0," *Wisconsin State Journal*, August 2, 1974.
11. Ron LeFlore, interview, October 23, 2020.
12. LeFlore with Hawkins, *One in a Million*, 144.
13. Mark Kram, "Still Alive and Kicking," *Sports Illustrated*, June 3, 1974.
14. Richard Goldstein, "Ralph Houk, Yankees Manager, Dies at 90," *The New York Times*, July 21, 2010.
15. Harwell, *Tuned to Baseball*, 21.
16. Joe Falls, *Joe Falls: 50 Years of Sports Writing* (Champaign, IL: Sports Publishing, 1997), 129.
17. Mike Conroy, "The Major's A Manager," *Soldiers*, April 1984.
18. Associated Press, "Ex-Convict LeFlore a Tiger Hero," *Honolulu Star-Bulletin*, August 5, 1974.
19. Larry Paladino, "Gates Brown: From Prison to Pro Baseball," *The San Bernardino County Sun*, July 8, 1974.
20. Rebecca M. Long, "Detroit's Field of Dreams: The Grassroots Preservation of Tiger Stadium" (thesis, Clemson University, 2012), 55, https://open.clemson.edu/all_theses/1371.
21. Falls, "From the Big House to the Big Leagues."
22. Bill Dow, "Where Are They Now: Former All-Star Ron LeFlore," *Baseball Digest*, June 2009.

23 Joe Falls, "An Era Has Ended . . . Tigers Must Trade," *Detroit Free Press*, August 5, 1974.

24 Mike Shropshire, "Rangers Floor Tigers, Lolich in 10th 6–4," *Fort Worth Star-Telegram*, August 25, 1974.

25 Tracewski, interview.

26 Richman, "LeFlore Knows Meaning of Freedom."

27 Jim Hawkins, "Odds Makers Off Base on Tigers, Growls Houk," *The Sporting News*, April 12, 1975.

28 Jim Hawkins, "Tiger Fans the Best? Acid Test Still Ahead," *Detroit Free Press*, August 26, 1974.

29 Jim Hawkins, "Campbell Sees Tiger Crisis as Springboard for Rise," *The Sporting News*, February 1, 1975.

30 Jim Kaplan, "American League East," *Sports Illustrated*, April 4, 1975.

31 Ron LeFlore, interview, November 20, 2020.

32 Larry Paladino, "LeFlore Wows 'Em With Background," *The Hillsdale Daily News* (Hillsdale, MI), March 10, 1975.

33 Joe Falls, "Gates Brown—A Guiding Light," *Detroit Free Press*, March 3, 1975; Wilson, *The Bird*, 92.

34 *Baseball*, episode 9, "9th Inning—Home," written by Geoffrey C. Ward and Ken Burns, directed by Ken Burns, aired on September 28, 1994 on PBS.

35 Rhiannon Walker, "The State of the Black Manager in Major League Baseball Would Disgust Jackie Robinson," *The Undefeated*, April 20, 2018, https://theundefeated.com/features/the-state-of-the-black-manager-in-major-league-baseball-would-disgust-jackie-robinson/.

36 Michael Strauss, "Tigers Subdue Yankees, 10–9," *The New York Times*, June 21, 1975.

37 Phil Hersh, "Oriole Items," *The Baltimore Evening Sun*, June 27, 1975.

38 "News Briefs," *The New York Times*, June 29, 1975.

39 Jim Hawkins, "Bowie's Decree Saved Writers—Sure It Did," *Detroit Free Press*, July 10, 1975.

40 Jim Kaplan, "Man on a Tightrope," *Sports Illustrated*, May 12, 1975.

41 Clotworthy, *Al Kaline's Last Bat Boy*, 176.

42 Clotworthy, interview.

43 Jim Hawkins, "Surging Tigers Reward Patient Houk," *The Sporting News*, July 26, 1975.

44 Scott Burnstein, "Detroit Tigers Traded LeFlore in '79 Partially Due to Ties to Frank Usher," *The Gangster Report* (website), May 26, 2015, https://gangsterreport.com/detroit-tigers-traded-leflore-in-79-partially-due-to-ties-to-frank-usher/.

45 *To Create a Select Committee on Narcotics Abuse and Control: Hearing Before the Committee on Rules and Administration*, United States Senate, 96th Congress, 2nd Session, on Senate Resolution 207 to Create a Select Committee on Narcotics Abuse and Control (U.S. Government Printing Office, 1980), 93.

46 Burnstein, "Detroit Tigers Traded LeFlore in '79."

Chapter 10

1 Birdsong, interview.

2 "Outside League Competition Feasible," *The Spectator* (Jackson Prison, Jackson, MI), July 24, 1975.

3 Robin Herman, "People in Sports: Ali's Attack: Gorilla Wordfare," *The New York Times*, August 27, 1975.

4 Staples and Herschlag, *Before the Glory*, 139.

5 Mickey Lolich with Tom Gage, *Joy in Tigertown: A Determined Team, a Resilient City, and Our Magical Run to the 1968 World Series* (Chicago: Triumph Books, 2018), 243.

6 Ron LeFlore, interview, May 15, 2021.

7 Ron Ishoy and Jim Hawkins, "LeFlore is 4 Years Older than He Says," *Detroit Free Press*, March 9, 1976.

8 Jim Hawkins, "Age Doesn't Matter with Tigers' LeFlore," *The Sporting News*, March 27, 1976.

9 LeFlore with Hawkins, *One in a Million*, 171.

10 Ken Fidlin, "From Big Slammer to Big O for LeFlore," *Ottawa Journal*, December 12, 1979.

11 Dow, "Where Are They Now."

12 Associated Press, "LeFlore Really 23 Going on 28," *Lansing State Journal*, March 9, 1976.

13 Hawkins, "Age Doesn't Matter."

14 Jim Hawkins, "Taking Up Defensive Slack Houk's Toughest Tiger Task," *The Sporting News*, March 6, 1976.

15 Ron LeFlore, interview, August 16, 2020.

16 Vern Plagenhoef, "LeFlore May Cry Tomorrow," *The Grand Rapids Press*, April 24, 1976.

17 Ron LeFlore, interview, August 16, 2020.

18 Benagh, "The Slugger Who Came in from the Cold."

19 United Press International, "LeFlore: Game Comes Before Grief," *Orlando Sentinel*, April 24, 1976.

20 "Six Released in LeFlore Case," *The Chapel Hill News* (Chapel Hill, NC), April 25, 1976.

21 Jim Hawkins, "Varney Not Awed by LeFlore," *Detroit Free Press*, May 8, 1976.

22 Jim Hawkins, "Look Out DiMagg . . . Here Comes LeFlore," *Detroit Free Press*, May 16, 1976.

23 Seth Poho, "1976: The Year 'The Bird' Took Over Baseball," Baseball Essential, https://www.baseballessential.com/news/2016/07/05/1976-year-bird-took-baseball/ [link no longer available], accessed on May 15, 2021.

24 Wilson, *The Bird*, 66.

25 Jim Hawkins, "Hitting Streak Makes LeFlore a Celebrity," *Detroit Free Press*, May 28, 1976.

26 Pete Swanson, "Baseball," *The Evansville Press*, May 30, 1976.

27 "What They Are Saying," *The New York Times*, March 31, 1976. For Ron's stats, see "League Leaders," *Detroit Free Press*, May 29, 1976.

28 Jim Hawkins, "LeFlore's 30-Game Skein Longest in A.L. Since '49," *The Sporting News*, June 19, 1976.

29 Swanson, "Baseball."

30 Curt Sylvester, "Meditation Helping LeFlore Ease Tension," *Detroit Free Press*, May 28, 1976.

31 Brian Bragg, "LeFlore 'Just Trying to Make Contact,'" *Detroit Free Press*, May 27, 1976.

32 Brian Bragg, "Ron's Reward: Fans' Cheer," *Detroit Free Press*, May 29, 1976.

33 Larry Keith, "A Tiger Burning Bright," *Sports Illustrated*, June 7, 1976.

34 Hawkins, "Hitting Streak Makes LeFlore a Celebrity."

35 Keith, "A Tiger Burning Bright."

36 "A.L. Flashes," *The Sporting News*, June 12, 1976.

37 Jim Hawkins, "Bird Swoops Down on the O's, 4–0," *Detroit Free Press*, July 4, 1976.

38 Joe Falls, "LeFlore Knows Just Where He's Going," *Detroit Free Press*, July 14, 1976.

39 LeFlore with Hawkins, *One in a Million*, 16.

40 Lowell Reidenbaugh, "Insult Added to Injury: A.L.'s Sad All-Star Fate," *The Sporting News*, July 31, 1976.

41 Ron LeFlore, interview, August 16, 2020.

42 Joe Falls, "Frustrated Fans Are Down on Houk," *Detroit Free Press*, September 25, 1976. For the complete Earl Wilson story, see Red Smith, "Bob Woolf Behind Closed Doors," *The New York Times*, September 6, 1976.

43 Butsicaris, interview.

44 Smith, "Bob Woolf Behind Closed Doors."

Chapter 11

1 "Hawkins on Baseball Hall of Fame Ballot," *Superior Telegram* (Superior, WI), July 19, 2012, https://www.superiortelegram.com/news/hawkins-on-baseball-hall-of-fame-ballot.

2 Paladino, interview.

3 Hawkins, interview.

4 Bill Brown, in an interview with the author, March 26, 2021.

5 Hawkins, interview.

6 Joseph Durso, "Tigers' Fidrych Out 2 Months With Torn Cartilage in Knee: Tigers Lose Fidrych for Two Months," *The New York Times*, March 31, 1977.

7 Ron LeFlore, interview, August 9, 2020.

8 Jim Hawkins, "Will 2-Day Benching Help LeFlore?", *Detroit Free Press*, June 12, 1977.

9 Jim Hawkins, "LeFlore First 200-Hit Tiger in 22 Seasons," *The Sporting News*, October 29, 1977.

10 Jim Selman, "'Breakout' Makes Good Reading," *The Tampa Tribune*, March 13, 1978.

11 Joe Falls, "LeFlore's Story a Real Shocker," *The Sporting News*, March 11, 1978.

12 Jeff Greenfield, "Nonfiction in Brief," review of *Breakout* by Ron Leflore with Jim Hawkins, *The New York Times*, March 12, 1978.

13 Samuel Simons, "Breakout: From Prison to the Big Leagues," review of *Breakout* by Ron Leflore with Jim Hawkins, *Library Journal*, February 1, 1978, 380–1.

14 Tom McEwen, "The Reincarnation of Ron LeFlore," *The Tampa Tribune*, March 31, 1978.

15 Ron LeFlore, in an interview with the author, October 30, 2021.

16 "It's Time to Meet Some Mothers Whose Hands Rocked the Cradles of Celebs," *People*, May 15, 1978.

17 Hawkins, interview.

18 Eli Zaret, Denny McLain, and Bob Page, hosts, *No Filter Sports*, podcast, "Episode 64: The Legend of Ron LeFlore? You Ain't Heard These Stories!" Aired on August 19, 2019, http://www.nofiltersportspodcast.com/2019/08/19/episode-64-the-legend-of-ron-leflore-you-aint-heard-these-stories/ [access no longer available], accessed on August 9, 2020.

19 Bettelou Peterson, "Ron LeFlore Turned Kunta Kinte into a Baseball Fan," Special Pullout Section, *Detroit Free Press*, September 24, 1978.

20 Jim Hawkins, "Grand Slam! LeFlore Movie Draws Raves," *Detroit Free Press*, September 7, 1978.

21 Brian Bragg, "Hollywood Comes to Tiger Stadium to Film Ron's Story," *Detroit Free Press*, May 21, 1978.

22 Larry Paladino, "Actor LeVar Burton Swings into New Role," *Lexington Herald* (Lexington, KY), May 25, 1978.

23 LeVar Burton, "LeVar Burton at Motor City Comic Con 2017," interview by Julie Hinds, *Detroit Free Press*, Posted by Romain Blanquart on May 20, 2017, https://www.freep.com/videos/entertainment/2017/05/20/levar-burton-motor-city-comic-con-2017/101921726/.

24 Tom Henderson, "'See You in the Movies' Comes True for Billy Martin, Al Kaline & Crew," *Detroit Free Press*, May 23, 1978.

25 Mark Orr, in an interview with the author, July 10, 2021.

26 Doom, "Ron LeFlore's Unlikely Journey."

27 Paladino, "Actor LeVar Burton Swings into New Role."

28 Ron LeFlore, interview, August 16, 2020.

29 Jim Hawkins, "Maybe Now LeFlore Can Get Back to Baseball," *Detroit Free Press*, June 11, 1978.

30 Hawkins, "Maybe Now LeFlore Can Get Back to Baseball."

31 Ron LeFlore, interview, November 20, 2020.

32 Honorable Kenneth McClintock-Hernández, in an interview with the author, September 18, 2022.

33 Tom Sherry, in an interview with the author, November 26, 2021.

34 Hawkins, "Grand Slam!"

35 "Ratings Ryan: Weekly Nielsen Ratings: 1978–79 TV Season (UPDATED)," Ratings Ryan, http://www.ratingsryan.com/2022/01/weekly-nielsen-ratings-1978-79-tv-season.html, accessed in April 2024. The website where I retrieved the data is no longer available on the internet as of May 22, 2024.

36 Ron LeFlore, interview, August 16, 2020.

Chapter 12

1 Dan Holmes, "Faithful Soldier Moss Stepped Aside for Sparky in '79," *Vintage Detroit Collection*, May 14, 2012, https://www.vintagedetroit.com/blog/2012/05/14/faithful-soldier-moss-stepped-aside-for-sparky-in-79/.

2 Sparky Anderson with Dan Ewald, *They Call Me Sparky* (Chelsea, MI: Sleeping Bear Press, 1998), 163.

3 Anderson with Ewald, *They Call Me Sparky*, 151.

4 Leonard Koppett, *The Man in the Dugout: Baseball's Top Managers and How They Got That Way* (New York: Crown, 1993), 333.

5 Anderson with Ewald, *They Call Me Sparky*, 162.

6 Harwell, *Tuned to Baseball*, 25.

7 Peter Golenbock, *The Forever Boys: A Second Chance to Star Again* (South Orange, NJ: Summer Game Books, 2014), 68.

8 Irwin Cohen, in an interview with the author, April 7, 2021.

9 Bill Brown, interview.

10 Mick McCabe, "Where's LeFlore? The Plot Thickens," *Detroit Free Press*, July 25, 1979.

11 Bill Brown, interview.

12 Fred T. Smith, *Fifty Years with the Tigers* (Published by author, 1983), 236.

13 Brian Bragg, "Sparky Gets a Few Media Beefs Off His Chest," *Detroit Free Press*, July 26, 1979.

14 Harwell, *Tuned to Baseball*, 209.

15 Jim Hawkins, "Highway Sparky Leads Out of Town," *Detroit Free Press*, July 22, 1979.

16 "Woman Sues LeFlore for Stopping Support Payments," *Jet*, February 22, 1979.

17 Nathan Michael Corzine, *Team Chemistry: The History of Drugs and Alcohol in Major League Baseball* (Champaign, IL: University of Illinois Press, 2016), 100.

18 Patrick Harrigan, *The Detroit Tigers: Club and Community, 1945–1995* (Toronto: University of Toronto Press, 1997), 191.

19 Ron LeFlore, interview, March 13, 2022.

20 Ron LeFlore, interview, August 16, 2020.

21 Brian Flanigan and Jack Kresnak, "Southfield Man Held in Beheadings," *Detroit Free Press*, October 14, 1979.

22 Burnstein, "Detroit Tigers Traded LeFlore."

23 Flanigan and Kresnak, "Southfield Man Held in Beheadings."

24 The conversation derives from two sources: Allen Abel, "Bus Squad Shuffle LeFlore's Addition Unsettles Expos," *The Globe and Mail* (Toronto, Ontario, Canada), March 3, 1980; and Michael Farber, "LeFlore Runs on His Record," *Montreal Gazette*, March 29, 1980. As for the Bowie Kuhn note, it is located in the Bowie K. Kuhn collection, National Baseball Hall of Fame and Museum, Cooperstown, NY, Series VI, "Administrative and Misc. Commissioner Files," Sub-Series 3, "Misc. Files," Box 16, Folder 6 (Security).

25 Jim Hawkins, "LeFlore's Shocked, Hurt by Trade," *Detroit Free Press*, December 8, 1979.

26 Associated Press, "Ex-Tiger Crushed by Transaction," *Ottawa Citizen*, December 8, 1979.

27 "LeFlore, Rodriguez Swapped by Tigers" *The New York Times*, December 8, 1979.

28 Mick McCabe, "Rodriguez, LeFlore Deals Draw Fans' Ire," *Detroit Free Press*, December 8, 1979.

29 George Puscas, "Tigers Prove It Again: They Refuse to Compete," *Detroit Free Press*, December 8, 1979.

30 Donald Kaul, "Message to Detroit's Lions, Pistons, Red Wings, Tigers: I Quit," *Detroit Free Press*, May 4, 1980.

31 Donna Urschel, "Stinky Protest," *Detroit Free Press*, December 11, 1979.

32 Ian MacDonald, "Expos See Swift LeFlore Leading 1980 Flag Push," *The Sporting News*, December 22, 1979.

33 "LeFlore Runs Wild Against Cards," *The Globe and Mail* (Toronto, Ontario, Canada), June 7, 1980; and "Expos' Lee Beats Cardinals as LeFlore 'Steals' the Show," *Montreal Gazette*, June 7, 1980.

34 "A Leg Up on the League Lead," *Sports Illustrated*, July 14, 1980.

35 Michael Strauss, "Mets Lose Opener, Then Top Expos, 4–3," *The New York Times*, August 5, 1980.

36 Warren Cromartie, in an interview with the author, July 27, 2022.

37 Ian McDonald, "LeFlore Sparkles in Opener as Expos, Mets Split Double," *Montreal Gazette*, August 5, 1980.

38 Alex Belth, "Inside *Inside Sports*: The Oral History," *The Sunday Long Read*, January 28, 2018, https://sundaylongread.com/2018/01/28/inside-inside-sports-the-oral-history/; and Jerry Knight, "*Inside Sports* Goes on the Block," *The Sun/The Daily Herald: The Sunday Paper* (Biloxi, MS), November 8, 1981.

39 Bill Lee, in an interview with the author, October 29, 2020.

40 Danny Gallagher, *Never Forgotten: Tales about Ron LeFlore, Ron Hunt and Other Expos Yarns from 1969–2004* (Toronto: Scoop Press, 2021), 102.

41 Alain Usereau, *The Expos in Their Prime: The Short-Lived Glory of Montreal's Team, 1977–1984* (Jefferson, NC: McFarland, 2013), 174.

42 Jim Hawkins, "Ron LeFlore: Season with Expos 'Greatest Year of My Career,'" *Toronto Sun*, February 26, 2013, https://torontosun.com/2013/02/26/ron-leflore-season-with-expos-greatest-year-of-my-career.

43 Kenny Brown, in an interview with the author, January 2, 2025.

44 Michael Farber, in an interview with the author, October 18, 2020.

45 Joe Lapointe, "Late Again: LeFlore Scoring for Expos but Can't Stop Missing Games," *Detroit Free Press*, August 14, 1980.

46 Ted Blackman, "LeFlore Can't Duck Attack on Expos," *Montreal Gazette*, September 4, 1980.

47 Mark Ribowsky, "The Inside Track: Ron LeFlore," *Inside Sports*, September 1980.

48 Jackie Robinson, *I Never Had It Made: An Autobiography* (New York: HarperCollins, 1995), 47.

49 Ribowsky, "The Inside Track: Ron LeFlore."

50 "Dawson Is Not in Accord with LeFlore Racial Views," *The Globe and Mail* (Toronto, Ontario, Canada), August 30, 1980.

51 Cromartie, interview.

52 Michael Farber, "Expo 'Rednecks and Militants' Laugh Together," *Montreal Gazette*, September 6, 1980.

53 Blackman, "LeFlore Can't Duck Attack on Expos."

54 "'Nigger' LeFlore Blasts Expos," *Ottawa Citizen*, August 28, 1980; and Canadian Press, "'Racist': LeFlore Attacks Montreal," *Vancouver Sun*, August 29, 1980.

55 "Fans prejudiced, Montreal's LeFlore quoted as saying," *The Globe and Mail* (Toronto, Ontario, Canada), August 29, 1980.

56 "I Was Misquoted—LeFlore," *Vancouver Sun*, September 11, 1980.

57 Ron LeFlore, interview, July 24, 2022.

58 "10/4/80 Phillies at Expos," October 4, 1980, Posted on February 3, 2017, by Expos Classics, YouTube, https://www.youtube.com/watch?v=A7w8-r1gAJw.

59 Hawkins, "Ron LeFlore: Season with Expos."

60 Bob Ferguson, "Home Run by 'Super Sub' a Day Too Late for Expos," *Ottawa Citizen*, October 6, 1980.

61 Dick Williams with Bill Plaschke, *No More Mr. Nice Guy: A Life of Hardball* (Orlando: Harcourt Brace Jovanovich, Publishers, 1990), 222.

62 Farber, interview.

63 Cromartie, interview.

64 Hawkins, "Ron LeFlore: Season with Expos."

65 Allen Abel, "LeFlore Digs Into McHale," *The* [Toronto] *Globe and Mail*, October 7, 1980.

66 Usereau, *The Expos in Their Prime*, 102.

67 Williams, *No More Mr. Nice Guy*, 222.

68 "Interview of John McHale" by Alain Usereau (a transcript was provided to the author by Usereau).

69 Andy McCue, *Stumbling Around the Bases: The American League's Mismanagement in the Expansion Eras* (Lincoln, Nebraska: University of Nebraska Press, 2022), 25.

70 Robert Markus, "Ron LeFlore: Can the White Sox Harness the Wild Horse?," *Chicago Tribune*, April 12, 1981.

71 Joe Goddard, "LeFlore Credits Lau for Power Display," *The Sporting News*, May 17, 1982.

72 Bob Markus, "LeFlore Declares: 'I Can Play Center,'" *The Sporting News*, January 2, 1982.

Epilogue

1 Gallagher, *Never Forgotten*, 103.

2 Dick Weiss, "Vitale: Carnival Barker of College Hoops," *Philadelphia Daily News*, January 6, 1988.

3 Golenbock, *The Forever Boys*, 71.

4 Butsicaris, interview.

5 Karalla III, interview.

6 Emily LeFlore, in an interview with the author, November 20, 2020.

7 Emily LeFlore, interview.

8 Steven Krasner, "Ex-Con LeFlore Seeks Return to Baseball via Umpire School," *The Providence Journal* (Providence, RI), February 18, 1988.

9 Golenbock, *The Forever Boys*, 60.

10 Jim DeRosa, in an interview with the author, July 23, 2022.

11 Ron LeFlore, interview, November 20, 2020.

12 David Shepardson, "He's Destitute, Ex-Tiger Says: Seized after Tiger Stadium Closing, LeFlore Claims Poverty in Battle over Child Support," *The Detroit News*, September 29, 1999.

13 Associated Press, "LeFlore Spends Night in Jail," ESPN.com, September 28, 1999, http://a.espncdn.com/mlb/news/1999/0928/82972.html, accessed on November 16, 2024.

14 "LeFlore Arrested For Being Deadbeat Dad," *New York Post*, September 29, 1999.

15 Bill Brown, interview.

16 Ron LeFlore, interview, October 30, 2021.

17 "Ron LeFlore," BaseballReference.com, https://www.baseball-reference.com/players/l/lefloro01.shtml, accessed on November 2, 2024.

18 Rod Carew (@RodCarew_29), "He hit a one hop line to the SS [shortstop] and beat it out. I couldn't believe my eyes," Twitter (now X), May 19, 2021, accessed on June 10, 2021 (link not available; post possibly deleted).

19 Tom Gage, *The Big 50: The Men and Moments That Made the Detroit Tigers* (Chicago: Triumph Books, 2017), 298.

20 Zaret, McLain, and Page, *No Filter Sports*, "Episode 64."

21 Bruce Fretts, "Paul Giamatti, a Baseball Commissioner's Son, Makes His Own Calls," *The New York Times*, June 23, 2016, https://www.nytimes.com/2016/06/24/movies/paul-giamatti-a-baseball-commissioners-son-makes-his-own-calls.html.

22 Mike Shannon, *Everything Happens in Chillicothe: A Summer in the Frontier League with Max McLeary, the One-Eyed Umpire*, (Jefferson, NC: McFarland & Company, 2004), 182.

23 Jim Hawkins, "Former Montreal Expos Star Ron LeFlore Down But Not Out," *Toronto Sun*, February 26, 2013, https://torontosun.com/2013/02/26/former-montreal-expo-ron-leflore-down-but-not-out.

24 Karen Kozy, "See the Movie, Meet the Legend," digital file attachment in email to the author, June 25, 2021.

25 Dave Mesrey, in an interview with the author, December 15, 2024.

26 Dave Mesrey, in an interview with the author, April 28, 2021.

27 Dave Mesrey, in an interview with the author, April 27, 2021.

28 Orr, interview.

29 Mark Dehem, text message to Dave Mesrey, August 17, 2019.

30 Mesrey, interview, April 28, 2021.

BIBLIOGRAPHY

Books

Anderson, Sparky, with Dan Ewald. *They Call Me Sparky*. Chelsea, MI: Sleeping Bear Press, 1998.

Bak, Richard. *Turkey Stearnes and the Detroit Stars: The Negro Leagues in Detroit, 1919–1933*. Detroit: Wayne State University Press, 1994.

Berlin, Ira. *The Making of African America: The Four Great Migrations*. New York: Viking, 2010.

Betzold, Michael, John Davids, Bill Dow, John Pastier, and Frank Rashid, eds. *Tiger Stadium: Essays and Memories of Detroit's Historic Ballpark, 1912–2009*. Jefferson, NC: McFarland & Company, 2018.

Boykin, Ulysses W. *A Hand Book on the Detroit Negro*. Detroit: Minority Student Associates, 1943.

Clotworthy, Dennis. *Al Kaline's Last Bat Boy*. Pickney, MI: Wynwidyn Press, 2014.

Corzine, Nathan Michael. *Team Chemistry: The History of Drugs and Alcohol in Major League Baseball*. Champaign, IL: University of Illinois Press, 2016.

Darden, Joe T., Richard Child Hill, June Thomas, and Richard Thomas. *Detroit: Race and Uneven Development*. Philadelphia, PA: Temple University Press, 1987.

Falls, Joe. *Joe Falls: 50 Years of Sports Writing*. Champaign, IL: Sports Publishing, 1997.

Foster, Terry. *100 Things Tigers Fans Should Know & Do Before They Die*. Chicago: Triumph Books, 2013.

Gage, Tom. *The Big 50: The Men and Moments that Made the Detroit Tigers*. Chicago: Triumph Books, 2017.

Gallagher, Danny. *Never Forgotten: Tales about Ron LeFlore, Ron Hunt and Other Expos Yarns from 1969–2004*. Toronto: Scoop Press, 2021.

Golenbock, Peter. *The Forever Boys: A Second Chance to Star Again*. South Orange, NJ: Summer Game Books, 2014.

Groch, Dick, and Bill Lajoie. *Baseball: The Major League Way*. Dubuque, IA: Kendall Hunt Publishing Company, 1976.

Harrigan, Patrick. *The Detroit Tigers: Club and Community, 1945–1995*. Toronto: University of Toronto Press, 1997.

Harwell, Ernie. *Tuned to Baseball*. South Bend, IN: Diamond Communications, Inc. 1985.

Herr, Richard. *Inside-Outside: To Be Continued*. Bloomington, IN: iUniverse, 2011.

Koppett, Leonard. *The Man in the Dugout: Baseball's Top Managers and How They Got That Way*. New York: Crown, 1993.

LeFlore, Ron, with Jim Hawkins. *One in a Million: The Ron LeFlore Story*. New York: Warner Books, 1978.

Lolich, Mickey, with Tom Gage. *Joy in Tigertown: A Determined Team, a Resilient City, and Our Magical Run to the 1968 World Series.* Chicago: Triumph Books, 2018.
Martin, Billy, and Peter Golenbock. *Number 1.* New York: Dell, 1980.
Masters, Todd. *The 1972 Detroit Tigers: Billy Martin and the Half-Game Champs.* Jefferson, NC: McFarland & Company, 2010.
McRae, Earl. *The Victors and the Vanquished.* Toronto: Amberley House Limited, 1981.
Mee, Bob. *Ali and Liston: The Boy Who Would Be King and the Ugly Bear.* New York: Skyhorse Publishing, 2010.
Myrdal, Gunnar. *An American Dilemma: The Negro Problem and Modern Democracy.* New York: Harper and Brothers, 1944.
Pennington, Bill. *Billy Martin: Baseball's Flawed Genius.* New York: Houghton Mifflin, 2015.
Perkins, Useni Eugene. *Home Is a Dirty Street: The Social Oppression of Black Children.* Chicago: Third World Press, 1991.
Raper, Arthur F. *The Tragedy of Lynching.* Chapel Hill, NC: University of North Carolina Press, 1933.
Remnick, David. *King of the World: Muhammad Ali and the Rise of an American Hero.* New York: Random House, 1998.
Robinson, Jackie. *I Never Had It Made: An Autobiography.* New York: HarperCollins, 1995.
Shannon, Mike. *Everything Happens in Chillicothe: A Summer in the Frontier League with Max McLeary, the One-Eyed Umpire.* Jefferson, NC: McFarland & Company, 2004.
Silberman, Charles E. *Criminal Violence, Criminal Justice.* New York: Random House, 1978.
Sinha, Anup, and Bill Lajoie. *Character Is Not a Statistic: The Legacy and Wisdom of Baseball's Godfather Scout Bill Lajoie.* Xlibris Corporation, 2010.
Smith, Fred T. *Fifty Years with the Tigers.* Published by the author, 1983.
Staples, Billy, and Rich Herschlag. *Before the Glory: 20 Baseball Heroes Talk About Growing Up and Turning Hard Times into Home Runs.* Deerfield, FL: Health Communications, 2007.
Sugrue, Thomas J. *The Origins of the Urban Crisis: Race and Inequality in Postwar Detroit.* Princeton, NJ: Princeton University Press, 2014.
Usereau, Alain. *The Expos in Their Prime: The Short-Lived Glory of Montreal's Team, 1977–1984.* Jefferson, NC: McFarland & Company, 2013.
Williams, Dick, with Bill Plaschke. *No More Mr. Nice Guy: A Life of Hardball.* Orlando: Harcourt Brace Jovanovich, Publishers, 1990.
Wilkerson, Isabel. *The Warmth of Other Suns: The Epic Story of America's Great Migration.* New York: Random House, 2010.
Wilson, Doug. *The Bird: The Life and Legacy of Mark Fidrych.* New York: Thomas Dunne Books, 2013.
Wolff, Rick. *What's a Nice Harvard Boy Like You Doing in the Bushes?* Englewood Cliffs, NJ: Prentice Hall, Inc., 1975.
Zinsser, William. *Spring Training.* Pittsburgh, PA: University of Pittsburgh Press, 2003.

Newspapers and Magazines

The Evansville Courier & Press

(includes articles from *The Evansville Press*, which, in 1998 was discontinued as a separate newspaper from the *Evansville Courier*).

Johnson, Dave. "When Cell Door Opened, LeFlore Took Off, Never Looked Back." June 20, 1999.
Swanson, Pete. "LeFlore like Bob Hayes." July 28, 1974.
Swanson, Pete. "Baseball." May 30, 1976.
Tuley, Tom. "Ex-Convict Flying Free with Triplets." July 23, 1974.
Tuley, Tom. "Those Flying Feet." July 27, 1974.
Tuley, Tom. "Detroit Eyes Watch Trips End Home Stand." July 31, 1974.
Tuley, Tom. "Triplets Rest." August 1, 1974.

Detroit Free Press

"Detroit Heavy Casts Eyes on Gloves Crown." March 4, 1956.
"League Leaders." May 29, 1976.
"LeFlore Batting 1.000." July 9, 1973.
"Two Arraigned in Extortion Plot." December 21, 1968
Bragg, Brian. "LeFlore 'Just Trying to Make Contact'." May 27, 1976.
Bragg, Brian. "Ron's Reward: Fans' Cheer." May 29, 1976.
Bragg, Brian. "Hollywood Comes to Tiger Stadium to Film Ron's Story." May 21, 1978.
Bragg, Brian. "Sparky Gets a Few Media Beefs Off His Chest." July 26, 1979.
Dow, Bill. "Fernandez Paved Way as Tigers' First Latino Position Player." August 1, 2015.
Dow, Bill. "Jim Leyland on How to Speed Up the Game: Get in the Batter's Box!" July 28, 2020.
Falls, Joe. "Tigers Get the Razz from the Laughing Fans." July 27, 1974.
Falls, Joe. "An Era Has Ended . . . Tigers Must Trade." August 5, 1974.
Falls, Joe. "Gates Brown – A Guiding Light." March 3, 1975.
Falls, Joe. "Frustrated Fans Are Down on Houk." September 25, 1976.
Falls, Joe. "LeFlore Knows Just Where He's Going." July 14, 1976.
Flanigan, Brian, and Jack Kresnak. "Southfield Man Held in Beheadings." October 14, 1979.
Hawkins, Jim. "Tigers Call Up Whiz Kid LeFlore." August 1, 1974.
Hawkins, Jim. "How Baseball Saved Ron LeFlore." August 2, 1974.
Hawkins, Jim. "Tiger Fans the Best? Acid Test Still Ahead." August 26, 1974.
Hawkins, Jim. "Bowie's Decree Saved Writers—Sure It Did." July 10, 1975.
Hawkins, Jim. "Varney Not Awed by LeFlore." May 8, 1976.
Hawkins, Jim. "Look Out DiMagg . . . Here Comes LeFlore." May 16, 1976.
Hawkins, Jim. "Hitting Streak Makes LeFlore a Celebrity." May 28, 1976.
Hawkins, Jim. "Bird Swoops Down on the O's, 4–0." July 4, 1976.

Hawkins, Jim. "Will 2-Day Benching Help LeFlore?" June 12, 1977.
Hawkins, Jim. "Maybe Now LeFlore Can Get Back to Baseball." June 11, 1978.
Hawkins, Jim. "Grand Slam! LeFlore Movie Draws Raves." September 7, 1978.
Hawkins, Jim. "Highway Sparky Leads Out of Town." July 22, 1979.
Hawkins, Jim. "LeFlore's Shocked, Hurt by Trade." December 8, 1979.
Helms, Matt, and Brian Murphy. "Big Hearted Bar Owner Served Sports Legends." November 21, 1996.
Henderson, Tom. "'See You in the Movies' Comes True for Billy Martin, Al Kaline & Crew." May 23, 1978.
Ishoy, Ron, and Jim Hawkins. "LeFlore Is 4 Years Older Than He Says." March 9, 1976.
Kaul, Donald. "Message to Detroit's Lions, Pistons, Red Wings, Tigers: I Quit." May 4, 1980.
Lapointe, Joe. "Late Again: LeFlore Scoring for Expos But Can't Stop Missing Games." August 14, 1980.
McCabe, Mick. "Where's LeFlore? The Plot Thickens." July 25, 1979.
McCabe, Mick. "Rodriguez, LeFlore Deals Draw Fans' Ire." December 8, 1979.
Peterson, Bettelou. "Ron LeFlore Turned Kunta Kinte into a Baseball Fan." September 24, 1978.
Prato, Lou. "Tales of Booze, Bets, and Brawls at America's No. 1 Bar for Superjocks." September 21, 1975.
Puscas, George. "Tigers Prove It Again: They Refuse to Compete." December 8, 1979.
Ricke, Tom. "Vito Giacalone Gets His First Jail Term." December 6, 1968.
Shanahan, Edward. "The Needle that Costs Detroit $40 Million Yearly." February 15, 1970.
Sylvester, Curt. "Tigers Fulfill His 'Dream' – Sign Ex-Jackson Prisoner." July 3, 1973.
Sylvester, Curt. "Meditation Helping LeFlore Ease Tension." May 28, 1976.
Urschel, Donna. "Stinky Protest." December 11, 1979.

Montreal Gazette

Blackman, Ted. "LeFlore Can't Duck Attack on Expos." September 4, 1980.
"Expos' Lee Beats Cardinals as LeFlore 'Steals' the Show." June 7, 1980.
Farber, Michael. "LeFlore Runs on His Record." March 29, 1980.
Farber, Michael. "Expo 'Rednecks and Militants' Laugh Together." September 6, 1980.
McDonald, Ian. "LeFlore Sparkles in Opener as Expos, Mets Split Double." August 5, 1980.

The New York Times

Daley, Arthur. "The Dismissal of Billy Martin." September 4, 1973.
Durso, Joseph. "Tigers' Fidrych Out 2 Months with Torn Cartilage in Knee: Tigers Lose Fidrych for Two Months." March 31, 1977.
Fretts, Bruce. "Paul Giamatti, a Baseball Commissioner's Son, Makes His Own Calls." June 23, 2016. https://www.nytimes.com/2016/06/24/movies/paul-giamatti-a-baseball-commissioners-son-makes-his-own-calls.html.

Goldstein, Richard. "Ralph Houk, Yankees Manager, Dies at 90." July 21, 2010.
Greenfield, Jeff. "Nonfiction in Brief." Review of *Breakout*, by Ron Leflore with Jim Hawkins. March 12, 1978.
Herman, Robin. "People in Sports: Ali's Attack: Gorilla Wordfare." August 27, 1975.
"LeFlore, Rodriguez Swapped by Tigers." December 8, 1979.
"News Briefs." June 29, 1975.
Smith, Red. "Bob Woolf Behind Closed Doors." September 6, 1976.
Strauss, Michael. "Tigers Subdue Yankees, 10–9." June 21, 1975.
Strauss, Michael. "Mets Lose Opener, Then Top Expos, 4–3." August 5, 1980.
United Press International. "Tigers Dismiss Martin for 'Policy' Infractions." September 3, 1973.
"What They Are Saying." March 31, 1976.

The Sporting News

"A.L. Flashes." June 12, 1976.
Falls, Joe. "LeFlore's Story a Real Shocker." March 11, 1978.
Hawkins, Jim. "Bleak Message to Tiger Fans: 'Bite the Bullet.'" January 18, 1975.
Hawkins, Jim. "Campbell Sees Tiger Crisis as Springboard for Rise." February 1, 1975.
Hawkins, Jim. "Odds Makers Off Base on Tigers, Growls Houk." April 12, 1975.
Hawkins, Jim. "Surging Tigers Reward Patient Houk." July 26, 1975.
Hawkins, Jim. "Taking Up Defensive Slack Houk's Toughest Tiger Task." March 6, 1976.
Hawkins, Jim. "Age Doesn't Matter with Tigers' LeFlore." March 27, 1976.
Hawkins, Jim. "LeFlore's 30-Game Skein Longest in A.L. Since '49." June 19, 1976.
Hawkins, Jim. "LeFlore Speeded Bat Pace by Waiting." June 26, 1976.
Hawkins, Jim. "LeFlore First 200-Hit Tiger in 22 Seasons." October 29, 1977.
MacDonald, Ian. "Expos See Swift LeFlore Leading 1980 Flag Push." December 22, 1979.
Reidenbaugh, Lowell. "Insult Added to Injury: A.L.'s Sad All-Star Fate." July 31, 1976.
Spoelstra, Watson. "Tigers Are Red-Faced on Dead-End Street." March 6, 1971.
Swanson, Pete. "Hernandez and Hill Spark A.A. Talent Gush to Majors." October 5, 1974.
Zier, Patrick. "LeFlore: No Run of the Mill Farmhand." July 27, 1974.

San Francisco Examiner

Associated Press. "NY Asked to Outlaw Or Suspend Boxing." February 6, 1961.
"Dead Fighter's Spartan Mates at Rite Tonight." May 19, 1961.
Grieve, Curley. "Sports Parade." March 16, 1961.
Muller, Eddie. "80 Olympic Stars Invade S.F." May 17, 1960.
Muller, Eddie. "Rodriguez Winner by Unanimous Decision." November 29, 1960.
Muller, Eddie. "Shadow Boxing: Martin Seeks Recognition as State Champion Today." December 16, 1960.
Muller, Eddie. "Shadow Boxing: Campbell's Future on Line in Rematch with Medrano." May 14, 1961.

Muller, Eddie. "Ring Injury Proves Fatal." May 17, 1961.

Sports Illustrated

"A Leg Up on the League Lead." July 14, 1980.
Kaplan, Jim. "American League East." April 4, 1975.
Kaplan, Jim. "Man on a Tightrope." May 12, 1975.
Keith, Larry. "A Tiger Burning Bright." June 7, 1976.
Kram, Mark. "Still Alive and Kicking." June 3, 1974.
Leggett, William. "Anyone Finding Fountain of Youth, Call Detroit." November 26, 1973.

Miscellaneous Newspapers, Including Online Versions of Articles

"C.R. Astros Lose 10–2." *The Gazette* (Cedar Rapids, IA), July 8, 1973.
"Campbell in Coma; Hope Growing Dim." *Spartan Daily* (San José State University), May 17, 1961.
"Clinton Pilots Plan Workout Thursday." *The Times-Democrat* (Davenport, IA), April 18, 1973.
"Dawson Is Not in Accord with LeFlore Racial Views." *The Globe and Mail* (Toronto, Ontario, Canada), August 30, 1980.
"Fans Prejudiced, Montreal's LeFlore Quoted as Saying." *The Globe and Mail* (Toronto, Ontario, Canada), August 29, 1980.
"Hawkins on Baseball Hall of Fame Ballot." *Superior Telegram* (Superior, WI), July 19, 2012. https://www.superiortelegram.com/news/hawkins-on-baseball-hall-of-fame-ballot.
"LeFlore Arrested for Being Deadbeat Dad." *New York Post*, September 29, 1999.
"LeFlore Runs Wild Against Cards." *The Globe and Mail* (Toronto, Ontario, Canada), June 7, 1980.
"I Was Misquoted – LeFlore." *Vancouver Sun*, September 11, 1980.
"Indiscriminate." *Spartan Daily* (San José State University), May 18, 1961.
"'Nigger' LeFlore Blasts Expos," *Ottawa Citizen*, August 28, 1980.
"Outside League Competition Feasible." *The Spectator* (Jackson Prison, Jackson, MI), July 24, 1975.
"Six Released in LeFlore Case." *The Chapel Hill News* (Chapel Hill, NC), April 25, 1976.
"Tigers Entertain Cards." *The Tampa Tribune*, July 11, 1974.
"Tigers Host BoSox, 3,500 Expected." *The Tampa Tribune*, April 15, 1974.
Abel, Allen. "Bus Squad Shuffle LeFlore's Addition Unsettles Expos." *The Globe and Mail* (Toronto, Ontario, Canada), March 3, 1980.
Associated Press. "Boxer's Death Probe Seeks Other Causes." *St. Petersburg Times*, May 18, 1961.
Associated Press. "Ex-Convict LeFlore a Tiger Hero." *Honolulu Star-Bulletin*, August 5, 1974.

Associated Press. "LeFlore Really 23 Going on 28." *Lansing State Journal*, March 9, 1976.
Associated Press. "Ex-Tiger Crushed by Transaction." *Ottawa Citizen*, December 8, 1979.
Associated Press. "Bill LaJoie Dies; He Really Knew Talent." *Public Opinion* (Chambersburg, PA), January 1, 2011.
Bowen, Mel. "Medrano Will Substitute for Campbell in SC Bout." *Santa Cruz Sentinel*, January 27, 1961.
Canadian Press. "'Racist': LeFlore Attacks Montreal." *Vancouver Sun*, August 29, 1980.
Cohen, Irwin. "Rapping with Ron LeFlore." *Baseball Bulletin* [monthly newspaper], May 1975.
Doom, Jimmy. "Ron LeFlore's Unlikely Journey from Prison to the Detroit Tigers Honored 45 Years After His Big-League Debut." *Detroit Metro Times*, August 14, 2019.
Duffy, Tom. "Lakeland Has Eyes on Division Title." *St. Petersburg Times*, April 26, 1974.
Ferguson, Bob. "Home Run by 'Super Sub' a Day Too Late for Expos." *Ottawa Citizen*, October 6, 1980.
Fidlin, Ken. "From Big Slammer to Big O for LeFlore." *Ottawa Journal*, December 12, 1979.
Gage, Tom. "Tiger Trail Blazers Still Are Standing Tall Today." *The Detroit News*, March 2, 2010.
Gergen, Joe. "They Sure Weren't Much as Players, but McIlvaine, Leyland Are Now." *Newsday*, July 31, 1988.
Hawkins, Jim. "Ron LeFlore: Season with Expos 'Greatest Year of My Career.'" *Toronto Sun*, February 26, 2013. https://torontosun.com/2013/02/26/ron-leflore-season-with-expos-greatest-year-of-my-career.
Hawkins, Jim. "Former Montreal Expos Star Ron LeFlore Down But Not Out." *Toronto Sun*, February 26, 2013. https://torontosun.com/2013/02/26/ron-leflore-season-with-expos-greatest-year-of-my-career.
Hawley, Tom. "Fryman Stifles Brewers, 2–0." *Wisconsin State Journal*, August 2, 1974.
Hersh, Phil. "Oriole Items." *The Baltimore Evening Sun*, June 27, 1975.
Kassal, Bentley. "Letter to the Editor." *New York Daily News*, December 24, 1960.
Kelley, Ken. "From Jackson Prison to Center Field: Ron Comes Home." *Ann Arbor Sun*, 3 (15), July 17–July 31, 1975.
Knight, Jerry. "*Inside Sports* Goes on the Block." *The Sun/The Daily Herald: The Sunday Paper* (Biloxi, MS), November 8, 1981.
Krasner, Steven. "Ex-Con LeFlore Seeks Return to Baseball via Umpire School." *The Providence Journal* (Providence, RI), February 18, 1988.
Masini, Kay. "The Question: Where Do We Go From Here?" *The News-Herald-Palladium* (Benton Harbor, MI), September 24, 1969.
McEwen, Tom. "The Reincarnation of Ron LeFlore." *The Tampa Tribune*, March 31, 1978.
Milsom, Tom. "Jackson Prison Outbreaks Unlikely." *Battle Creek Enquirer* (Battle Creek, MI), October 10, 1971.
Paladino, Larry. "LeFlore Wows 'Em with Background." *The Hillsdale Daily News* (Hillsdale, MI), March 10, 1975.
Paladino, Larry. "Gates Could Pinch Hit as Preacher Man Too." *The Times Herald* (Port Huron, MI), July 6, 1974.

Paladino, Larry. "Gates Brown: From Prison to Pro Baseball." *The San Bernardino County Sun*, July 8, 1974.
Paladino, Larry. "Actor LeVar Burton Swings into New Role." *Lexington Herald* (Lexington, KY), May 25, 1978.
Phipers, Todd. "Harry Campbell Loses Fight for Life." *Spartan Daily* (San José State University), May 17, 1961.
Plagenhoef, Vern. "LeFlore May Cry Tomorrow." *The Grand Rapids Press*, April 24, 1976.
Richman, Milton. "LeFlore Knows Meaning of Freedom." *Beckley Post-Herald and Register* (Beckley, WV), April 20, 1975.
Richman, Milton. "Ron LeFlore: 'Inside' Story." *The Evening Sentinel* (Carlisle, PA), March 17, 1978.
Selman, Jim. "On Their Second Chance." *The Tampa Tribune*, June 18, 1974.
Selman, Jim. "'Breakout' Makes Good Reading." *The Tampa Tribune*, March 13, 1978.
Shepardson, David. "He's Destitute, Ex-Tiger Says: Seized after Tiger Stadium Closing, LeFlore Claims Poverty in Battle over Child Support." *The Detroit News*, September 29, 1999.
Shropshire, Mike. "Rangers Floor Tigers, Lolich in 10th, 6–4." *Fort Worth Star-Telegram*, August 25, 1974.
United Press International. "Arrest Five Detroit Men on 'Juice' Racket Charge." *Petoskey News-Review* (Petoskey, MI), May 14, 1968.
United Press International. "LeFlore: Game Comes Before Grief." *Orlando Sentinel*, April 24, 1976.
Weiss, Dick. "Vitale: Carnival Barker of College Hoops." *Philadelphia Daily News*, January 6, 1988.
Wilkinson, Budd. "Billy Martin Has a Tough Role in Film about Baseball Player." *The Arizona Republic* (Phoenix, AZ), August 5, 1980.

Miscellaneous Magazines

"Ex-Con Ron LeFlore Does His Time in Tiger Stadium Now." *People*, September 30, 1974.
"Ex-Olympic Boxer Dies of 'Massive Blood Clot.'" *Jet*, June 1, 1961.
"It's Time to Meet Some Mothers Whose Hands Rocked the Cradles of Celebs." *People*, May 15, 1978.
"Woman Sues LeFlore for Stopping Support Payments." *Jet*, February 22, 1979.
Allen, Maury. "From Prison Cage to Batting Cage." *Sports Today*, April 1975.
Benagh, Jim. "The Slugger Who Came in from the Cold (of a Prison Cell)." *Popular Sports: Baseball*, May 1978.
Dow, Bill. "Where Are They Now: Former All-Star Ron LeFlore." *Baseball Digest*, June 2009.
Falls, Joe. "From the Big House to the Big Leagues." *Popular Sports*, May 1975.
Hemphill, Paul. "Ron LeFlore, Flying Tiger." *Sport*, August 1975.
Ribowsky, Mark. "The Inside Track: Ron LeFlore." *Inside Sports*, September 1980.
Simons, Samuel. "Breakout: From Prison to the Big Leagues." Review of *Breakout*, by Ron Leflore with Jim Hawkins. *Library Journal*, February 1, 1978.

Interviews

Napolun Birdsong
Bill Brown
Kenny Brown
Mel Butsicaris Jr.
Dennis Clotworthy
Irwin Cohen
Warren Cromartie
James Derosa
Bill Dow
Michael Farber
Gary Gilette
Jerry Green
Jim Hawkins
Ray Herbert
Philip Hersh
Betty Holden
Frank Howard
Tracy Irwin
James Karalla III
Steve Kemp
Karen Kozy
Joe Lapointe
Bill Lee
Emily LeFlore
Ron LeFlore
Honorable Kenneth McClintock-Hernández
Dave Mesrey
Mark Orr
Larry Paladino
Frank Rashid
Tom Sherry
John Sinclair
Anup Sinha
Dick Tracewski
Tom Tuley
Linda Walter
Al Usereau

Other Website Articles

Associated Press. "LeFlore Spends Night in Jail." *ESPN.com*, September 28, 1999. http://a.espncdn.com/mlb/news/1999/0928/82972.html.

Belth, Alex. "Inside *Inside Sports*: The Oral History." *The Sunday Long Read*, January 28, 2018. https://sundaylongread.com/2018/01/28/inside-inside-sports-the-oral-history/.

Burnstein, Scott. "Detroit Tigers Traded LeFlore in '79 Partially Due to Ties to Frank Usher." *The Gangster Report*, May 26, 2015. https://gangsterreport.com/detroit-tigers-traded-leflore-in-79-partially-due-to-ties-to-frank-usher/.

Gagnon, Dave. "Gates Brown." Society for American Baseball Research, accessed on September 29, 2024. https://sabr.org/bioproj/person/gates-brown/.

Hill, Benjamin. "Gimenez's Time in Clinton Goes Beyond Ball." *MILB.com*, June 3, 2015. https://www.milb.com/news/gcs-128334908.

Holmes, Dan. "Faithful Soldier Moss Stepped Aside for Sparky in '79." *Vintage Detroit Collection*, May 14, 2012. https://www.vintagedetroit.com/blog/2012/05/14/faithful-soldier-moss-stepped-aside-for-sparky-in-79/.

Keenan, Jimmy, and Frank Russo. "Billy Martin." Society for American Baseball Research. https://sabr.org/bioproj/person/billy-martin/ (accessed on October 10, 2024).

Moore, Kimberly C. "Tigers' Willie Horton Recalls Segregated Lakeland, Gives Thanks for Progress." *Lakeland Now*, January 20, 2023. https://www.lkldnow.com/tigers-willie-horton-recalls-segregated-lakeland-gives-thanks-for-progress/.

Pearlman, Jeff. "Nearly 45 Years Ago, Ron LeFlore Went from Prison to the Big Leagues." *The Athletic*, June 28, 2018. https://www.nytimes.com/athletic/411275/2018/06/28/nearly-45-years-ago-ron-leflore-went-from-prison-to-the-big-leagues/.

Poho, Seth. "1976: The Year 'The Bird' Took Over Baseball." *Baseball Essential*, May 15, 2021. https://www.baseballessential.com/news/2016/07/05/1976-year-bird-took-baseball/ [link no longer available].

Rice, Stephen V. "Ed Katalinas." Society for American Baseball Research. https://sabr.org/bioproj/person/ed-katalinas/ (accessed on October 11, 2024).

Russo, Frank. "Billy Martin." Society for American Baseball Research. https://sabr.org/bioproj/person/billy-martin/ (accessed on October 10, 2024).

Smith, Leanne. "Peek Through Time: From Bountiful Gardens to 'Ponderosa,' Jackson Prison Farms Were Fruitful." *Michigan Live*, June 4, 2014. https://www.mlive.com/news/jackson/2014/06/peek_through_time_from_lush_ga.html.

Sternberg, Gerald. "One in a Million: Kermit Smith and the Ron LeFlore Story." *Michigan State University Football Players Association News*, February 2, 2021. https://msufpa.com/one-in-a-million-kermit-smith-and-the-ron-leflore-story/.

Other Sources

"10/4/80 Phillies at Expos." October 4, 1980, posted on February 3, 2017, by Expos Classics, YouTube. https://www.youtube.com/watch?v=A7w8-r1gAJw.

BaseballReference.com. "Ron LeFlore." https://www.baseball-reference.com/players/l/lefloro01.shtml (accessed on November 2, 2024).

Burns, Ken, dir. *Baseball*. Episode 9, "9th Inning – Home." Aired on September 28, 1994 on PBS.

Burton, LeVar. "LeVar Burton at Motor City Comic Con 2017." Interview by Julie Hinds. *Detroit Free Press*, posted by Romain Blanquart on May 20, 2017. https://www.freep.com/videos/entertainment/2017/05/20/levar-burton-motor-city-comic-con-2017/101921726/.

Carew, Rod (@RodCarew_29). "He Hit a One Hop Line to the SS [shortstop] and Beat it Out. I Couldn't believe My Eyes." Twitter (now X), May 19, 2021 (accessed on June 10, 2021).

Eaton, Adrienne, John Knox, Frank Sudia, et al. *A History of Jackson Prison: 1920–1975*. Ann Arbor: University of Michigan, 1979.

"Field of Dreams." April 1992, posted on January 22, 2014, by Kiners Korner / SportsTalkNY, YouTube. https://www.youtube.com/watch?v=xDeQ8wJdZW0.

Karalla, Jimmy, to Jimmy Butsicaris. April 11, 1973. Provided by Tom Sherry's personal collection.

Kuhn, Bowie, to unknown. Memorandum with the heading "Security Review." November 29, 1979. Found in the Bowie K. Kuhn collection, National Baseball Hall of Fame and Museum, Cooperstown, NY, Series VI, "Administrative and Misc. Commissioner Files," Sub-Series 3, "Misc. Files," Box 16, Folder 6 (Security).

"Letter from a Detroit Tigers Representative (Unnamed) to Frank Scott." August 19, 1961. Goldin Auctions, Lot #9. https://goldinauctions.com/Historically_Significant_Lot_of_Letters_to_General-lot5337.aspx [link no longer available] (accessed on July 1, 2015).

Long, Rebecca M. "Detroit's Field of Dreams: The Grassroots Preservation of Tiger Stadium." Thesis, Clemson University, 2012. https://open.clemson.edu/all_theses/1371 (accessed November 26, 2024).

Ratings Ryan. "Ratings Ryan: Weekly Nielsen Ratings: 1978–79 TV Season (UPDATED)." Accessed in April 2024. http://www.ratingsryan.com/2022/01/weekly-nielsen-ratings-1978-79-tv-season.html. The website where I retrieved the data is no longer available on the internet as of May 22, 2024.

"Ron LeFlore?" Spartan Tailgate [forum]. https://247sports.com/college/michigan-state/board/93/Contents/ron-leflore-136174337/?page=1 (accessed on September 27, 2019).

To Create a Select Committee on Narcotics Abuse and Control: Hearing Before the Committee on Rules and Administration. United States Senate, 96th Congress, 2nd Session, on Senate Resolution 207 to create a Select Committee on Narcotics Abuse and Control. Washington: U.S. Government Printing Office, 1980.

"Trip to Pennsylvania - Prior to Major League Baseball All-Star Game - Detroit Tigers Outfielder." July 13, 1976. Roll #B0656. White House Photographs, White House Photographic Collection, Gerald R. Ford Presidential Library. https://www.fordlibrarymuseum.gov/sites/default/files/pdf_documents/library/whphotos/b0656_nlgrf.jpg.

Zaret, Eli, Denny McLain, and Bob Page. *No Filter Sports*, podcast. "Episode 64: The Legend of Ron LeFlore? You Ain't Heard These Stories!" Aired on August 19, 2019. http://www.nofiltersportspodcast.com/2019/08/19/episode-64-the-legend-of-ron-leflore-you-aint-heard-these-stories/ (accessed on August 9, 2020).

INDEX

Page numbers in *italics* refer to photographs, n indicates a note.

A&P (grocery chain) 36
Aaron, Henry "Hank" 67, 137, 148, 168, 179
Albany Senators 71
Ali, Muhammad 22, 70
Amarillo Gold Sox 99–100
An American Dilemma (Myrdal) 7
Anderson, Sparky 217–20, *223*, 232
Atlanta Braves 137, 148, 179
Atlanta Crackers 71
Atlanta Federal Penitentiary 71
The Autobiography of Malcolm X 203

Baldwin, Billy 111, 112
Balkan American Community Center, Troy, Michigan 251–2, *253*
Ball Four (Bouton) 198, 203
Baltimore Orioles
    1972 season 77
    1973 season 113
    1974 season 147–8, 150–2
    1975 season 154, 158
    1976 season 181, 185
    signing Lajoie 99
    spring training location 116
Banks, Ernie 148
Baylor, Don 150
Berle, Milton 74
Berlin, Ira 3
Berra, Yogi 145, 181
Big Brothers of America 168
Birdsong, Napolun 60, 67–8, 167
Black Bottom neighborhood, Detroit 6
Black Panthers 49
Blackman, Ted 234
Blessitt, Ike 256
Blue, Vida 200, 245
Blyleven, Bert 159
Bolden, Will and Georgia (great-grandparents) 2
Bonds, Bobby 160n, 201
Boston Red Sox
    1974 season 131
    1975 season 154, 158, 160, 163
    1978 season 208
    Giamatti as fan 249
    integration 148
    player records 181
    scouting Fidrych 178
Bouton, Jim 198, 203
Breakout (Ron LeFlore memoir); *see also One in a Million*
    book tour 201–2, 204
    contents 202–4, 212n
    co-writer choice 195–6
    Detroit Tigers goodwill tour 79n
    Hawkins' interviews of Ron 196–9
    reviews 202
    Ron's promotion to Detroit Tigers 132n
    royalties 214
    sales vi, 201–2
Brewster Recreation Center (later Brewster-Wheeler Recreation Center) 15
Briggs, Walter 148
Briggs Stadium 74, 99; *see also* Tiger Stadium
Bristol Tigers 103
Brock, Lou 125, 134–5, 228

Bronfman, Charles 234
Brooklyn Dodgers 102, 148, 230
Brown, Bill 194, 219, 248
Brown, Ike 85, 86, 150
Brown, Jim 31
Brown, Kenny 39–40, 187, 231
Brown, Larry 39
Brown, William James "Gates" 72
   1963 season 149
   1974 season 142, 148
   1975 season 153, 162
   advice for Ron vi, 148, 244
   career overview vi
   Detroit Tigers 1973 goodwill tour 80
   as Detroit Tigers coach 247
   as hitting instructor vi
   prison time vi, 71–2, 80, 89
   welcoming Ron to Detroit Tigers 142
Brown family 39–40
Bruce (co-conspirator) 43–6
Bruton, Bill 149
Buffalo Bills 66
Burnstein, Scott 165
Burroughs, Jeff 164
Burton, LeVar vi, 204–*10*, 252
Butsicaris, Jimmy 73–5, 81–2, 85, 191–2, 214, 244
Butsicaris, Johnny 73–5, 191
Butsicaris, Mel 191–2, 242, 257
Butsicaris, Mel, Jr. 63
Butsicaris, Meleti 73
Bybee, Vern 26, 27

California Angels 173, 201
Campbell, Harry (brother)
   advice for Ron 15–17
   army service 17, *18*
   boxing 15, 17, 22–28, 31
   childhood in Memphis 3, 4, 7
   death 26–9
   Detroit gangs 10, 12
   idolized by Ron 15
   living conditions in Detroit 9–10
   marriage and son 24
   Olympics 2–3, *23*, 43
   punching ability 9–10
   San José State University 17
   teenage move to Detroit 9
Campbell, Jim *191*
   1974 season 130
   Anderson hired as manager 217–18
   Black players and 148, 150, 151
   Breakout (Ron LeFlore memoir) 202–4
   contract negotiations 190
   Detroit Tigers 1973 goodwill tour 80
   ensuring Ron avoided negative elements 165, 191, 244
   Evers and 123
   frugality 116
   Houk hired as manager 145–6
   Lolich trade 170
   Martin (Billy) and 113, 115
   Moss hired/fired as manager 217
   Ron requesting tryout 69
   Ron traded to Montreal Expos 223–4, 223n
   Ron's age inaccuracy 171, 172
   Ron's complaints about 232
   Ron's contract 220, 222–3
   Ron's probation 156
   Ron's promotion to Majors 134, 135, 144
   on Ron's super star potential 154
   Ron's tryout 88–90
   spring training 116, 119
   spring training rules 117
   suspicions about Ron 221
Campbell, Marvin (brother)
   childhood in Memphis 3, 4, 7
   death 256
   Detroit gangs 10, 12
   living conditions in Detroit 9–10
   San José State University 23
   teenage move to Detroit 9
Capone, Al 165
Carew, Rod 201, 249
Carlos, John 91
Carter, Gary 225, 227
Carter, Jimmy 211–13, 212n

INDEX

Casey (childhood friend)   187
Cash, Norm
   1971 season   77
   1974 season   115
   One in a Million (movie adaptation of Ron's memoir)   206–7
   retirement   153
   Ron's tryout   85
   suspicions about Ron's honesty   139
Cavanagh, Jerry   74
Cedar Rapids Astros   105–6
Central State University, Wilberforce, Ohio   92
Chamberlain, Wilt   74
Chambliss, Chris   183
Chicago Cubs   235
Chicago White Sox   83, 177–8, 239–40, 243
Chrysler stamping plant   44
Cincinnati Bengals   70
Cincinnati Reds   71, 100, 127, 217
Clay, Cassius; *see* Ali, Muhammad
Clemente, Roberto   152
Cleveland, Reggie   131
Cleveland Indians
   1973 season   113
   1976 season   173, 179
   1978 season   209, 211
   Evers' career   123
   Robinson (Frank) as manager   157
   Veeck as owner   239
Clinton, Iowa   107
Clinton Pilots   96, 98, 99, 101–12, *110*, 127
Clotworthy, Dennis   139, 164
Cobb, Ty   135, 153, 188, 200, 211
Cohen, Irwin   219
Colbert, Nate   154
Coleman, Joe   161
Collins, John Norman   92n, 197–8
Colschen, Fritz   111
Cromartie, Warren   225, 229, 233, 237

Dalton Farms   53–4
Daugherty, Duffy   66
Davis, Tommy   150
Dawson, Andre   225, 227, 229–30, 233

Decatur Commodores   98, 104, 105
Dee's bar   44–6
Dehem, Mark   254
DeRosa, Jim   246
Derry, Tom   252–3
Desmond, Vince   81–2
Detroit, Michigan
   automobile industry   4–6
   Black Bottom neighborhood   6
   Black population   5, 6, 21
   ethnic ghettos   5
   gangs   10–11
   Great Depression   6–7
   Great Migration   3–4
   heroin   34
   living conditions for Black residents   6–8, 77
   Paradise Valley neighborhood   6
   population decline   21
   population growth   5
   quality of public schools   21
   racial segregation   5–7
   riots (1943)   7
   riots (1967)   40–*2*, 49, 77
Detroit Diesel   40, 53
Detroit Historical Museum   252–6
Detroit Lions   74
Detroit Police Department   20, 24, 36, 40–*2*
Detroit Red Wings   74
Detroit Stars   148
Detroit Tigers; *see also* Tiger Stadium; *specific players*
   1958 season   148
   1968 World Series   73, 75, 90, 130–1, 169
   1971 season   77
   1972 season   77–8, 112
   1973 goodwill tour   79–83, 79n
   1973 season   78, 81, 83–4, 89–90, 112–13
   1974 season   115–16, 130–3, 137–44, 147–8, 150–3
   1974 spring training   116–18
   1975 season   153–4, 158–64

INDEX

1975 spring training   154, 156–7
1976 season   173–87, 189–90
1976 spring training   169–71, 178–9
1977 season   199–201
1977 spring training   199
1978 season   205–9, 211
1978 spring training   vi
1979 season   217–22
1981 spring training   240
1984 World Series   244
Anderson's policy changes   218
Black players, history of   148–50
Briggs Stadium   74
Brown (Gates) signed by   71–3
contract negotiations   190–1
Fidrych drafted by   178
finances   133
Houk hired as manager   116, 145–6
integration   118, 148–9
Lajoie as scout   101
Martin (Billy) as manager   73, 75–8, 112–13
Martin (Billy) fired   113, 115
Moss hired/fired as manager   217
off-season instruction in Puerto Rico   169
players' suspicions about Ron's honesty   139
Ron promoted to   132–5
Ron signed by   96–8
Ron traded to Montreal Expos   221–4, 223n, *226*
Ron's contract   137–8, 189–90, 220, 222–3
Ron's MLB debut   137–42
Ron's prison release   95–6
Ron's tryout request   69, 82–3
Ron's tryouts   82–91
segregated spring training facilities   118–19
spring training rules   116
white-centric ecosystem   196
Detroit Wheels   96
DiMaggio, Dom   180, 183, 183n

DiMaggio, Joe   131, 180
Doby, Larry   72, 149, 239
Doom, Jimmy   253
Dunedin, Florida   115, 124, 156

Emmett (co-conspirator)   43–6
Eric (friend)   34–5
Evansville Triplets   112, 125–32, 134, 178, 217
Even, Dan   111
Evers, Walter Arthur "Hoot"   123–5, 130, 134, 135, 248

Falls, Joe
   on 1974 season   130
   on *Breakout* (memoir)   202
   on Houk   146
   as "institution"   194–5
   on Ron   152, 156, 188
Farber, Michael   233, 237
FBI (Federal Bureau of Investigation)   221
Feller, Bob   129
Fernández, Chico   149
Fetzer, John   117, 163, 181
Fidrych, Mark "the Bird"
   1976 All-Star Game   185–6, *189*
   1976 season   178–80, 185–8
   1976 spring training   178–9
   1977 season   199
   1978 season   209, 211
   drafted by Detroit Tigers   178
   Evansville Triplets   178
   Go Bird Go! (memoir)   194, 203
Fingers, Rollie   245
Fishkin, Ken   222–3, 239, 242
Florida Southern College   170
Ford, Gerald R.   186–7, *189*
Ford, Henry   5
Ford, Whitey   145
Ford Motor Company   5
Foster, Roxanne   256
Fowler, Art   85, 87
Fox, Pete   180

INDEX

free agency 157, 170–1
Freehan, Bill
   1974 season 116, 130, 142
   1975 All-Star Game 161
   1975 season 153, 162
   1976 season 185
   as Detroit Tigers coach 247
   groin injury 130
   One in a Million (movie adaptation of Ron's memoir) 205–7
   retirement 199
Fryman, Woodie 140–1, 153

Gage, Tom 249
Garagiola, Joe 125
Garnett, Joseph, Jr., photo by *250*
Garrabrout, Sara 221–2, 232, 242, 243, 245
Gehrig, Lou 71, 179, 181
Giacalone, Anthony 37, 63–4, 165
Giacalone, Vito 63–4, 165
Giamatti, A. Bartlett 249
Giamatti, Paul 249
Gibson, Kirk 218
Gimenez, Ray 105–7, 111
Glynn, Ed 107, 112
Go Bird Go! (Fidrych memoir) 194, 203
Great Depression 1–2, 6–7
Great Migration 3, 5–6
Green, Jerry 89, 139
Greene, Doc 75
Grimsley, Ross 151
Groch, Dick 98, 109
Guerrero, Johnny 24
Gutiérrez, César 150

Hadden, Sandy 223n
Haley, Alex 203
Harding, Reggie 59
Harrison, Gus 56–7
Harwell, Ernie 79–82, 79n, 86, 146, 220, 247
Hatfield, Fred 127, *127*, 129, 132, 134, 135
Hawkins, Jim "Hawk"
   on 1973 season 90
   on 1975 season 154
   2013 interview with Ron 251
   Breakout (Ron LeFlore memoir) 79n, 195–9, 201–3, 212n
   career overview 193–4
   competitive nature 193–4
   Go Bird Go! (Fidrych memoir) 194, 203
   on Houk's arrest 161
   Jackson Prison visit 196–8
   on Roberts 154n
   on Ron's 1977 season 200
   on Ron's 1978 season 210
   Ron's age inaccuracy 171
   Ron's complaints about 232
   on Ron's hitting streak (1976) 177, 179
   on Ron's promotion to Majors 133, 138
   at Ron's tryout 88, 99
Hernandez, Keith 130
Herr, Richard 66
Hersh, Phil 161, 163, 163n
Hiller, John 153, 184, 199
Hillsdale College 66
Hitsville U.S.A. 33
Hoffa, Jimmy 37
Holtzman, Ken 151
Home Is a Dirty Street (Perkins) 14
Horton, Willie 150
   1963 season 149
   1969 season 149–50
   1971 season 160
   1973 goodwill tour 80
   1974 season 130, 133, 148
   1975 season 153, 158, 159, 162, 164
   1976 season 170, 173, 185, 188
   2019 meeting with Ron 251–2, *253*
   advice for Ron 150, 164, 248
   as Detroit Tigers coach 247
   Hawkins and 194
   as Howard's roommate 82
   inside-the-park home run 160
   off-season instruction in Puerto Rico 169

protest of Tigers not promoting Black and Hispanic players   149–50
  racism faced by   118–19
  Ron's tryout   85, 86
  spring training   118–19
  traded by Detroit Tigers   199
Houk, Harold   144
Houk, Ralph   *147*
  1961 World Series   145
  1962 World Series   145
  1966 season   146
  1974 season   138–40, 144
  1975 season   158, 160–3
  1975 spring training   154
  1976 season   176–90
  1977 season   199–200
  1978 season   207
  advice for Ron   164
  arrest   161, 163, 163n
  background   144–5
  Detroit Tigers contract   188
  faith in Ron   248
  on Fidrych   185
  Hawkins and   193
  hired as Tigers' manager   116, 145–6
  managing Ron   146
  on Mantle   185
  as New York Yankees manager   145, 146
  One in a Million (movie adaptation of Ron's memoir)   207, 209
  patience   146, 165, 218
  playing career   144, 145
  retirement   217
  Ron compared to other great players   181
  Ron's age inaccuracy   172
  Ron's devotion to   190
  on Ron's learning baseball   184–5
  Ron's MLB debut   138–40
  Ron's promotion to Majors   134, 135, 144
  on Ron's speed   153
  Second World War   144–6
  team rules   151
  violent temper   146, 161, 162
Howard, Elston   157

Howard, Frank   80–2, 85, 86, 88
Humphrey, Hubert   76
Humphrey, Terry   154
Hunter, Jim "Catfish"   157

Indianapolis Indians   127–8
Inside Sports magazine   230–5, 238
Ionia, Michigan   37–9
Irwin, Tracy   253–4
Ishoy, Ron   171

Jackson, Liz   257
Jackson, Reggie   168, 201, 215
Jackson Prison; *see* State Prison of Southern Michigan
James, Art
  1975 season   158, 159n
  Clinton Pilots   107, 109, 111, 112, 115
  Dunedin, Florida   115
Johnny (co-conspirator)   43–6
Johnson, Alex   180
Johnson, Perry   47, 49–50, 64, 83, 93, 95
Johnson, Rafer   22

Kaiser, Bob   112
Kaline, Al "Mr. Tiger"
  1955 season   200
  1961 hitting streak   178, 180, 181
  1971 season   77
  1974 season   115, 134, 140–4, 151–2
  character traits   141
  comparisons to   154, 154n
  as Detroit Tigers coach   247
  Lakeland speaking engagements   156
  mentoring Ron   142, 151–2, 244, 248
  One in a Million (movie adaptation of Ron's memoir)   205–7
  on racial discrimination   118
  retirement   153
  Ron's MLB debut   140–2
  Ron's tryout   85, 88
  3,000 hits club   152
Kane, Martin   196
Kansas City Athletics   76
Kansas City Royals   152, 162

Karalla, James III   63, 64
Karalla, James "Cokey", Sr.   62–3
Karalla, James "Jimmy", Jr.
  athleticism   63
  childhood   62–3
  faith in Ron   248
  impact on Ron's baseball career   62, 64, 68, 73, 75, 81–2, 86
  imprisonment   64
  lawsuit against Ron   243
  life after prison   165
  Mafia ties   63–4, 86
  Ron's age inaccuracy   172
Karras, Alex   74
Kassal, Bentley   25
Katalinas, Ed
  Evers and   123
  Lajoie and   101
  as liaison to MLB concerning Ron   96, 98
  on Ron's promotion to Majors   126
  Ron's tryouts   88–9, 91
  on Tigers' need for speed   135
Kaul, Donald   224
Keller, Edward   27
Kemp, Steve   208, 245
Key West Conchs   122
Kincade, Georgia; *see* LeFlore, Georgia Kincade
Kincade, Gerald (grandfather)   2, 4, 7, 9, 28
Kincade, Henrietta (grandmother)   2, 4, 7, 9, 13, 28
Kingman, Dave   235
Kuenn, Harvey   169
Ku Klux Klan   124
Kuhn, Bowie   96, 97, 223n, 232–3, 235

La Russa, Tony   239–40
Lajoie, Bill
  with Anderson   *223*
  as baseball fanatic   99
  Evers and   123
  faith in Ron   248
  impact on Ron's career   96, 98–9, 101–3, 108, 223

informing Ron he'd been traded   221–2
playing career   99–100
Ron's contract   222
Ron's tryouts   87–8, 90–2
as scout   99–101
teaching career   100
Lakeland, Florida   116–19, 124, 126, 156, 199
Lakeland Tigers   117, 119–27, 134
Lamont, Gene   143–4
Lane, Marv   131, 138, 140
Lane, Richard "Night Train"   92
Lapointe, Joe   256
Lastreto, Don   26–7
Lee, Bill   231, 245
LeFlore, Georgia (daughter)   242
LeFlore, Georgia Kincade (mother)
  1976 All-Star Game   186
  athleticism   2–3, 31
  Breakout (Ron's memoir)   203
  death   256
  on difficulties of parenting   19, 33
  domestic service positions   4, 8
  family background   2
  fearlessness   12–13
  financial difficulties   9, 203
  Gerald's death   174
  Gerald's upbringing   39
  giving Ron news of former accomplices   115
  with grandson, Gerald, Jr.   *215*
  homes   39, 195–6
  living conditions in East Detroit   7–9
  marrying John LeFlore   3
  in Memphis   2–4
  move to Detroit   4, 7
  restaurant jobs   8, 56
  Ron's childhood misbehavior   11, 14, 24
  Ron's education   31
  Ron's generosity after signing with Detroit Tigers   96, 162
  Ron's release from prison   96

Ron's robbery trial   46
Ron's teenage robberies and   36
son Harry's boxing   23
son Harry's death   27–8
Tiger Stadium closure   247
unaware of Ron's drug use   35
visiting Ron in prison   56
LeFlore, Gerald (brother)   176
   addiction cycle   174
   attending Ron's Tigers' games   148
   birth   7
   childhood   7–9, 16, 19–20
   children   174, *176*, *215*, 216
   death   174–6, 174n–5n
   drug trade   38–9, 174
   Ron's concern for   38–40
   teenage years   38–9
   visiting Ron in prison   56
LeFlore, Geraldine (aunt)   1, 3, 4
LeFlore, Gerald, Jr.   174, *176*, *215*
LeFlore, John, Jr. (father)   84
   1976 All-Star Game   188
   abusing family   10, 19, 36
   alcoholism   8, 10, 19
   artistic talent   1
   auto industry job   4, 8
   death   243
   Detroit Diesel job   40
   Detroit gangs and   12
   ethnic heritage   1
   fearlessness   1–2, 12
   Gerald's death   175
   as Harry's boxing coach   15
   homes   39, 195–6
   leaving South   1–3
   living conditions in East Detroit   7–9
   marrying Georgia   3
   move to Detroit   3–4, 7
   Ron's celebrity status   *214*
   Ron's childhood misbehavior   24
   Ron's Detroit Tigers tryouts   84, 85, 90–1
   Ron's drug use and   35–6
   Ron's early release from prison   96
   Ron's education   31

Ron's generosity after signing with Detroit Tigers   96, 162
Ron's teenage robberies   36
unemployment   8
visiting Ron in prison   56
Zenith factory job   4
LeFlore, John (son)   243
LeFlore, LaRonda (daughter); *see* Lewis, LaRonda
LeFlore, Ronald Alexander, Jr. (son)   232, 242, 243
LeFlore, Ronald "Ron"; *see also* State Prison of Southern Michigan
   age inaccuracies   98, 171–2, 203, 212, 212n
   baseball career
      1974 season   116, 132–3, 137–44, 147–8, 150–3
      1974 spring training   117
      1975 season   153–6, 158–64
      1975 spring training   156–7
      1976 All-Star Game   186–8, *189*
      1976 season   173–88
      1976 spring training   169–70
      1977 season   199–201
      1977 spring training   199
      1978 season   209
      1978 spring training   vi
      1978 trade rumors   209
      1979 season   218–22
      1980 season   226–32, 234–7
      1981 season   239–40
      1981 spring training   240
      1982 season   240, 243
      agents   190, 192, 199, 204, 222–3, 239, 242, 254
      as bad influence on young players   238
      as baseball instructor   245–6
      career overview   248–9
      Chicago White Sox contract   239, 240
      clashes with Anderson   218–20, 232
      Clinton Pilots   96, 98, 99, 101–12, *110*

Detroit Tigers contract 137–8, 189–90, 220, 222–3
Detroit Tigers tryout 82–91
in Detroit Tigers uniform *155*
drug use impacting 220, 231–2, 240
in Dunedin, Florida 115, 156
elevated to Majors 121
Evansville Triplets 126–30, 132, 134
fielding skills 108–9
hitting streak (1976) 177–85, 183n, 186
Houk as ideal manager 146
Inside Sports interview 230–5, 238
inside-the-park home run 159–60
Kaline comparisons 154, 154n
knee injuries and surgery 163–4, 188, 195, 199
Lakeland speaking engagements 156
Lakeland Tigers 119–26, 134
legacy 248–52
meeting Billy Martin 82–3
mentored by Kaline 142, 151–2
as minor league manager 246–7
MLB debut 137–42
Montreal Expos contract 226
offseason in Dunedin, Florida 113, 115, 156
offseason in Puerto Rico 168–9, 180, 242
promotion to Detroit Tigers 132–5
released by Montreal Expos *228*
Ron LeFlore Baseball Camp 246
Senior Professional Baseball Association 245
shaking hands with security guard *212*
signing autographs *214*
signing with Detroit Tigers 96–8
stealing home 229, 229n
stolen-base record 228, 230, 237, 249

Tiger Stadium closure 247
Tracewski and 119–21
traded to Montreal Expos 221–6, 223n, *226*
Breakout (memoir) vi, 79n, 132n, 195–9, 201–4, 212n, 213
celebrity status *214*, 215–16
character traits
  fashionable style 41, 97, 204, 215
  fearlessness 13, 16–17
  intelligence 51
  not heeding advice vi
  self-sabotage 230–5, 238, 242, 248
  toughness 40, 44, 46
  trust issues 248
childhood
  athleticism 15–16, 18, 19, 24, 31
  birth 7
  culinary interests 8
  education 11–14, 17
  fearlessness 13, 16–17
  gang run-in 11–12
  idolizing brother Harry 15, 17
  living conditions in East Detroit 7–10
  misbehavior 13–14, 16, 19–20, 24
  risk-taking 20
  substance abuse 16
drug use
  arrests 240
  childhood 16
  cocaine 37, 220, 231–2, 242
  counseling for 245
  heroin 34–5, 37, 43, 50, 55, 203, 260
  impacting baseball career 220, 231–2, 240
  marijuana 16, 204, 220
  in memoir 202, 203
  post-baseball life 242, 244, 245
  in prison 59–60
  teenage years 34–7
family
  advice from brother Harry 15–17
  brother Gerald's death 174–7
  brother Harry's death 28–9

children   168, 176, 216, 220, 232, 242, 243, 245
child support payments   220, 245, 247–8, 251
concern for brother Gerald   38–40
on father's alcoholism   10
on father's artistic talent   1
on father's fearlessness   1–2
on his aunt (Geraldine)   4
girlfriends   124 (*see also* Garrabrout, Sara; Lewis, Deborah; Zafer, Emily)
life after baseball
   amputation of leg   251
   automobile accident   244
   health problems   251
   MLB Alumni Legends Game   *250*
   Sarasota life   241–4
   signing autographs   246, 247, 251–2, *253*
   as skycap   241–2, 245
marriage (*see* Zafer, Emily)
musical tastes   162
off-field troubles: drug arrest   240
   failure to pay child support   247–8, 251
   FBI investigation   221
   gun charge   243
   hangers-on   243–4
   Mafia friends   165, 221
   as target of exploitation   216
One in a Million (movie adaptation of Ron's memoir)   205–*10*, 212–16, 249
One in a Million fortieth anniversary screening   252–6
parole obligations   109–11, 156
philanthropy   168, 209–12
on racism in Montreal   233–5
teenage years: cocaine use   37
   crimes committed   35–7, 41–6, 115
   heroin use   34–7
   high school sports   31–4, 36
   incarceration   37–8
   jobs   36, 40, 44, 53

looting during Detroit riots   41–2, 204
transcendental meditation   181
Lemanczyk, Dave   142
Lemon, Chet   245
Lewis, Alvin "Blue"   70
Lewis, Charles   18–20, 24
Lewis, Deborah
   Gerald LeFlore's death and   175
   marriage and widowhood   168
   pregnancy and motherhood   168, 177, 216, 220
   raising Gerald's children   216
   relationship with Ron   168, 176, 211, 216
   Ron's child support payments   220, 245, 247–8
Lewis, LaRonda (daughter)   177, 220, 245, 247, 256
Leyland, Jim
   as Clinton Pilots' manager   102–5, 107–9, 111–12
   as Evansville Triplets' manager   112
   faith in Ron   248
   "fiery" temper   103
   as Montgomery Rebels' manager   112
   playing career   103
Lima, S. R.   31
Lindell AC (Detroit bar)   73–6, 81, 85, 86, 213–14, 256
Liston, Sonny   69–70
Lolich, Mickey
   1968 World Series   169
   1974 season   116, 152
   1975 season   153, 161, 162
   Hawkins and   194
   traded to Montreal Expos   169–70
Lopopolo, Sandro   22, *23*
Los Angeles Dodgers   134, 168
Louis, Joe   15
Lynn, Fred   160

McClintock-Hernández, Kenneth   213
McHale, John   225, 226, 234, 238

McLain, Denny 76–7, 169
McRae, Norm 150
Maddox, Elliott 229
Mafia 37, 62–4, 74, 165
Major League Baseball (MLB)
   Black managers 157–8
   former prisoners as players 70–1
   odds of becoming an MLB
      player 61–2
The Making of African America
   (Berlin) 3
Malcolm X 203
Mankowski, Phil 112
Mantle, Mickey
   1961 season 145
   1962 season 145
   drawing crowds 185
   Kaline comparison 141
   LeFlore comparison 181
   as Lindell AC patron 74
   Martin friendship 76, 77
   power and speed 153
   Stanley comparison 131
Manuel, Jerry 182
March of Dimes 211
Maris, Roger 145, 179
Martin, Billy
   alcoholism 112, 113
   Butsicaris (Jimmy) and 73, 75–6, 81–2
   career pattern 112
   Detroit Tigers' 1973 goodwill
      tour 80–3
   as Detroit Tigers' manager 73, 75–8, 80–90, 112–13
   explosive personality 76, 112–13, 146
   fired by Detroit Tigers 113, 115
   as Lindell AC patron 73, 75, 76, 86
   marriages 73
   meeting Ron LeFlore 82–3
   as New York Yankees' manager 182
   One in a Million (movie adaptation of
      Ron's memoir) 207, *210*
   playing career 76
   Ron's tryout 82–90
   as Texas Rangers' manager 130, 152
   "winaholic" attitude 218
Martin, Dean 74
Martinez, Tippy 183
Masters, Todd 78
Matlin, Lew 79–83, 98
Maurice (gang member) 11–12
Mayagüez Indians 169
Mays, Willie 148
Medrano, Al 25–7
Memphis, Tennessee 2–3, 7, 13, 28
Menendez, Jules 25
Mesrey, Dave 252–5
Meyer, Danny 116, 131–3, 154n, 170
Miami Orioles 122
Michigan State University 47, 65, 66, 70
Michigan Training Unit (MTU) 37–9
Miller, Dave 125
Milwaukee Braves 137
Milwaukee Brewers
   1973 season 89
   1974 season 137–44, 147
   1975 season 159
   1976 season 173, 185
   1979 season 219
   farm system 126
   scouts 69
Minnesota Twins 76, 84, 89, 159–60, 201
minor league baseball 61–2, 70–1; *see
   also specific teams*
Missouri State Penitentiary 69–70
Money, Don 140
Montgomery Rebels 112, 125, 126
Montreal Expos
   1975 spring training 157
   1979 season 225
   1980 season 226–32, 234–7
   Ron traded to 221–6
   Ron's contract 226
   Ron's racism accusations 233–5
Moore, Charlie 140
Moreno, Omar 235–7
Morris, Jack 199
Morton, Bubba 149

Moss, Les 217, 218
Motown Records 33
MTU (Michigan Training Unit) 37–9
Muller, Eddie 26
Mullin, Pat 72
Munson, Thurman 153, 182, 183
Murder Row (crime family) 165
Murphy, Turner 24, 36
Murray, Eddie 122
Myrdal, Gunnar 7

National Advisory Committee on
    Juvenile Justice and Delinquency
    Prevention 212–13
Negro League 85
Nelson, Jo, photo by *29*
Nettles, Graig 182
Nettles, Jim 131
Neudecker, Jerry 183
New York Mets 229–30, 234
New York Yankees
    1961 World Series 145
    1962 World Series 145
    1966 season 146
    1968 World Series 75
    1973 season 81
    1974 season 137, 153
    1975 season 154, 158, 160, 160n
    1976 season 181–5
    1977 season 201
    Houk's career 116, 144, 145
    Hunter signing with 157
    Martin's career 76, 182
    player records 178–81
    Sing Sing games 71
    spring training location 116, 119
Newburgh Night Hawks 246
Nitti, Frank; *see* Usher, Frank Lee
Norman, Fred 225
Northrup, Jim
    1974 season 115, 131, 142
    1975 season 153
    off-season instruction in Puerto
        Rico 169

One in a Million (movie adaptation of
    Ron's memoir) 205–6
    traded to Montreal Expos 153
    welcoming Ron to Detroit Tigers 142

Oakland A's
    1972 season 77, 112
    1974 season 151
    1975 season 160n
    1976 season 173
    1977 season 200
    Hunter's free agency 157
    interest in Ron 92
    off-season instruction in Puerto
        Rico 168
Office, Rowland 225
Oglivie, Ben 131, 140, 170, 173
Ohio State Reformatory, Mansfield 71–2
Oklahoma 89ers 129
Olivet College 128
Olympia Stadium, Detroit 74, 216
Olympics (1960) 22–3, *23*, 43
One in a Million (movie adaptation of
    Ron's memoir); *see also* Breakout
    airing 213–15
    cast vi, 204–*8*, *210*
    filming 205–*8*
    fortieth anniversary screening 252–6
    title 249
The Origins of the Urban Crisis
    (Sugrue) 21
Orr, Mark *208*, 254
Overmire, Frank "Stubby" *121*–3, 125,
    134, 135, 248

Paige, Satchel 239
Paladino, Larry 133
Palmer, Jim 158
Parrish, Lance 199
Pennington, Bill 77
Perkins, Useni Eugene 14, 41–2
Philadelphia Phillies 157, 235–6
Phillips, Jess 70
Pitts, Edwin "Alabama" 70–1

INDEX

Pittsburgh Pirates   71, 150, 168, 235, 236
Puerto Rico, Winter League   168–9, 181, 242
Puscas, George   224

Quad City Angels   112

Raines, Tim   238–9
Ramos, Bobby   236
Rangel, Valentin   24
Redmond, Wayne   150
reserve clause   170
Ribowsky, Mark   230–4
Rice, Jim   245
Richman, Milton   vi
Rickey, Branch   102
Rivera, Jim   71
Roberts, Leon   131–4, 154n, 162
Robinson, Brooks   113
Robinson, Frank   157
Robinson, Jackie   102, 148, 157–8, 196, 230, 233
Robinson, Rachel   233
Rodríguez, Aurelio   77, 80, 115, 142, 218, 222
Rogers, Steve   227, 229
Rojas, Cookie   162
Ron LeFlore Baseball Camp   246
Roots (miniseries)   204, 205
Rose, Pete   183n, 236
Rudolph, Wilma   22
Rugh, Elana   255
Ruhle, Vern   128, 161
Ruth, Babe   71, 181

St. Claire, Mr. (parole officer)   110–11
St. Louis Cardinals   116, 119, 130, 134, 227, 228
St. Petersburg, Florida   246
St. Petersburg Cardinals   122
St. Rose of Lima   31–2
Sarasota, Florida   241–5
Saunders, Frank   196
Savas, Sheryl, photo by   *48*

Schatzeder, Dan   222
Schmidt, Mike   235, 236
Schultz, Joe   159–60
Scott, George   140–1
Scott, Rodney   225, 227, 229
Second World War   4, 117, 123, 144–5
Selman, Jim   125, 202
Senior Professional Baseball Association   245
Shakers (Detroit gang)   11–12
Shannon, Mike   249–50
Sharon, Dick   131
Sherry, Tom   213
Silberman, Charles E.   49
Sinclair, John   49, 256
Sing Sing Correctional Facility, New York   71
Slaton, Jim   138–40
Smith, Kermit   65–7
Snider, Duke   230
Southern Michigan Prison; *see* State Prison of Southern Michigan
Speier, Chris   229, 236
SPSM; *see* State Prison of Southern Michigan
Stanley, Mickey
  1968 World Series   130–1
  1973 season   131
  1974 season   130–1, 134
  1975 season   153, 161
  1976 season   173, 176
  1976 spring training   170
  1977 season   199
  advice for Ron   248
  fielding prowess   131
  injury   121, 134
  Ron's tryout   88
State Prison of Southern Michigan (SPSM)   46–69
  African American inmates   47, 49
  athletes, privileges for   64
  baseball team revamped   167–8
  daily routine   52
  Dalton Farms   53–4

Detroit Tigers goodwill tour 79–82, 79n
Diagnostic Center 50–1
Georgia's visits to Ron 56
guards 49–50, 57, 197
Honor Block 50, 64, 93
Karalla's incarceration 62, 64, 68, 73
Lewis boxing at 70
Phillips in 70
rape as rampant 58
Ron as football coach 92
Ron attacked by guards 57
Ron becoming better person 92–3
Ron in Slammer 57
Ron in solitary confinement (the Hole) 54–7, 205–6
Ron playing baseball 66–9, 73, 104, 128
Ron playing basketball 51, 59
Ron playing football 65–6
Ron playing softball 65
Ron sentenced to 46
Ron witnessing acts of violence 58
Ron's arrival 50–1
Ron's desire for early release 58–60, 66–7
Ron's drug use 59–60
Ron's early release 95–6
Ron's education 60
Ron's exercise regimen 55–6, 59
Ron's furloughs 83–4, 90
Ron's GED 93
Ron's jobs 52–4, 59–60
Ron's return visits 167, 196–8
size 47
The Spectator (newspaper) 67, 69, 167
sports amenities 64–5, 92
warden (*see* Johnson, Perry)
Staub, Rusty
  1976 All-Star Game 186
  1976 season 170, 184, 186
  1977 season 200
  1978 season 208
  1979 season 218
  let go by Tigers 222
  traded to Detroit Tigers 169
Steinbrenner, George 145
Stengel, Casey 145
Studio 54, New York City 215
Sudberry, Bob 82
Sugrue, Thomas J. 21
Sutherland, Gary 143–4, 151, 162, 173, 179
Swanson, Pete 129, 132
Sylvester, Curt 98

Tampa Tarpons 122, 124, 126
Taylor, Tony 85, 86
Tempesta, John 46
Texas Rangers 130, 152, 164, 175–6
Thomas, Lou 24
Thompson, Jason 186, 188, 200, 209, 218
Tiant, Luis 158
Tiger Stadium 74, 206–7, *212*, 247
TigerTown, Lakeland, Florida 103, 117–19, 156
Till, Emmett 13
Tracewski, Dick "Trixie" 86, 87, 119–21, *120*, 153
Trammell, Alan 199, 209, 217
Trudeau, Justin 228
Trudeau, Pierre Elliott 228, 230
Tuley, Tom 128–9, 132, 133
Tulsa Oilers 130
Tuned to Baseball (Harwell) 79n
Tyler, Gerald 106, 107

Usher, Frank Lee (Frank Nitti) 165, 221

Valentine, Ellis 225, 229
Veeck, Bill 239
Virdon, Bill 109
Virgil, Ozzie 118, 148
Virgil, Ozzie, Jr. 237
Vitale, Dick 241–2

Wagner, Mark 112
Walker, Tom 154

Washington, Claudell   160n
Washington, Dinah   92
Washington Senators   80
Waterloo Royals   111
West, Joe   169
Whitaker, Lou   199, 209
White, Frank   162
White, Jerry   229
White Panthers   49
Williams, Dick   225, 226, 231–2, 236–8
Williams, Ted   88, 181
Wills, Maury   134–5, 168
Wilson, Earl   149, 190
Winter Haven Red Sox   122
Wisconsin Rapids Twins   112

Wood, Jake   118, 149, *149*, 153
Woods, Ron   149
Woolf, Robert "Bob"   190, 192, 199, 204, 222
World Football League   96
World War II   4, 117, 123, 144–5
Wright, Clyde   142, 143

Young, Bill   22
Young, Coleman   97

Zachry, Pat   229
Zafer, Emily   243–5, 247, 252–5
Zaret, Eli   204
Zenith   4